FRAGILE BULLY

Understanding Our Destructive Affair
with Narcissism in the Age of Trump

LAURIE HELGOE, PhD

DIVERSION
BOOKS

To Mom and Dad

Diversion Books
A Division of Diversion Publishing Corp.
443 Park Avenue South, Suite 1004
New York, New York 10016
www.DiversionBooks.com

The views expressed in this book are the author's own and do not represent
the policies or positions of the Ross University School of Medicine.

For more information, email info@diversionbooks.com

Book design by Elyse Strongin, Neuwirth & Associates.

First Diversion Books edition March 2019.
Paperback ISBN: 978-1-63576-545-8
eBook ISBN: 978-1-63576-544-1

Printed in the U.S.A.

3 5 7 9 10 8 6 4 2

ACKNOWLEDGMENTS

I am grateful to all who have taught me, including those who generously offered their stories for this book. Thanks to my agent, Jessica Faust, and editors Lia Ottaviano and Keith Wallman, who loved this book and shepherded it through. To Nancy Selfridge, thank you for believing in the value of this project and for your ongoing support. Thanks to Paul L. Wachtel for breaking the bonds of polarized thinking and laying the foundation for this book. And to Barron, my first-editor-in-residence, thank you for being as good an editor as you are a husband. I love you.

CONTENTS

FOREWORD

Paul L. Wachtel

It is difficult to escape how powerfully this book addresses the central problem of our current political life. Its title resonates with what we see every time we turn on the television news or open a newspaper. We are all challenged to find our stance with regard to the fragile bully who seeks to dominate and, at the same time, to feed his neediness and prop up a self always on the verge of imploding.

But for many people, the problem of the fragile bully is not just "out there"—on the newsfeed or even in the impact of policies that make us increasingly vulnerable and at odds with each other. It is a problem even closer to home. It is in the bedroom, in the phone call to mother, in the interaction with our child's teacher, in the office, and, for some, in our relation to *ourselves*.

It is rare for a book to weave together successfully the intimately psychological and the broadly social and cultural. It is even rarer to do so with graceful prose, wit, vivid narrative, and a sense of personal intimacy with the author, of sitting across the table from her and having a real conversation. This is what Laurie Helgoe has accomplished, with both a light hand and deep seriousness.

Helgoe's canvas is broad ranging. She moves easily from ancient myths to today's headlines, from examples that every reader will find familiar to scholarly and authoritative summaries of the literature of psychoanalysis and psychological research. She probes the depth of individual experience, explores the dynamics of couples and families, and makes plain how all of this derives both from the powerful impact of our earliest experiences and from the equally powerful impact of our current interactions and current social and cultural context. In her hands, there is no contradiction in this complex web of causality, just a rich tapestry of interwoven threads that create a life.

This seemingly effortless linkage between the intimately psychological and the broadly social and cultural is one of the great achievements of this book. All too often these are treated as separate realms and explored in separate silos. Helgoe breaks down those silos, offering us an integrative account of people whose internal world and actual daily experiences continually and reciprocally shape each other.

The book is especially sharp and perceptive in its account of the ironic, often self-perpetuating patterns that are elicited in interacting with the combination of aggression and vulnerability that characterizes narcissistic personality dynamics. Helgoe articulates the different forms such dynamics can take and the different pulls that each form, each balance between these two poles, can exert. Many readers will experience both a shock of recognition—a sense that she "gets it"—and, at the same time, a fresh perspective that can help to recenter and find alternatives.

Those alternatives are not easy to reach and harder still to maintain. The emotions stirred by *both* the aggression *and* the vulnerability lead us, repeatedly, to respond in ways that keep the pattern going even when we think we are working to change it. In this, Helgoe is a steady, strong, yet gentle guide, providing useful examples of how one can begin to interact in ways that have at least a chance of having a different outcome.

Importantly, Helgoe does not take the easy path of making the fragile bully a villain. Through moving examples from her own life, she shows how, not infrequently, these are people we *love*, people who can hurt us *because* we also love them, and so we get caught in the trap over and over, sometimes in the very effort to "save" them. She shows how the trap we get caught in, in interacting with them often, catches them as well, causing pain in all parties.

At the same time—and important in the current political era—she does not absolve behavior that is destructive or place all narcissists on the same moral plane. Some narcissists deal with their fragility and inner emptiness in ways that are so externally directed, so compulsively driven to deny their doubts, so prodigiously lacking in even the most fundamental empathy for others, that their path is almost exclusively strewn with the pain of others. Such is the current denizen of the White House, and Helgoe makes no excuses for him.

But she does insist—correctly in my view—that the problem is never *just* in the damaged personality of the single individual. As she puts it, "As much as narcissism looks like a solo act, it is better understood as a dance." In Trump's case, it is a dance in which tens of millions of people are participating, people who address (and often simultaneously exacerbate) their own needs and insecurities through identification with someone who—however insincerely and hollowly—seems to say "I am strong and I will look out for you," and who express the anger that arises from their frustrations and feelings of being left behind through a voice that seems to make acceptable feelings that once had to hide in the shadows.

As Helgoe illustrates aptly and with keen insight throughout this book, escaping from the trap is not easy. Narcissistic patterns are like flypaper. Each step we take to extricate ourselves is as likely to entrap us further. When the absence of empathy that is one of the toxins of the narcissistic way of life seeps into the body politic, it becomes easier to divide the world into "us" and "them" and to discard concern for the feelings and point of view of those who we see as "them." This just perpetuates our divisions and the erosion of empathy that is both the source and the result of those divisions. If we are really to get off the flypaper and back to a normal, thriving society, we need *more* empathy, not less. We need to work to change our politics, but we also need to understand the needs, hurts, perceptions, and aspirations of those who have been vulnerable to getting caught in the web of a fragile bully. And we need to work to create a society in which their needs—not just material needs, but needs for respect, needs to be heard, needs to belong—are genuinely met.

I wish this book were not as timely as it is. But at least the current (hopefully temporary) crisis we face has contributed to prompting a book that will have value for struggling individuals, couples, and families long after the current baleful era is over. Written with wit, wisdom, and empathy, *Fragile Bully* is a map to the exit ramps on a highway that can look like an endless closed circle.

—Paul L. Wachtel, PhD
Distinguished Professor of Psychology,
City College of New York

INTRODUCTION

FRAG·ILE ˈfrajəl, ˈfraˌjīl/ (adjective): easily damaged, broken, or harmed.

BUL·LY ˈbo͝olē/ (noun): a person who threatens to hurt someone, often forcing that person to do something.

FRAGILE BULLY (noun): a person who repeatedly threatens and intimidates others—passively or aggressively—into feeding his or her grandiose self, while remaining convinced that he or she is the victim: narcissist.

"The story changes, but one thing remains the same," Christina told me. "He is always the victim, and he is always the hero." Christina and I were sharing a breakfast meeting to talk about the book I was writing—and her story.[1] Christina had been with Jim twelve years and loved him, but, more and more, hated him. She was tired. Even as his bullying escalated, she told me, it was hard to walk away: "I thought of him as an orange. Like a navel orange, bumpy and bruised on the outside. If I could just peel the skin off, I could get to this delicious, juicy, fresh inside."

The archetypal narcissist is a crazymaker, at once needy and aggressive, desperate for love and yet rejecting of it, fragile child and bully. The relationship contract with the narcissist requires emptying the self and assuming the role of mirror and echo.

Christina had fallen into a destructive dance with a fragile bully, a vicious circle in which attempted solutions fed the problem. He saw her efforts to repair their interactions as evidence that she hated him, which hooked her into trying harder, which further aroused his paranoia. This is the maddening paradox of engaging a narcissist. We see the potential and we see the problem, and both are intoxicating. For Christina, the potential was the kind and heroic man to whom she'd been given exclusive access. The problem—his blocked potential—was a special challenge entrusted to her. Jim was a generous and lovable man who consistently lied to her but had never been physically abusive—until he inflicted a blow that required her to undergo brain surgery. He was now out of her house but not out of her mind. The intoxicating pull was still there. They were talking every day.

The fragile bully paradox is at the heart of pathological narcissism. Jim seemed vulnerable, misunderstood, and deserving of special consideration. He also was "full of himself" and more than willing to sacrifice truth and loyalty in favor of attention and power. And when Christina confronted his lies, Jim made himself her victim, pressuring her to abandon her own interests and protect him.

As much as destructive narcissism consumes relationships, American culture has a particular talent for feeding the beast. Where there is narcissism, there is drama, and reality TV is ready to capture it.

Divas with big jewelry and dyed hair, so-called victims whose attacks on others are always justified, spew venom to the camera. Slighted bullies.

Commentators with their authoritative take on the world get more and more room to openly insult the object of their commentary. Bullies only defending their positions.

A billionaire tycoon flaunts his power over his celebrity staff, barking out "You're fired!" as the recurring punchline. Bully by virtue of position.

Said tycoon becomes presidential candidate in an election marked by low blows justified as self-defense, and the drama of the fragile bully finds a home in the White House.

It is convenient to sit back and watch the narcissistic displays, admiring or cringing, but doing no more than reacting. As much as problematic narcissism looks like a solo act, it is better understood as a dance. To see ourselves as above narcissistic needs, while dehumanizing those who openly display these needs, is to walk right into the dance. In fact, a recent study showed that viewers who indulge in media showcases for narcissism, such as reality TV and political talk shows, tend to score higher on a scale measuring narcissism.[2] And though President Trump has been an easy focal point for anxieties about narcissism, we can only single him out when we forget that he is a freely elected representative, or when we ignore studies that show increasing levels of narcissism among U.S. presidents or disregard the immense appeal of narcissistic drama.[3]

Whatever part we may play in the dance, narcissism is us. And while our culture exhibits an increased tolerance for destructive narcissism, that is only part of the story. Contemporary research by Craig Malkin and his colleagues affirms what pioneers like Heinz Kohut first recognized: narcissism does not need to be unhealthy, and the absence of narcissism is as debilitating as its destructive counterpart.[4] The problem is, destructive narcissism is designed to captivate, and in our society, it seems to be getting a good deal of traction.

How do we restore health to a society that indulges the destructive forces of narcissism? How do we contend with our own appetites for narcissistic drama? How do we deal with the fragile bullies in our lives—and in ourselves? These are the questions that inspired me to write this book.

Why I Wrote *Fragile Bully*

After the 2016 election, when articles on narcissism were displacing political discourse, I felt like I was observing something very familiar. I was in the middle. A man who came to be our leader, a man I knew would be in my life for better or for worse, elicited feelings—for me and for many—that I had experienced before. These were uncomfortable feelings: shock, embarrassment, rage, sometimes disgust and contempt, sometimes fascination. I also felt uncomfortable about the retaliations against this man and protective of those who loved and supported him. He reminded me, in some ways, of a man I loved and supported.

That man was my father, and while he would not be a fan of Twitter, he was prone to rants. His narcissistic personalization of issues, from politics to art preferences, made discussion of differences both toxic and dangerous. Dad used his family as a sounding board for his tirades about CBS, which he dubbed the "Communist Broadcasting System." And he easily shifted to victim mode when challenged. This man could also be warm and funny and was the one who encouraged my aspirations and praised my accomplishments. I felt every emotion on the spectrum in relation to him. As a girl, I admired his intellect and creativity, even as I sensed and defended his fragility. As a woman, I learned to expect more, and my protectiveness gave way to anger and resentment. Eventually, after specializing in personality as a psychologist, undergoing a personal analysis, and benefitting from the softening influence of time, narcissism loosened its hold on our relationship. But I wasn't alone in my relationship to my dad. I have nine siblings, and as I observed their relationships to him—some loyal and idealizing, some combative, others caretaking—I realized that these roles had their own shifts and evolution. My mother was more quietly present, and the significance of her role took me much longer to appreciate.

Fast forward to 2016. As I read post-election Facebook and Twitter feeds, I was catapulted back to my childhood home and the futile interactions I observed there. As I read rants and observed friends and family members vying for the correct take on the situation, everything seemed personal, and the reactions too easily became vicious. What stood out to me is how our attempts to contend with the combination of fragility and aggression only fed the fragility and aggression. Responses to narcissism perpetuated narcissism. I saw people moving in predictable dance steps. And even as they complained about the state of affairs, they stayed right on tempo.

Fragile Bully: Understanding Our Destructive Affair with Narcissism in the Age of Trump looks at what happens when the fragile bully dynamic gains power in a relationship and in a culture. Until we recognize our participation in the dynamic, we are powerless to change the steps.

A Preview

You likely picked up this book because "fragile bully" sparked something in you—a memory, a current struggle, the image of a difficult person in your life. While the concept of the fragile bully will not account for every instance of narcissism, I believe it gets to the crux of the reflexive, repetitive, and destructive patterns that characterize relationships governed by narcissism. The book is divided into three parts. Part I reviews the various ways we talk about narcissism and introduces the fragile bully and his frequent counterpart, Echo. In this context, "bully" refers not just to direct forms of intimidation but also passive maneuvers, such as threatening self-harm or oppressing others with martyred outbursts. Part II discusses the vicious circles, or destructive dances, that emerge in the fragile bully's relationships. We look closely at six of these dances, show how they play out in relationships and in public discussions, and explore how to change the steps. Part III explores the losses we encounter when we let go of familiar patterns and how we can begin—as individuals and as citizens—to engage responsibly and authentically, rather than reflexively.

PART
I

1

NARCISSISM BY MANY NAMES

Fear of a name increases fear of the thing itself.
–J. K. ROWLING

Narcissism is easier felt than defined. We sense it through our own responses: fascinated and curious, shocked and irate, helpless, used, riveted. We feel bullied yet compelled to hang around—either to take care of the bully or to try to win the losing battle. We freely respond with the label "narcissist," often in retaliation, and those labeled don't seem to care anyway. Sometimes the label seems our only defense against that person in our life we can't seem to reach—and also can't seem to ignore. But what is narcissism anyway? Beyond the basic association with "self-absorption," the word conjures a myriad of meanings. At once, narcissism is a developmental phase, a personality trait existing on a continuum, and a full-fledged psychiatric disorder. This chapter looks at two divergent ways of understanding narcissism, starting with the healthy and natural and proceeding to the diagnostic extreme of pathological narcissism. (In Chapter 2, we'll explore the murky and complex in-between.)

Necessary Narcissism

Inflated narcissism is normal—for babies and toddlers. The infant enters the world in survival mode and is necessarily self-centered. The world *should* revolve around this new being. Baby cries, someone responds. A sucking, "rooting" reflex produces the breast or bottle. Caregiver pulls away the soiled source of discomfort and gently provides a soft, fresh diaper. The fearful, flailing baby calms as the caregiver swaddles her in a tight blanket. In healthy development, the infant sees others as extensions of the self, picking up each cue and responding—a symbiosis of need and satiation.

These early caregiver responses assure the infant that she is safe: she can trust the world to sense her need and respond in turn. But the dance of narcissism takes on new significance as the infant begins to develop a sense of self. As the philosopher Martin Buber stated, "Man becomes an I through a thou." When another, independent person mirrors and responds to us, we see our own reflection and internalize a sense of who we are. Adults naturally mirror and mimic the self-discovering toddler. I recall my sixteen-month-old son, sitting in a high chair, surrounded by his extended family at a reunion. He started waving his hands up and down, and without missing a beat, the family chorus below him responded with the same gesture. Delighted and empowered, he squealed with satisfaction, and the dance of expression and response continued.

These simple mirroring responses help the growing child construct a sense of self. It is as if the toddler notes, "So *that's* what I'm doing. That's how I look, how I sound." This crucial feedback may be denied when parents are too preoccupied with their own concerns to mirror the child, or when they are threatened by the child's growing competence and independence. According to Heinz Kohut, whose theory of self psychology focused on the importance of mirroring, the optimal response is an empathic one: one that tunes into and reflects the child's experience. Gradually, through the "thou," the child becomes an "I," constructing an internalized representation of the self.

And even more gradually, the child begins to separate what is self and what is other and learns to relate to others as an independent participant. Developmental researcher and psychoanalyst Margaret Mahler saw this awakening to the self as so central, she called it the "psychological birth" of the child.[1]

For Mahler, who took psychoanalytic study to its source by directly observing mother-child interactions, healthy narcissism peaks along with the toddler's radical assertion of independence—first steps. She observed with some surprise that healthy toddlers took their first steps *away from* rather than *toward* the primary caregiver. Now able to explore the world on his own, the little one basks in a heady feeling of competence and invincibility. Others cheer him on, and he revels in the spotlight. Mahler observed, "The child is exhilarated by his own capacities—he wants to share and show...he acts as though he were enamored of the world and with his own grandeur and omnipotence."[2]

Until he falls. He crashes and cries, seeks security in mommy or daddy, gets up, reclaims his power, and the process repeats. Knocked, over and over again, between invincibility and powerlessness, the healthy child eventually strikes a compromise. He is not omnipotent, nor is he completely helpless.

This is the dance of healthy developmental narcissism. Reconciling narcissistic yearnings with human limitations is a challenging, and often lifelong, task. As we come to terms with our own limits, we also learn that others cannot perfectly meet our needs—they are limited too, with needs of their own.

Psychologically healthy adults can still access that heady, "top of the world" feeling, but they aren't blinded by it. We see healthy narcissism in the form of ambition, self-confidence, and a sense of personal effectiveness. Malkin describes healthy narcissism as the ability to view oneself through "*slightly* rose colored glasses."[3] Individuals with this type of narcissism approach new goals with confidence, often overestimating the ease with which they will fulfill the task. Yet, like the two-year-old taking first steps, these lofty dreams can be the very fuel propelling psychologically healthy adults through life's inevitable falls and scrapes. On the other hand, narcissistically impaired individuals have the lofty dreams but are less able to tolerate the humbling effects of reality. They may deny, avoid, or distort those realities, or conversely, suffer intense shame and self-punishment.

The Disorder

At the other extreme from healthy narcissism is the diagnosis of Narcissistic Personality Disorder (NPD) or, more broadly, pathological narcissism. The most recent version of the Diagnostic and Statistical Manual of Mental Disorders (DSM-5) describes NPD as "a pervasive pattern of grandiosity, need for admiration, and lack of empathy."[4] Let's look at each of these elements separately.

Pervasive pattern implies that the symptoms are not just phase-related, such as adolescent self-preoccupation, or situation-specific, such as the high one might feel in response to an adoring audience. The narcissistic pattern becomes most noticeable in adult relationships, but a recent analysis of longitudinal data found that certain childhood traits, such as social attention getting, lack of stable self-esteem, and the need for control predicted narcissistic psychopathology in adulthood.[5]

All personality disorders come with their own "pervasive pattern." In contrast to other mental health disorders, personality disorders are a product of an individual's *adaptation* woven into the fabric of his or her character. This is why individuals with personality disorders often do not experience distress or a desire to change. For example, people who suffer from Obsessive-Compulsive Disorder typically feel intense distress about their symptoms, even as they feel compelled to engage in the problematic behaviors. By contrast, people exhibiting features of the related *personality disorder*—Obsessive-Compulsive Personality Disorder—are often comfortable with, or even proud of, their attention to order and rules and may criticize those who don't conform to their standards.

For the individual with NPD, the features of *grandiosity* and *need for admiration* represent two sides to what has been called the "narcissistic paradox."[6] The grandiose individual feels superior and special. She vastly overestimates her capacities, denies human vulnerabilities, and assumes only special people are able to comprehend her. This self-inflation tends to push others aside and cast them as dispensable admirers. On the other hand, her need for admiration exposes vulnerability, revealing a lacking sense of self and the need for constant reassurance and praise from those in her world. This paradox is central to the fragile bully dynamic we'll be discussing in this book. Though the "need for admiration" criteria suggests vulnerability, critics have noted that the current DSM diagnostic criteria neglect the more fragile presentations of a subgroup of narcissists. Those who drafted the fifth revision of the DSM in 2013 proposed an alternative NPD diagnosis for research purposes, and this version better acknowledges the dual nature of narcissism.[7] However, because so much of available research uses the current criteria, existing data may both underrepresent and oversimplify the disorder.

The final basic feature, *lack of empathy*, is described in the DSM-5 as an unwillingness to "recognize or identify with the feelings and needs of others."[8] This need to be separate from others stems from grandiosity; however, lack of empathy may also relate to the narcissist's excessive neediness. In the latter case, empathy, which would put the focus on someone else, interferes with the narcissist's need for others to constantly focus on and mirror him. The talent of the narcissistic person to turn everything around and make it "about them" exempts them from practicing empathy toward others.

The DSM-5 goes beyond this general description to outline specific criteria, introducing related features such as "interpersonally exploitative," "sense of entitlement," and "envious of others or believes that others are envious of him or her."[9] If five out of nine listed criteria are evident "in a variety of contexts," the diagnosis may be applied.

If you are nodding as you think of people who fit this description, you may assume NPD is common. Researchers who have tested samples resembling the general population have found the contrary. A systematic review of studies looking at the prevalence of NPD in the general population found an average estimate of 1.06%, meaning only one in about one hundred people meet the criteria for NPD.[10] If we focus in on the U.S. population, two large studies revealed contrasting results: one was unable to find anyone in their sample who met all the conditions for the diagnosis, while another found that NPD described 6.2% of their sample.[11] Men are more likely to meet the criteria than women, and narcissism is more common among extraverts than introverts. However, as we've discussed, the criteria used for NPD in these studies is based on DSM criteria emphasizing the grandiose features of narcissism. Grandiosity is more socially condoned for men, and, as an outward-directed trait, is more associated with extraversion. When research incorporates "vulnerable" forms of narcissism—which we will discuss later in this chapter—more women and introverts meet the criteria.[12]

When the Lack of a Problem Is the Problem

Though the DSM-5 provides a useful diagnostic template, pathological narcissism may be present without the diagnosis of NPD. To receive a psychiatric diagnosis, one has to present as sick—the person either feels bad or has a life that isn't working. People with personality impairments, especially those of a narcissistic variety, don't usually feel sick—though the people around them may feel quite ill. The personality dysfunction may disrupt the person's life and relationships, but the one with the problem often seems the most oblivious of trouble. Franz Alexander offered a useful distinction between disorders that locate the problem within—*autoplastic disorders*—and those that locate the problem outside the person—*alloplastic disorders.*[13] Whereas autoplastic disorders like depression and anxiety disorders create suffering in the diagnosed person, personality disorders represent a way of defending against, or walling-off, the distress that might be imposed by life and relationships. The disorder may be the very thing holding the person together—while at the same time holding that person in dysfunctional patterns and away from help. Pathological narcissism is not a temporary ailment but rather a reliable way of being in the world. It is *ego-syntonic.* The ego—referring here to the executive function of the personality—is in on it. Far from feeling a need to change, the afflicted person may revel in the very characteristics that cause distress to others.

Interestingly, a large, nationally representative study by Stinson and his associates found a significant negative relationship between NPD and dysthymic disorder—a chronic form of depression—among their study subjects.[14] Narcissism seems to repel depression. In fact, therapists see it as a positive sign when a narcissistic person feels distress and motivation to change. Like an alcoholic who "hits bottom," a hurting narcissist has the best chance of seeking help.

Though our conversations tend to isolate and focus on its pathological extreme, narcissism comes in many varieties and intensities. In the next chapter, we'll explore these complexities along with a model for understanding how they relate— the fragile bully matrix.

2

THE FRAGILE BULLY MATRIX

The Matrix is everywhere. It is all around us. Even now,
in this very room. You can see it when you look out your
window or when you turn on your television.

–MORPHEUS, *The Matrix* (1999)

The proliferation of articles on narcissism reveal our fascination with the subject, while our discussions of narcissists tend to cut them off from the rest of humanity. When people use the word "narcissist," they conjure a certain image: puffed chest, bold, showy, big talker—probably male and probably an extravert. In other words, a grandiose narcissist. We also tend to see narcissism as a pathology rather than what it is: a quality of personality we all exhibit in varying degrees. Narcissism becomes pathological only at its extremes, when it either defines the personality or is notable for its absence. More and more, clinicians and researchers are revealing that narcissism comes in more than one variety and in a range of intensities. Understanding narcissism means seeing where each of us falls within the complex matrix of these dimensions.

The Two Sides of Narcissism

A review of the literature on pathological narcissism reveals a number of different classifications, some with three subtypes, and some with four or more.[1] But when we look at these various systems, we find that they tend to cluster into two general categories.

First, we have the commonly recognized "overt," exhibitionistic, aggressive, "phallic" form of narcissism. Some have labeled this type an "oblivious" narcissist, noting the lack of sensitivity he or she exhibits toward the needs and feelings of others. Though there are likely many variations on the theme, these descriptions fall best into the category of *grandiose subtype* and most closely match our stereotypic image of the narcissist as well as the DSM diagnosis.

The second group of characteristics fit what many experts have identified as the *vulnerable subtype*, sometimes referred to as "covert" or "introverted" narcissism. In contrast to the oblivious presentation of the grandiose narcissist, vulnerable narcissists are hypersensitive to what others think of them. Rather than using bullying and aggression, they maintain control over relationships through their fragility. Both subtypes share a propensity toward self-absorption—they just express this tendency differently. In 2003, researchers at Penn State found validation for the grandiose and vulnerable subtypes in a nonclinical but symptomatic sample.[2]

The question remains: are these subtypes distinct or two sides of the same phenomenon? The short answer seems to be "yes." While studies have found distinct features for the two subtypes, such as differences in self-esteem and introversion-extraversion, shared features are also evident.[3] Miller and his associates identified a common trait of "interpersonal antagonism," encompassing characteristics such as lack of empathy, entitlement, distrust and reactive anger, while Krizan and Herlache use the term "entitled self-importance" to describe the unifying feature.[4] Controversies remain regarding whether the grandiose and vulnerable subtypes distinguish *people* within the spectrum of narcissism or whether the spectrum exists within individual narcissists.

In their review of the literature, researchers from the University of Graz in Austria observe that the answer to this question varies based on the population studied. They note that in the general population, grandiosity and vulnerability appear unrelated, while, among those studied in clinical settings and diagnosed with narcissistic disorders, grandiose narcissism is consistently associated with vulnerability.[5] These researchers tested this observation empirically and found that grandiose and vulnerable features converge at the pathological end of the narcissistic spectrum. Similarly, Jordan and his associates found that, at the highest levels of narcissism, subjects reported high self-esteem but revealed low unconscious self-regard.[6] "Fragile" and "bully" seem to be a particularly volatile combination.

Rather than viewing subtypes independently, it is helpful to think of the way the two poles—the opposites of "bully" and "fragile"—work in concert, with the proportion of each varying across individuals, but also manifesting differently *within* individuals. At one pole, we have narcissists who appear all bully—unaffected by others, able to charm and manipulate, more sociopathic than true narcissist. The fragility of these narcissists has more to do with a corrupt psychological structure than with acknowledged vulnerability. Essential pieces, such as a grounded, reality-based sense of self, are missing. Though the bully who requires constant worship appears strong, the demand for this narcissistic feeding reveals a weakness of the self.

At the other pole, we have someone extremely needy and vulnerable, holding interpersonal challenges at bay by hiding behind fragility. Gabbard described these "hypervigilant" narcissists as "quietly grandiose."[7] The bullying at this extreme is less obvious but comes via psychological blackmail: "If you expose any lack in me, you'll hurt me." The slightest criticism plunges the vulnerable narcissist into a well of shame. The shame itself becomes part of the narcissist's emotional ammunition removing any focus on the person communicating the complaint. This passive bullying can be particularly insidious, leaving others with a feeling of being "slimed"—as if forced to carry the narcissist's need or emotion in place of their own.

We can conceptualize a continuum between those who fit neatly into the grandiose and vulnerable subtypes. Between the narcissist who appears vulnerable or fragile and the outwardly, or "overtly," aggressive narcissist, we find fragile bullies exhibiting various combinations of grandiose and vulnerable characteristics:

Fragile ————————Fragile Bully————————Bully
(passive bully)   (fragile structure)

In the middle, we find the common pattern in which the narcissist leads with aggression but suddenly becomes fragile when others fire back. The alchemy of fragile and bully creates numerous problems for relationships—from coddling and enabling to knee-jerk combativeness—and we'll discuss these in detail in Part II of this book.

Humanizing Narcissism

With any psychiatric condition, the very discussion of the problem can create further problems, such as stereotyping and stigmatizing people who fit the description and creating sickness via labeling. Narcissism seems particularly prone to this dehumanizing influence. There are a number of reasons for this. First, people with narcissistic disorders, by investing in grandiose identities, often project to the world a caricature rather than a real and fallible human being. Interactions feel like performance, stories are larger than life, and sentiments are laid on too thick. Even a vulnerable narcissist can seem unreal by out-martyring everyone else. In an effort to cast themselves as special, narcissistic individuals dehumanize themselves, and we go along for the ride. The inflated presentation somehow frees us to ridicule and parody them, or, conversely, to pity them. We cannot take a caricature seriously, nor can we hold it accountable.

Second, the restrictiveness of the NPD diagnosis, while necessary to avoid misuse of the label, makes it easy to project all problematic narcissism onto the diagnosed few. And these diagnosed few only capture the more overtly grandiose end of the fragile-bully continuum. Developers of the DSM-5 noted that present personality disorder diagnoses represent a "categorical perspective," which looks at diagnostic categories as qualitatively different from what is seen in normal functioning. If we see people with NPD in a different category than those without the disorder, it is easier to neglect the subtler manifestations of problematic narcissism—the ways any of us can get caught up in looking good at the expense of others, for example.

Third, the label "narcissist" and the armchair diagnosis of NPD often become a defense and a retaliation for those trying to navigate a relationship with a self-focused individual. In these cases, the dehumanizing tendency may serve a protective function. With narcissism comes exploitation, haughtiness, and lack of empathy—a maddening combination that leaves those hurt grasping for a weapon. People who felt helpless in the wake of the Trump election could, by wielding the diagnosis, at least temporarily experience some feeling of power and control.

Finally, even mildly narcissistic individuals can make us uncomfortable, especially if we feel conflicted about our own desires for attention and adulation. Better to see that person as impaired than to face our own competitive or envious feelings.

The tendency to project narcissism outward was observed in a series of studies looking at perceptions of national character of Americans as a group.[8] Researchers, using measures of grandiose narcissism, found that Americans rated "Americans in general" as significantly more narcissistic than they perceived themselves to be. This externalization tendency was not observed when people rated themselves vs. typical Americans on criteria for Avoidant Personality Disorder. Narcissism seems to have a "hot potato" effect—amplified in others while minimized in ourselves.

A number of theorists and researchers have worked against these tendencies, looking at narcissism in its subtler manifestation. Malkin assigns a numerical value to the level of narcissism manifested by individuals, from someone unable to self-enhance—zero—to someone who puts self above all others and exploits others—a ten.[9] He places health in the middle of the continuum, at healthy narcissism, rather than at the narcissism-free end.

This way of understanding narcissism is consistent with our growing understanding that most psychiatric symptoms are ubiquitous, problematic when dominant but most often manageable—and sometimes beneficial. For example, the Yerkes-Dodson curve demonstrates that an optimal, moderate level of anxiety is necessary for motivation.[10] Too little anxiety equates with boredom; too much interferes with functioning. Even one of the deficits associated with schizophrenia—the inability of the brain to filter out irrelevant information—is, at more manageable levels, beneficial. The ability to produce freer mental associations is an aspect of divergent thinking, the "out of the box" vision essential to creativity. Though the developers of the DSM-5 retained the categorical approach to personality disorder diagnoses in order to maintain continuity for clinical practice, they too proposed a dimensional model as an alternative for future use. This approach, according to the authors, looks at mental disorders as "maladaptive variants of personality disorders that merge imperceptibly into normality."[11]

When we see mental disorders as rough edges of our shared humanity, we're less likely to cut ourselves out of explanations of society's ills. Narcissism does not just belong to those we call "narcissists," and the absence of narcissism is not necessarily a virtue. The field of psychoanalysis has long understood the continuity that we are increasingly recognizing in our diagnostic models. We'll look at these contributions further in the next chapter.

Current models are accounting for the emerging research on the topic, while making room for the complexity of narcissistic phenomena. Malkin's Narcissism Spectrum Scale captures the low-to-high spectrum of narcissism and the Narcissism Spectrum Model is a recent example of systems that account for variations in grandiosity and vulnerability within the narcissistic personality.[12]

How do we bring this understanding together in a cohesive framework? Perhaps science fiction can provide a wider model.

The Fragile Bully Matrix

In the 1999 movie *The Matrix*, we learn that what looks like real life is an illusion, a system that both provides people security and makes them dependent. Narcissism has much in common with this condition: it provides people a reliable, yet illusory, way of engaging with the world while keeping them dependent on maintaining the illusion. Perhaps coincidentally, I found a matrix to be the easiest way of illustrating the

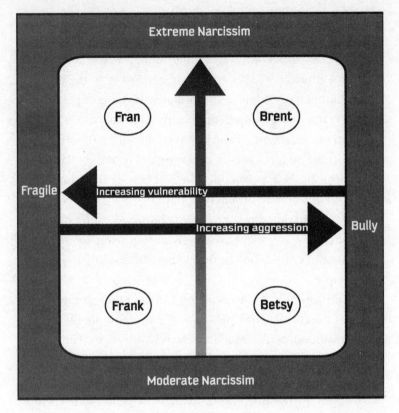

Figure 1

various manifestations of narcissism. Figure 1 incorporates the fragile-bully spectrum with the problematic end of Malkin's narcissism continuum.

Brent has a severe level of narcissism and leans toward the "bully" end of the fragile bully dynamic. He is located in the upper right portion of the matrix. He likely meets the criteria for NPD, though he probably won't be diagnosed unless he seeks treatment to complain about others in his life. He directs his narcissism, aggressively, into the world. He idealizes and seeks the favor of high-status people and rewards those who feed his inflated self by allowing them in his "in" circle. However, when others fail to respond to him approvingly, he becomes openly hostile and aggressive. Those who challenge him become his targets—and he willingly uses mocking and humiliation to punish them for not showing him the proper reverence. Brent invokes whatever methods necessary to keep Brent on top, from lying to intimidation and possibly even physical aggression.

Betsy also leans to the bully side of the fragile-bully spectrum, but she is located at the lower right corner of the matrix, exhibiting a more moderate level of narcissism. When with friends, she frequently hogs the spotlight and listens poorly. If someone doesn't mirror her enthusiasm or says they need to go when she's talking, she can react impulsively with an angry stare or a flippant comment, but her aggressive maneuvers are more benign and short-lived than Brent's. She may even occasionally catch herself and laugh at her own behaviors.

At the fragile side of the matrix, we have Fran and Frank. Fran, sitting in the upper left side of the matrix, has a severe level of narcissism, but she expresses it through her vulnerability. If her partner asks anything of her, the implication that she lacks in any way is too much for her to bear, and she breaks into tears. She complains that she is never good enough, and that she might as well give up, and may go so far as to threaten suicide. What makes her impairment severe is her ability to trap others into focusing exclusively on her feelings and continually bolstering her sense of self, even as she neglects the needs and feelings of others.

Frank, located in the lower left corner of the matrix, has a more subtle form of vulnerable narcissism. Like Fran, he is hypersensitive to criticism. If his partner hints at a possible fault in him, he becomes quiet and depressed and comments on how he can't ever seem to meet her needs. His apparent distress causes her to back off and remind him of his positive qualities. Even as he keeps her at a distance this way, he has some awareness of what he's doing and regrets the disconnection. He wants to be able to hear his partner but is afraid. Can he tolerate his partner's honesty?

These examples each favor one side of the fragile-bully spectrum, but in the coming chapters we will encounter many examples from the middle where narcissism moves in a dance between aggression and vulnerability.

Diagnosing Culture

Earlier, we discussed a series of studies looking at Americans' ratings of Americans on measures of grandiose narcissism.[13] While Americans rated Americans in general as highly narcissistic, they didn't let themselves entirely off the hook, putting themselves and acquaintances, on average, in the moderately narcissistic range. Not only did Americans see narcissism as an American attribute, this view was shared by raters from other countries, including China, Turkey, the UK, and the Basque area of Spain.

According to the DSM-5, a personality disorder is a pervasive and inflexible pattern "that deviates markedly from the expectations of the individual's culture."[14] But what if the expectations of the culture are inherently unhealthy? What if the narcissistically impaired fit in just fine and some are hugely successful?

And what if one of those people becomes the nation's president?

Psychiatrist Allen Frances, who originally drafted the DSM criteria for narcissism, famously argued that President Trump is a "world class narcissist, but he's not mentally ill."[15] To be mentally ill, a person needs to show signs of distress or impairment. Far from sources of distress or societal maladjustment, Donald Trump's grandiose declarations and antagonistic behaviors seemed key to his success. Frances argues in his book, *The Twilight of American Sanity*, that Trump's rise is a symptom, not the sole cause, "of a world in distress."[16]

Other mental health professionals have suggested that the psychopathology in our midst *is* Donald Trump. In the book, *The Dangerous Case of Donald Trump*, twenty-seven prominent mental health experts broke with restrictions on assessing a public figure in order to warn the public of Trump's dangerous capabilities.[17] In addition, petitions by scores of mental health professionals—one with more than 70,000 signatures at the time it closed—declared Trump mentally ill and unfit to lead and called for his removal from office.[18]

These two perspectives comprise a healthy and vigorous debate on the role of mental health professionals. On one side, experts warn against the weaponizing of psychiatric diagnoses, or the use of these diagnoses to further political aims. On the other side, professionals argue that it is untenable to expect trained professionals to withhold their observations when public health is at risk. They also cite our ethical duty to warn when we determine that someone poses a danger to themselves or others.

Though this debate can appear as polarized as the ones on the political floor, there are important areas of agreement. Most mental health professionals, including this author, agree that we cannot formally diagnose a public figure without conducting a first-hand clinical evaluation. Determining mental illness is not even the main point. While voicing a variety of perspectives, contributors to *The Dangerous Case of Donald Trump* are careful to point out that presidents suffering from mental illness can lead effectively.[19] Abraham Lincoln, who suffered greatly from depression, faced some of the nation's gravest challenges with courage and wisdom.[20] The authors focus instead on the question of dangerousness, as well as a concern also voiced by Frances: Is there something larger at play? Have we skewed our sense of what is acceptable and trustworthy? Psychohistorian Robert Jay Lifton uses the term "malignant normality" to describe the collective desensitization to, and acceptance of, what is dangerous and destructive.[21] I'm not so sure that we accept the displays we are viewing as normal—some find Trump refreshing because he's *not* conventional. However, content we find disturbing is often, at the same time, compelling, entertaining, and tantalizingly addictive—and too easily comes to register as acceptable.

Where these two perspectives seem to agree is that there is something not right—even dangerous—about what we have come to accept as the status quo.

Mental health diagnoses are culture-bound. Even if the expectations of one's culture promote excessive self-focus and feelings of entitlement—a point argued by authors Christopher Lasch in 1979, and Jean Twenge and W. Keith Campbell in 2009—those expectations will set the standard of health for diagnosticians.[22] Lasch, who points to trends such as the human potential movement, the advertising industry's promotion of consumption and envy, and the theatrics of politics, argues that American society had become "the society of the spectacle," promoter of narcissism.[23] Based on their analysis of data from generations of students who had taken the Narcissistic Personality Inventory (NPI) while in college, Twenge and Campbell cite a dramatic increase in narcissism scores between the mid-1980s and 2008.[24] The authors blame increasing rates of narcissism on cultural trends such as parenting practices emphasizing children's specialness separate from achievement, easy access to credit, and the new media's "transmission of narcissism."

Malkin has challenged the significance of the above data, noting that (a) the NPI does not distinguish healthy and unhealthy narcissism, and (b) college students have naturally higher—and transient—levels of narcissism.[25] Also, authors arguing for a culture of narcissism generally confine their discussions to the grandiose form of narcissism. Vulnerable narcissism doesn't seem to hold as much social capital in the United States as its grandiose counterpart.

It seems safe to conclude that narcissism, at least in its grandiose form, is woven into the character of our society—and that this is not all bad. We have the "right" to pursue individual happiness, and we thrive on capitalism, which promotes aggression and self-enhancement. At our best, we are an incredibly generative and productive society. We are also a democratic nation with checks and balances on power.

But some would argue that destructive narcissism is gaining on democracy. Back in the '70s, Lasch observed the way President Kennedy created a sense of crisis to justify increased executive power. He wrote, "No other president exemplified so completely the subordination of policy to national prestige, to the appearance and illusion of national greatness."[26] As we reflect on President Trump's "Make America Great Again" campaign, Lasch's comment seems naïve. While we're tempted to see Trump as a narcissistic outlier, there is evidence that his rise is part of the trend observed by Lasch. A retrospective analysis of U.S. presidents from Washington to G.W. Bush shows an increasing prevalence of grandiose narcissism.[27] The authors found that high levels of grandiose narcissism predicted both positive and negative leadership qualities. However, the study also found that when vulnerable narcissism—the formula for a fragile bully—entered the picture, presidents were more likely to engage in unethical behaviors and to sacrifice effective policy in service of political success.

If we agree that our society accepts and rewards problematic narcissism, and we know that we cannot *diagnose* a narcissistic disorder unless an individual noticeably deviates from what society expects, we have to conclude that pathological narcissism is underdiagnosed in our culture. It is right to be conservative about parceling out diagnoses, but it is time to resolve the split between the diagnosed few and the cultural promotion of narcissism. Narcissism is typically not as dramatic as seen in our chosen narcissist mascots—even when that mascot is a president—nor is it as benign as self-perceptions suggest.

In the next chapter, we look at narcissism, not as an isolated disorder but as a dynamic, living system, which is fed, and potentially transformed, through our interactions—through the dance of narcissism.

3

NARCISSUS ON THE COUCH

I think that the overcoming of a hypocritical attitude toward
narcissism is as much required today as was the overcoming
of sexual hypocrisy a hundred years ago.

–HEINZ KOHUT, 1972,
"Thoughts on Narcissism and Narcissistic Rage"

Though the ancient myth of Narcissus tells of the ills of excessive self-focus, the clinical understanding of narcissism is a recent invention. Some would say that narcissists are a recent invention, spawned by increased self-focus in modern society, but there are plenty of figures in history and literature to suggest that representatives of the disorder were alive and kicking before the terminology came around. The field of psychoanalysis, popularized by Sigmund Freud in the early 1900s, started the conversation about pathological narcissism. But it wasn't until the 1960s and '70s, as psychoanalysis evolved into new forms, namely self-psychology and object relations theory, that therapists started to crack the code for how to deal with the people that people didn't want to deal with.

The Couch, Revisited

Popular images of psychoanalysis—the patient on the couch and the silent analyst seated behind and out of sight—have not caught up with developments in the broader field of psycho-analytic psychotherapy. Rather than the old model of hosting sessions four or five times a week, today's analytic therapists typically meet with patients from one to three times a week and often work within constraints imposed by health insurance. Instead of reclining on a couch, the patient usually sits across from the therapist, with chairs angled out to allow the patient to escape the therapist's gaze.

However, even in traditional psychoanalysis, the function of the couch is not to create distance but—quite the opposite—to allow patients the comfort and freedom to express themselves without censorship, to share feelings about the analyst without interference, and to promote an intimacy between the analyst and the inner experience of the patient. Far from being untouched and distant, the analyst likewise is trained to access his or her own responses and feelings and to use them to make real and healing connections with the patient. I recall a moment in my own analysis when I was complaining about my husband's expectations. Rather than nodding her head and supporting my perception, my analyst shared with me, "I think I might be feeling a little of what your husband experiences." We had a strong enough relationship for her to share with me the way I was reproducing an old story of my resistance to parental expectations, both with my husband and with her. Her disclosure was hard for me to hear, but it helped me see something that others were likely unwilling to tell me.

This experience speaks to another misconception about psychoanalytic work: the idea that the analyst reinforces narcissism. That may be true of an inexperienced or poorly trained practitioner, and it is a potential trap in any kind of therapy. To simply support and empathize with the woes of the patient can inadvertently condone destructive patterns.

This willingness of therapists to analyze their own responses is especially important when working with personality disorders. As we've discussed, those in a relationship with someone with a personality impairment are often the ones who feel the impact of the disorder. Personality disorders do not exist in isolation. A person's interactions in their formative years may produce problems, but ongoing interactions keep those problems alive. This is why psychoanalysts are required to go through psychoanalysis themselves: analysts have the potential to do much good, but they can also do great harm if they act without self-awareness. Analysts in training expose themselves to the same psychological scrutiny that their patients will experience. In addition, the practicing analyst not only looks at each patient's "transference"—the projection of longstanding patterns into the analytic encounter—but is also required to monitor how she responds and projects her own patterns— the "countertransference"—onto that relationship.

Let's look at an example. Stewart comes to therapy with complaints about people in his life who just don't seem to "get" him. He is sure the therapist, a well-respected expert in the field, will understand him and help him figure out how to explain himself to others. The therapist may have any number of reactions depending on his own psychological makeup. For example, he could get hooked by the patient's flattery and feel ready to show the patient that he is indeed the only one who can understand him. Conversely, he might feel hostile toward the patient, sensing his arrogance and wanting to knock him down a notch. If he acts on these responses, the therapist misses an opportunity to learn more about the patient's world and use the information therapeutically. He simply becomes another person in the patient's world who dances right in step with the disorder. In my psychoanalytic work with patients, I frequently comment on my own reaction and invite the patient to look at it with me: what is happening here that is making me want to react this way? A potential toxic and destructive interaction becomes a study tool for us to work with.

How To Make a Narcissist

For most psychiatric disorders, the answer to the question of cause, of nature vs. nurture, is "yes." In other words, nature's raw material, or genetics, sets down a vulnerability to certain problems, while nurture—bad parenting or environmental trauma—can activate the vulnerability and produce psychiatric symptoms. Studies of the genetics and neurobiology of Narcissistic Personality Disorder are extremely limited but give some preliminary indication that deficits in the capacity for empathy may contribute to narcissistic psychopathology.[1] More than psychiatric conditions such as schizophrenia, however, the expression of problematic narcissism appears tied to the influences of parenting and culture. Narcissism expert Craig Malkin went so far as to conclude that narcissists are "made, not born."[2]

But how are narcissists made? If we put narcissism on the couch, or the comfortable chair, the answer may vary depending on who is doing the analysis.

Anyone studying the development of narcissism will encounter two key theorists: Heinz Kohut and Otto Kernberg. Both theorists helped to define Narcissistic Personality Disorder when it was first added to the psychiatric diagnostic nomenclature (*DSMIII*), and one reviewer noted that "these two authorities are the compass points by which all other theorists identify their own positions."[3] As with so many influential American psychoanalytic thinkers, both have roots in Freud's hometown of Vienna but had to flee Germany due to the Nazi invasion. Kernberg eventually landed in New York, Kohut in Chicago, and both forged new ground by working with patients even Sigmund Freud said could not be reached. While Freud had focused on neurotic disorders stemming from conflict over sexual and aggressive impulses—"Oedipal" stage conflicts—Kohut and Kernberg were part of a new cohort of analysts working with those who suffered disturbances in the nonverbal, pre-Oedipal phases of development. Both theorists founded new offshoots of the psychoanalytic method, approaches that involved more activity and involvement on the therapist's part. And both took on the challenge of understanding and treating the narcissistically impaired.

Better a Bully Than a Baby

I drew heavily on Kernberg's method during my predoctoral internship (which a fellow intern had dubbed "psychotherapy boot camp") at the Devereux Foundation in Pennsylvania. My training there involved providing twice-weekly psychoanalytic psychotherapy to adolescents categorized as "emotionally disturbed." These were students who would typically be considered ineligible for analytic therapy due to their impulsivity and severe conduct problems—students who had to be educated in a residential setting due to the same concerns. Though I was initially terrified, the combination of excellent supervision, the residential structure, and Kernberg's indirect guidance helped me stay anchored enough to help these troubled teens.

As I sat in my consulting office across from an angry and very large eighteen-year-old skinhead, I was grateful I had studied Kernberg. My client had suffered abuse, neglect, and an insecure home life, and now was set on intimidating and controlling everything and everyone he encountered. He wore large work boots, a shaved head, and a stare that carried an implicit threat. He was all bully with very little evidence of fragility.

The way to make a narcissist, according to Kernberg's model, is to provoke chronic frustration and rage in a developing infant. Think of the frustration you experience when you receive horrid treatment, and on top of that, those to whom you appeal for help respond vacantly, with no comprehension of what you're going through—even puzzled as to why you are complaining. Now imagine you are completely dependent on that treatment. It's all you've got. To remain isolated with this extreme vulnerability, this impotent rage, is intolerable. What to do?

When parents are chronically unresponsive and narcissistically preoccupied themselves, the infant is left frustrated, helpless—holding the burden of unanswered rage. The child's only avenue to relief is to project these markers of helplessness onto the caregivers: "I'm not enraged—they are. I'm the stable one." Relieved of rage but still vulnerable, the child finds refuge in the *grandiose self*.

The grandiose self holds the admired aspects of the self, along with the qualities of the idealized caretaker. This part of the self rejects any awareness of neediness or fallibility. When the child feels needy, the grandiose self transforms this feeling into boredom and emptiness. Rather than seeking care, the child learns to dominate interactions and seek excitement. No longer is the rageful infant crying out for recognition; she is bullying others she perceives as dangerous and feeding herself on the highs of grandiosity. For Kernberg, the aggression of the narcissist is a defense against intolerable need.

Because of the primitive and potentially destructive nature of the therapeutic transference, creating safety is central to Kernberg's methods. He emphasized the importance of the *therapeutic frame*. The frame can be likened to the tight, swaddling blanket that calms the cries of an agitated newborn.

Restrictions in the therapy—starting and ending on time, confidentiality, use of talk rather than action, and absence of extratherapeutic contact—assure both patient and therapist that aggressive impulses will not be allowed to destroy the therapy. By enforcing boundaries, the therapist is able to welcome the transference that causes most people in the patient's life to flee or retaliate. Kernberg's twice-weekly approach, *Transference-Focused Psychotherapy,* uses the therapy relationship as a window into the patient's internalized relationship template—or "object relations."[4] The whole field of *object relations theory* stems from the idea that we have objectified representations of people that we carry around in our heads, and that these inner "objects" end up causing more problems than the real people they represent. In addition to creating safety, the goal of transference-focused therapy is to loosen the rigidity of internalized object relations, in particular, by repairing the split between good/grandiose and bad/needy. According to Mahler, splitting is natural for the infant, who cannot yet reconcile the fact that the parent who is loving and nurturing can also be depriving.[5] Splitting protects ideal images of the self and others, even at the cost of preserving negative images in a primitive and sinister form. When I reminded my tough-looking client that my internship would be ending soon, I witnessed the split within him. He looked for a moment like a hurt child. Then the scowl came back, he stood and dug his hands into his jacket, walked out the door, and used his boot to kick a hole in the wall.

Mahler observed the challenge toddlers experience when trying to reconcile their needy selves with the grandiose, empowered self. One minute, the toddler brushes parents away declaring "do it myself!", and the next moment the little one erupts in frustration and helplessness at a task failed. Achieving *rapprochement,* the resolution of these opposites, is the psychological feat that separates healthier adults from those with severe personality disorders. No longer is the self—and the world—divided into the idealized "all good" and the devalued "all bad." That said, even healthy adults can regress to splitting to protect what they idealize. We see such regression in the current political climate, where both sides are reluctant to see wisdom in the opponent or weaknesses in their own points of view. In Part III, we'll return to the discussion of splitting to look at ways of mending our relational and cultural divisions.

Unrequited Narcissism

While Kernberg sees narcissism as a defense, Kohut regards narcissism as normal and healthy—only causing psychopathology when thwarted. Kohut, credited with the first use of the term "narcissistic personality disorder," based his entire theory—self psychology—on what he calls the "narcissistic line of development."[6] Like Kernberg, Kohut observes ways in which preoccupied parents fail to respond empathically to the developing child. But rather than viewing the grandiose self only as a defensive structure, Kohut sees grandiosity as the seedling of selfhood. A parent feeds this primitive self when delighting in and admiring the growing child. Marveling at the life one is raising is not the same as bragging or seeing that life only as an extension of oneself. Quite the opposite, this marveling is an early recognition that the child brings something of her own to the world. This is the gift of mirroring: to reflect the child back to the child.

According to Kohut, the infant requires a *selfobject*—someone experienced as part of the self but who is able to perform necessary functions for the self. These functions include: (a) mirroring and affirming the growing competence of the child, (b) soothing the child by allowing him to idealize and merge into the strength of the selfobject, and (c) allowing the child to experience a sense of belonging, or twinship, with the caregiver. This combination of parental support and strength resemble Diana Baumrind's description of "authoritative parenting," which has been widely studied and associated with better outcomes than either authoritarian (strong but not supportive) or permissive (supportive but not strong) parenting.[7] While empathic mirroring is essential, parents who try too hard may actually interfere with their child's development. According to Kohut, children benefit from "optimal frustration"—nontraumatic gaps in parental responding that allow the child to fill in these functions on her own. Instead of constantly looking to others for a nod of validation, the optimally frustrated child learns to self-validate and builds an internalized sense of self.

The way to make a narcissist, according to self psychology, is to deprive a child of competent selfobjects. Though there is not one straight route to producing a narcissist, caregivers who cannot or will not provide both mirroring and soothing put their children at risk for narcissistic fixation. For example, at the point when the child most needs affirmation and mirroring, narcissist-producing caregivers may be preoccupied with their own needs and unable or unwilling to empathically respond to the child. They may even exploit the child and look for her to mirror them, or to have the child perform so they look good. If such deprivation is pervasive, the child will emerge mirror-hungry and self-focused. Caregivers can also stunt development by shunning idealization by the child, assuring that the child's expectations of them remain low. In this way, they deprive the child of her developing sense of ideals and ability to rest in the caregivers' strength. Deprived of superheroes at this crucial stage, the child will enter the world with a sense of emptiness and hunger for idealization, perpetually holding out for a hero. Finally, depriving the child of a sense of belonging—a sense of being like mom or dad—can leave the future narcissist searching for an admired "twin" to affirm her identity. Early in Donald Trump's presidency, his apparent idealization of Vladimir Putin, whom Trump praised as a bold, fearless leader, had the flavor of a twinship transference. Putin also praised Trump, and the two were frequently dramatized in parodies as lovers. By the fall following the election, however, Putin sought to detach himself from this union, using language that reflected the intimacy of the perceived bond: "Trump is not my bride, and I'm not his groom."[8]

While the drive to meet unfulfilled selfobject needs dominates the narcissistic personality, obscuring development of relational capacities like empathy and mutuality, narcissistically healthy individuals can balance selfobject needs with relational responsibilities. They may still seek mirroring to validate their experiences but can also mirror the experiences of a friend in need. They may idealize the object of their love but can manage the imposition of reality when weaknesses are exposed. And they may find safety in identifications with people they admire without denying the other's independence and individuality.

Reinforcing Narcissism

Whether we see pathological narcissism as a defense or the result of developmental arrest, the psychodynamic view focuses on determinants in early childhood. With today's emphasis on cultural narcissism, is it possible for psychologically healthy individuals to *acquire* pathological narcissism?

According to the behavioral view of psychological problems, rewarding problematic behaviors perpetuates them. The past is not the determinant, but rather, the ongoing responses—rewards and punishments—meted out by the environment.

Robert B. Millman coined the term *acquired situational narcissism* to describe pathological narcissism brought on by privilege, fame, or wealth.[9] According to Millman, fans, media, and assistants, who feed the belief that the "star" is better and more worthy than others, can fuel even a slight tendency toward narcissism. This does propose a chicken-and-egg problem, however: do narcissists seek the kind of attention that reinforces narcissism, or does the attention itself create the narcissist?

In 1977, integrative theorist Paul L. Wachtel would answer "Yes" with his groundbreaking book, *Psychoanalysis and Behavior Therapy: Toward an Integration*. Wachtel interrupted the debate over causation with a "both-and" answer: causation occurs in a circle rather than a line, and the question of what comes first keeps us from seeing the whole problem.[10] Both childhood determinants and reinforcers in the present feed what he calls *vicious circles*. Someone with a narcissistic problem is likely to have issues from the past *and* to have all kinds of present-day reinforcers that assure he will remain a narcissist.

For example, the person stuck in a narcissistic cycle may protect her fragile self-image by intimidating others to praise and mirror her. Her intimidation may engage various vicious circles. In one, she "wins," getting the responses she desires, but without the independent volition of the other, the affirmation is empty. She soon feels alone and compelled to push for more, and on it goes. Or, her intimidation may provoke retaliation, affirming that she is a victim who needs to defend herself. The fragile and bully sides of the dynamic make it hard to exit the circle, and players increasingly enact stereotyped and dehumanizing roles.

We witnessed a prime example of such a circle in a stunt comedian Kathy Griffin staged to protest a comment Donald Trump had made about Megyn Kelly having "blood coming out of her wherever." Griffin posed with a fake, decapitated Trump head dripping with blood. Trump called the stunt

"Sick!" and referenced the difficulty his young son was having in response, and a chorus on both sides of the political fence shared his outrage. Chelsea Clinton admonished Griffin, as well. After stating that she was "merely mocking the Mocker In Chief," Griffin admitted she went too far and apologized. But the drama continued, with Griffin losing media contracts, receiving death threats, and shifting, as Trump had, from aggressor to victim. She tearfully—and somewhat accurately—stated that she had "lost everything." The loss was temporary, however, because in the world of celebrity, no publicity is bad publicity, and, sadly, the best publicity often comes with fragile bully drama.[11]

In that war of blood references, it is easy to lose the thread of causation. Griffin was reacting, but she was also starting something. And as tempting as it is to claim that Donald Trump imposed a narcissistic style onto the American people, the American people also empowered his efforts.

The vicious circles involving Trump have entered our living rooms, which allows us to witness, first hand, the magnetic pull of narcissistic dynamics. But there are other vicious circles, what I call "destructive dances," that may operate less visibly but engage us as powerfully. In Part II, we will name a variety of these dances and, for each, map the interactions that keep narcissism alive and unwell.

In the following chapters, we will meet the first partners in the dance—Narcissus and Echo—and extract that practical wisdom contained in their story.

4

NARCISSUS IS NOT ALONE: REVISITING THE MYTH

There's always another story. There's more
than meets the eye.

–W.H. AUDEN

L ong before psychoanalysts sought to explain pathological
narcissism, the myth of Narcissus provided rich insights
into the disorder. Recorded as part of the fifteen-volume
poem written by Ovid in 8 AD, the myth captures the frustration, hurt, and tragic realities known by anyone who has lived
with—or lived in the skin of—a narcissist.[1] Joseph Campbell
said that a myth is "the society's dream."[2] Let's look inside this
dream to unlock its wisdom. We'll start with the shorthand
version of the myth most of us know, and then we'll go to the
source for the whole story.

The familiar version of the myth goes something like this:

Narcissus is a physical specimen, a symbol of youth and perfection. Everyone he encounters falls in love with him. They fawn
all over him, flattering him and hungering for any indication
of his interest. Narcissus is not impressed. When suitors try to
get his attention, Narcissus dismisses their entreaties, and not

in a nice way. He is hostile and belittling. The spurned lovers want Narcissus to feel what they feel, so they curse the beautiful youth to fall in love with himself. When he sees his reflection in the pool, Narcissus does indeed feel what his suitors feel. He longs, aches to unite with that image. Unable to tear himself away, Narcissus eventually withers away and dies.

Even this surface treatment of the myth tells us much about the problem of narcissism and the dilemma of the fragile bully. We see the bully side of Narcissus as he rejects any hint of need. He projects his own neediness onto the admirers surrounding him and responds with disgust. Instead of engaging in a real relationship, he longs for his arrogant twin—the one he sees reflected in the pool. We see this tendency in grandiose narcissists. They often attach themselves to people they see as powerful and reflective of their own idealized selves while rejecting those they see as weak or needy.

The fragile side of Narcissus emerges with the curse, and he becomes plagued by the very neediness he despises. He longs for the idealized image of himself but is unable to possess and internalize it. This is the tragedy of the myth. Narcissus remains disconnected, addicted to the mirror. He cannot own and embrace himself enough to feel whole and genuinely connect with others. He becomes the spurned lover, attached to a grandiose image of himself he can never possess. The image, superficial and empty, creates only longing—never fulfillment.

In this common version, Narcissus is only a tragic figure, and he has no counterpart. Let's expand the myth and mine what is missing from its superficial rendering:[3]

Liriope, the divine river nymph, "whom once the river-god Cephisus clasped in his winding streams, and took by force under the waves," bears a child. The baby boy is so delicately formed, so beautiful, that his adoring mother asks the seer Tiresias, "Will he live to a ripe old age?" Tiresias answers: "Yes, if he does not discover himself." Liriope dismisses the prophecy, regarding it as a bundle of empty words. Instead, she revels in the baby's loveliness and lives on his radiance.

By age sixteen, Narcissus is a vision. Slender and proud, his cockiness only adds to his appeal. He entrances all he encounters, male, female, young, old. But no one can touch him. Used to a steady diet of admiration, he is unimpressed by their entreaties. More than that, the need he sees behind their longing repels him. He is fine with being admired, and thrives on that. But to be needed, to be in relationship, requires something of him. He will have nothing of it.

One day, a lovely mountain nymph, Echo, views the radiant youth "driving frightened deer into his nets," and she burns for him—"no differently than inflammable sulphur, pasted round the tops of torches, catches fire, when a flame is brought near it." Echo, fully embodied and engaging, has one limitation: her speech is restricted to the last words of others. So she follows him, waiting for words she can repeat.

At long last, Narcissus senses a presence near him and calls out, "Is anyone here?" Echo eagerly responds:

"Here!"

"Come to me!" says Narcissus. He sees no one and calls again, "Why do you run from me?"

"Why do you run from me?" Echo repeats.

Narcissus plants himself in place and proposes, "Here, let us meet together."

Thrilled, Echo replies, "Together," runs to him and, unable to contain her desire, throws her arms around his neck.

Pulling away, Narcissus responds, "Away with these encircling hands! May I die before what's mine is yours!"

Echo repeats, "What's mine is yours!"

Shamed, Echo withdraws into the woods, internalizing the feeling that once inspired hope. Her pining drains her of life. Body wasting, bones hardening into stone, only her voice remains.

Another voice can no longer bear Narcissus's cruelty. One of the spurned youths raises his hands in a plea to the Heavens: "May Narcissus love one day, so, himself, and not win over the creature whom he loves!"

Nemesis, Goddess of Vengeance, hears his plea and fulfills Tiresias's prophecy. Narcissus, hot and tired from hunting, sees a calm pool offering refreshment. As he tries to quench his thirst, another thirst grows. He sees himself.

He freezes to avoid scaring off the beautiful creature and lies prone to gaze upon him. Narcissus, now, is subject to the force that ensnared his lovers. He studies the shining eyes, the comely locks, the brush of color suggesting a response. The love is intense and immediate.

Like Echo before, Narcissus attempts to embrace his lover, trying to kiss the image hiding in the water, dipping arms under to hold the waiting body. Every time, the image flees leaving Narcissus empty.

Ovid narrates: "What you seek is nowhere, and if you turn away, you will take with you the boy you love. The vision is only shadow, only reflection, lacking any substance."

But Narcissus does not know what he sees. He refuses to leave his spot, even to eat or sleep. Finally, he cries out to the surrounding trees:

"What love, whose love, has ever been more cruel? I love him, but I cannot seem to find him! To make it worse, no sea, no road, no mountain, no city-wall, no gate, no barrier, parts us but a thin film of water…Come out, whoever you are! Where do you go when I am reaching for you? You promise, I think, some hope with a look of more than friendship. You reach out arms when I do, and your smile follows my smiling; I have seen your tears when I was tearful; you nod and beckon when I do; your lips, it seems, answer when I am talking."

As Narcissus laments, the mystery is revealed: "I know the truth at last. He is myself!" And now, his distress is complete. He resigns himself to death: "Let me look at you always, and in looking nourish my wretched passion!" Rending his garments, Narcissus is consumed by the fire of his own desire, his body gradually losing its color and strength. And, in the end when he beats his breast and cries out, "Alas!" you can hear Echo beating the shell of her body as she answers, "Alas!"

And even in Hell, Narcissus finds a pool to gaze in, again transfixed by his image.

Meanwhile, in the world above, his lovers mourn. But when they seek his body for the funeral pyre, they find nothing, "only a flower with a yellow center surrounded with white petals."

That lovely flower would carry the name "narcissus."

The Trophy Child

A detail often overlooked is that Narcissus is the product of a rape. Abandoned by his father, he lacks the guidance of a powerful river-god, a potential source of idealization and identification. Instead, Narcissus himself becomes the object of idealization. Liriope, taken by violence and also abandoned, finds refuge in this tiny symbol of perfection. Beautiful herself, she may see her own reflection in Narcissus. In fact, the Greek root of her name means "Face of the Narcissus."[4] We witness Liriope's vulnerability as she asks the wise Tiresias if Narcissus will live a long life. She is anxious to preserve her treasure, perhaps worried that Narcissus, like Cephisus, will abandon her.

There is an important line between the parental adoration Kohut describes and the way Narcissus is presented in the myth. Liriope needs him. I recall a professor of mine stating emphatically to his developmental psychology class, "*never* have a child to fulfill your own needs." Though humans always have their needs somewhere in the equation, I appreciated his point. Too many children become caretakers, brought to the world to fill a parent's emptiness, to fix a broken relationship, or even to "have what I didn't have." Liriope, impregnated through rape, has little choice about the conception. She was a trophy taken, then discarded, by Cephisus. However, she does have a choice about her relationship with her child, and this is where tragedy begets tragedy. Narcissus is never regarded as a helpless, undeveloped infant in need of care and guidance. He is born a trophy. The myth is that he is perfect. The grandiose self is his sole identity.

Lust and Hate

Readers of the myth quickly develop a hatred for Narcissus. He's pompous, rejecting, and full of himself. We can imagine this vicious circle starting early for the child. Idealizing mother responds to what is perfect about Narcissus, and he learns to deny what is not: the needy, undeveloped child. He invests in the trophy self that mother loves, and he becomes the object of attraction for all he encounters. Although he seems cruel, Narcissus's rejection of the need around him may be an important form of self-protection. As a trophy child, he has good reason to be wary of the hunger directed his way. Sadly, by rejecting others, he only arouses more need and, ultimately, hatred and vengeance, in place of empathy and care. What Narcissus gets is confirmation that others are only there to take from him and do not really care.

The myth exposes the reality that being envied and idealized is not the same as being loved. Like the Facebook posts that broadcast only our impressive selves, the purely admiring and envious responses we receive are both addicting and empty. It is telling that the phrase "I hate you!" has become a common compliment between women, following on the heels of a comment like "You look great!" Too often, admiration is a covetous emotion—"I want to be close to you because I want to take what you have."

Narcissus contributes to the destructive circle. He rejects all but the perfect mirror and banishes all who could help him grow. Those rejected give up on him and curse him to love only his reflection. They give him the fate he desires, while assuring that he will remain only a shell, a false self.

The Lover

We see one exception in Echo. She seems to seek a real relationship with Narcissus and loves him to the end. But Echo brings her own limitations to the interaction. She cannot speak for herself, while Narcissus cannot allow others to do more than echo and mirror him. Narcissists often find Echoes—people too scared to use their own voice who hide their own creativity behind that of a showman or diva.

But Echo makes a bold, potentially transforming move. She physically appears to Narcissus. He shoos her away, and her boldness instantly shrinks into shame. She willingly retreats while remaining captive to her love for him. This is the contract many strike with the narcissist: "I won't challenge you, but I'll hang around to echo you." In the myth, we have both the cursers and the echo, the haters and lovers—two contrasting responses to the fragile bully. Eventually, Echo withers away, losing her body—the vehicle for her independent desires. In the end, she is just a tired and weakened reverberation of the voices of others.

We often forget the Echoes that sustain narcissism. Because she is such an important counterpart, we'll explore her myth in depth in Chapter 6.

From Bully to Fragile

The myth of Narcissus best portrays the persona of a grandiose narcissist but also reveals the fragility inherent in grandiosity. The curse by the spurned youth fulfills Tiresias's prophecy: the tables are turned, and Narcissus feels the longing he had previously denied. He falls for the same rejecting young man others had fallen for. He falls for himself.

And he can't get enough. Narcissism has often been compared to an addiction, and we see these qualities in Narcissus's obsession with the mirror. He lusts after an ideal image of himself and makes this his sole focus. It is interesting that he neglects hunger and sleep—aspects of his human, needy self—in order to pursue this grandiose version of himself. We see similar sacrifices in addictions. Self-care is secondary to pursuit of the illusion offered by the drug or drink. Another hidden clue to this aspect of narcissism comes in the choice of flower that arose in his place. Though today "narcissus" is the genus for all varieties of daffodils, etymology sources note that the flower in the myth was a type of iris or lily that contained alkaloids with a sedating effect. The flower's name was associated with the Greek *narke*, meaning "numbness" or "narcotic."[5]

The narcotic effect of narcissism is what we experience when we live off the high of self-inflation while simultaneously starving ourselves. A performer who shapes her act to generate the most applause, while neglecting her authentic self-expression, may be caught in the sedating mirror. The workaholic, ever seeking more credentials or money or praise, while forgetting what he's working for, may be fixed on the sedating mirror. And the young woman who literally starves herself to achieve an illusion of physical perfection may be trapped in the sedating mirror.

From Thrill to Agony

Narcissus's desire to possess himself exposes the deficit in his development. He seeks himself because he does not yet "have" himself. The selective mirroring he received as a child left him dependent on external sources of validation. Even the reflection in the clear pool provides only superficial feedback.

Still, the awareness of himself is a beginning. Narcissus finally feels need. And for a while, his need is answered. The image in the pool mirrors him perfectly, smiling when he smiles, shedding a tear for each of his tears. For the first time, Narcissus feels the promise of friendship. He is no longer alone with himself, subject to the hunger of others. This beautiful being in the water is showing him his own emotions, making them tolerable. That reflection in the pool may be, for a moment, the parents he did not have—both heroic and attentive.

This stage in the myth can be likened to the early stage of psychoanalytic therapy, when patients often feel an intense love for the analyst. They may, for the first time, feel attended to and understood, recognizing intense idealization and longing.

But, for Narcissus, this thrill is short lived. Narcissus cries out in desperation as he realizes he cannot have this relationship because he is the reflection. In this, Narcissus is only partially correct. He can have a relationship with himself and can regard himself with empathy and love. But if that relationship is limited to an idealized projection, it will be as empty and fleeting as a reflection on the water's surface. What Narcissus cannot have is the perfect companion he imagined. And this loss is something we all must endure. Our parents are not perfect, we are not perfect, and there will be no perfect union. Narcissus now suffers the anguish of knowing that he cannot have this imagined companion, that he is indeed alone. He is at a crossroads. He can cling desperately to the illusory being, living off an empty addiction, or he can learn how to live with the real version of himself—the one who is both vulnerable and confident. As a whole person, he would then be equipped to seek relationships with other real and imperfect beings.

In my practice, I have witnessed both scenarios. Some patients demand that I be that perfect companion and leave therapy once the idealization wanes. Some jump from one therapist to another, as if looking for new pools to reflect them. Others allow the mirror to reveal more.

The Necessary Death

Almost as soon as Narcissus recognizes himself, he resigns himself to death. Though often interpreted as his tragic end, the myth has more secrets to reveal. At every turn in the myth, two realities are superimposed. At the crossroads, Narcissus goes both ways. He starves due to his addiction. He also goes deeper.

His death is a descent to Hell, which is often a metaphor for the descent into the unconscious. By finally knowing and admitting what he is looking for, he opens the way to inner exploration and self-possession. And death is the loss of illusion. He again finds a pool for his reflection, but this is an inside job. In order to grow, self-obsessed individuals must grieve the loss of the idealized self, the idealized other, and the idealized union and face the work of living with an imperfect self in an imperfect world. What may at first feel like Hell is the only truly life-giving option: real engagement.

Though Narcissus seems to be repeating his fate in the underworld, something changes. In the place of his earthly body, a flower grows—the narcissus. Flowers, a symbol of memory, point to the proper place for ideal love.

5

MEETING THE FRAGILE BULLY

I have huge pecs and a 9 pack.
—LEGO BATMAN

Let's indulge in a lighter depiction of narcissism. Meet Lego Batman.

Lego Batman has a nine pack instead of a six pack. He frequently saves the world and feeds off the attention of the grateful Gotham City residents. After his first rescue in the 2017 *Lego Batman* movie, he waves at his adoring fans, hops into his Batmobile and makes a quick stop at the orphanage where he showers the kids with Batman "merch" and advises them to work on their abs.[1] He feels threatened when the police commissioner appeals to him to work with her. He likes being the focus, the only one on the receiving end of the Bat Signal. His ego blinds him to what is best for his people.

While Lego Batman may be a benign version of a narcissist, he portrays a very real narcissistic dilemma. Attention keeps him together. It is what he knows. And having fans feels safer than having friends.

Look at Me!

Lego Batman looks good. His shiny bat suit shows ripples of muscles, and when he transforms into Bruce Wayne, the dark curl in his hair stays perfectly formed. He's a Lego figure, though, so his plasticity makes sense.

Those who know a fragile bully often describe an unreal quality evident in the first meeting:

> "She was so animated, so vibrant. It was as if I was looking through a filter that intensified all her colors."

> "I couldn't believe it. Was he for real? He said things I wouldn't even dare to think! I was embarrassed for him, appalled. But I couldn't stop listening."

> "She barely said a word, but there was such a pull to focus on her. I had a sense that if my attention abandoned her, she would fall apart—or take me apart."

> "His gaze—it went right through me. It was as if he had assumed control over my body. I would have done anything for him."

The reactions we have to a narcissist go beyond attraction. We may actually feel repelled, yet somehow compelled. Whatever we feel, there is a sense that we are responding to something that may be spectacular but bigger than it should be. Like the nine pack, it is overdone and oversold. False.

This is grandiosity. There's too much bravado in the voice, the list of important friends has ten too many, the claims— even when spoken in the language of pain and suffering— are too hard to believe. Even though Lego Batman's "good ideas tracker" registers that he's had 5,678,483 good ideas, compared to the big zero in the "everyone else" column, we doubt the data. Still, the narcissist is convincing, mostly because he believes the illusion so dearly himself. Flummoxed and fascinated, we hang out a little longer to see if the unbelievable might just be true.

While a narcissist may be dramatic, not all drama queens and kings are narcissists. There is a psychiatric diagnosis—histrionic personality disorder—for those whose emotionality and superficial bids for attention disrupt life and relationships.[2] Though a person can exhibit both histrionic and narcissistic characteristics, the fragile bully requires more than attention. The fragile bully requires devotion.

Often the initial attraction to a fragile bully is that he or she makes us feel special. We notice, "He's being a jerk to everyone else, but I'm different; I get him," or "She is so important, and she's giving me her full attention," or "Others have tried, but I'm the only one who can help him." But, while specialness is a benefit of the contract, the cost is hidden in the fine print. The fragile bully has demands.

Narcissistic Demands

So you're the lucky one having a one-on-one conversation with this dazzling or compellingly vulnerable personality. She charms you—and then you can't break away from the conversation. You need to go, but she won't let you. She keeps talking and looking you right in the eye, completely unresponsive to the fact that you are on your way to a meeting—and told her so. Now you really have to go, but she pulls nods and smiles out of you that betray your desire to leave. You finally emphasize that you absolutely have to go, now, and she looks stung, says, "Wow—always following the rules," turns and throws a "Whatever" over her shoulder before storming off.

Wait. What just happened? What happened is that you just got bullied. Not only did she insult you, but she also got inside you—perhaps even compelling you to want to run after her and assure her you were interested. This example demonstrates two important realities of the fragile bully dynamic.

First, the dynamic is familiar. You've probably experienced a version of this conversation, and maybe you've even played a version of the bully. Contrary to the popular view that narcissists comprise a distinct class, uniformly malignant, the fragile bully shows up in many forms and intensities. Some of us only regress to bullying tactics in certain circumstances or under stress; others seem perpetually poised to intimidate anyone in their path. And bullying, especially when paired with fragility, can be very subtle—holding someone in a conversation against their will, pressing for compliments, or even pouting until certain conditions are met.

Second, a fragile bully draws you closer. This is the baffling paradox of narcissism. A bully will intimidate you and make you want to run or defend yourself; a fragile bully intimidates you into defending *him*. He may do this in very aggressive ways —"If you challenge me, I'll punish you." Or he may use manipulation—"If you challenge me, I'll be devastated and injured." In both cases, the message is, "Stay put and echo me. I am more important/needy/victimized than you." So you set yourself aside and tend this vulnerable creature who happens to be bullying you.

As discussed in Chapter 1, fragile bullies line up all along the continuum, from the fragile (covert, vulnerable) end to the bully (overt, grandiose) extreme. Bullying becomes more subtle and less conscious as one moves toward the fragile end, and fragility becomes more subtle and less conscious as one moves toward the bully end. The vulnerable bully fronts with fragility but hooks others through passive-aggression and manipulation. The grandiose bully fronts with aggression, but vulnerability is the hook. In both cases, the hook is disguised—unseen but deeply felt. Child abusers often effectively use their own fragility to silence a victim. The victim is then not only afraid of retaliation but also worries about the abuser: "I can't tell anyone because it would hurt him too much."

The hurt we anticipate may be the break in their precarious sense of self. Before we meet the two variants of the fragile bully, let's look more closely at the injuries both types work so hard to avoid.

Narcissistic Injury

A narcissistic injury is a crack or break in the illusion of the grandiose self. It exposes, if even for a moment, the fallible human behind the illusion. Most of us have some grandiose notions about ourselves, but how much we invest in building and defending these notions will determine how much the exposure will hurt.

Decades before Kohut discussed narcissism, psychoanalytic theorist Karen Horney wrote about the problems with investing in one's idealized self while abandoning the real self. Such an arrangement—what Horney called the devil's pact—cuts the individual off from valuable sources of growth. By moving one's "center of gravity" from the real self to the ideal self, Horney explained, "the energies driving toward self-realization are shifted to the aim of actualizing the idealized self."[3] Actualizing the ideal requires controlling and manipulating—not considering or integrating—outside input. The narcissist "may speak incessantly of his exploits or of his wonderful qualities and needs endless confirmation of his estimate of himself in the form of admiration and devotion."[4] Because he has banished the real self, any recognition of it by others poses a serious threat. He is unable to laugh at himself in recognition, own up to transgressions, or join the human race of people who make mistakes. He must defend, defend, defend!

Cracks and scrapes imposed by reality and by the needs of others further self-realization. For healthy development, according to Horney, one requires both "the good will of others" and "healthy friction with the wishes and wills of others."[5] When both are available from childhood, narcissistic injuries do not feel so severe. We occasionally get knocked down a rung and may even sulk a little before coming to terms with our limitations, and then we either adjust expectations or work harder. We learn. We constantly negotiate that space between our ideal and real selves, and closing that gap is the essence of self-realization.

Sadly, the fragile bully closes off the negotiation. It's all or nothing, winner or loser, saint or demon. And when the absolute ideal is challenged, the fragile bully doesn't just feel stung—he feels devastated. The leak in the structure, the glimpse at a fault, releases waves of shame and humiliation. The aggressively inclined will shut it down ASAP using whatever means necessary, and the vulnerable bully will obsess over the injury at the exclusion of the needs of others.

Aggression and Narcissistic Rage

Lego Batman has poured vast resources into building and fortifying his Batcave, along with his top of the line Batmobiles, identity transformation station, and sophisticated computerized control center. The Bruce Wayne behind the suit is as flashy as Batman, but the flash and the fortifications prevent others—and himself—from meeting the boy who lost his parents and still wishes for a family. A break in his cover is not an option for Bruce. He says he needs it to fight crime, but we know he also needs it to fight off his own fragility. And, if threatened, he will do whatever it takes to restore the structure and security system and to keep intruders out.

Grandiose and aggressive narcissists are generally harder to connect to than the vulnerable ones. Yet Lego Batman's boldness is part of the pull. The offer is, "Identify with me, and you can hide behind my aggression." We've probably all had the experience of being weary of the bully who rages about *everything*—until he or she advocates an issue we care about. Then the bully is a hero. An aggressive spokesperson allows us to come off as more reasonable, while at the same time serving as a mouthpiece for our unspoken grievances. With Donald Trump, disenfranchised voters, those who had no voice, those tired of politics as usual, felt they now had not only a voice, but a voice that was booming and unstoppable. Even when the voice deviated from what they value—"He's a pig!" a Trump supporter I know declared—they felt he was someone who could get things done.

The internet provides a wealth of evidence that aggressive bullies attract followers. My youngest son, in his twenties, alerted me to an online world fueled by people who routinely lash out at followers. Take one online personality with more than a million followers, whom I'll refer to as "D." He sits behind a large desk adorned with his line of products, and his black cap and perfectly trimmed, pointy beard lend him a sinister appearance. He is known for hurling vile insults to anyone who criticizes his YouTube and Twitter channels, using the "n" word, inviting commenters to kill themselves, and laughing as he mocks them for "crying."

In one much-discussed exchange, another YouTuber suggested, in the context of a *positive* review, that D use a disclaimer in his video. D's retort was swift and extreme. He called the commenter "a fake piece of shit" and issued a string of videos ranting at the reviewer. In them, he started to build a case that the reviewer was a pedophile who was dating a thirteen-year-old.

As with any public figure, we have only publicly displayed behavior to go on. I cannot diagnose D because I have never met him, much less evaluated him. However, D's reaction exemplifies Kohut's description of *narcissistic rage* as a dispro-portionately severe reaction to a "seemingly minor irritant."[6]

The "irritant" might be as "seemingly minor" as the absence of a laugh in response to a joke, a compliment that lacks the desired enthusiasm, or a minor suggestion in a complimentary review. But for the fragile bully, what seems minor to others threatens to do major harm—to injure. And the injury is not just a temporary sting that quickly fades; it threatens the foun-dation of the grandiose self—the illusion that one is unique and perfect. While the vulnerable bully feels exposed and shamed, the grandiose bully fights against these feelings. He will not accept injury; he will, as Kohut describes, employ "a simple remedy: the active (often anticipatory) inflicting on others of those narcissistic injuries which he is most afraid of suffering himself."[7] D's barrage of insults and accusations have this sense of urgency. As Kohut puts it, "The narcissistically injured...cannot rest until he has blotted out a vaguely expe-rienced offender."[8]

The constant deflection of injury may explain why gran-diose narcissists tend to exhibit higher self-esteem than do vulnerable narcissists.[9] Some authors, such as Twenge and Campbell, argue that, far from having a masked self-esteem problem, grandiose narcissists think very highly of themselves. The authors reference studies that demonstrate that, even at an implicit or unconscious level, grandiose narcissists report good feelings about themselves.[10] Other studies reveal con-flicting findings,[11] and Malkin notes that high self-esteem is more related to healthy narcissism than to its pathological extreme.[12] But what does seem clear is that grandiose bullies are more likely than vulnerable types to deflect injury to their self-esteem. They get mad and they get even.

For the aggressive bully, a narcissistic injury is an emergency. The offender must take it back or regret dearly for offending. Like the evil queen of the legend, she'll train that mirror on the wall to tell her she's the greatest of all and will rage until the training is complete.

Defending herself, however, may not be enough. Horney also discussed the drive for "vindictive triumph"—the need to inflict shame and humiliation on anyone who challenges the narcissist's precarious superiority.[13] Though Horney said that this drive is often hidden and channeled as competitive strivings, one look at the volatile interactions on social media suggests that this defense has freer rein these days.

The aggressive bully is forever at battle, and narcissistic rage is a ready weapon.

The Vulnerable Bully

In contrast to the trigger-happy aggressor, the vulnerable bully wields aggression in a covert way, through neediness and manipulation of guilt. My father had this approach mastered. A tall, barrel-chested Norwegian who served as a Lutheran minister, he looked like a dark-haired angel in his cassock and white robe. He was a powerful preacher, and he inspired me. But his fragility emerged each Sunday after the church service. He would prod us for compliments, asking his children, "That was a terrible sermon, wasn't it?" We would reassure him, "No, Dad, it was great." But that wasn't enough. He would say, "Pretty lousy, then?" He wouldn't stop until we showered him with compliments. I was always frustrated by these exchanges because, while I was generally bored with church, I actually listened to his sermons, and he was good. Some sermons I enjoyed more than others, and I could have shared my true impressions with him if I had felt he could take it. But the more he manipulated me for compliments, the more I felt robbed of my ability to decide, and the more resistant I felt to giving him what he wanted. I'm sure he sensed that resistance, which only fueled his insecure bids for assurance. We were stuck in a vicious circle that left us both with less. It would be years before I would have the strength to respond differently and break us out of the circle, but that's a story for another chapter.

When the bully also wields fragility, we face an impossible dilemma. We can go along with the show, appeasing the bully while betraying ourselves. Or we can be honest and face the guilt of exposing and humiliating the bully. The ultimate demand of the fragile bully is to keep any competing needs and desires out of the conversation. For the fragile bully, getting his wish is the ultimate tragedy. He may go from his fans to a bat cave full of cool cars and commemorative plaques, but he'll remain deprived of real human interaction.

The Bullies We Can't See

The literature on narcissism is replete with examples of the aggressive extreme, but it's also important for us to be aware of more subtle instances of aggression—especially the kinds we use ourselves. The fact that we can so easily be pulled into malignant interactions—especially on social media—is evidence that we all have some capacity to bully. Sometimes it is harder to deal with seemingly benign instances of bullying that leave us growling with annoyance but ill-equipped to respond. I have an acquaintance who is generous and even self-deprecating in many realms, but when it comes to the books she has read, nobody gets to be at her level. She belittles readers of her less-favored literature, even if she is talking to those people. She also suffers extreme envy when others share their accomplishments. She bullies by passive-aggressively withholding any kind of response to the speaker and "pouting" until the focus turns to her. She is a kind person much of the time, a grandiose bully in the arena of literature, and a vulnerable bully when she feels threatened by the accomplishments of others.

Though you may not identify with the shiny, showy narcissist, you will likely see yourself in these pages. You may start to notice garden-variety narcissism in your actions: the way you fish for compliments and collect likes, the way you admire your compassionate response to a friend's distress rather than actually attending to your friend, the fifteenth take of your selfie to capture that stunning, "natural" pose. You may even notice your inner fragile bully: the one who pressures others to affirm your specialness.

Just as I was completing this chapter, an interaction with my husband shined a mirror on a fragile bully response of my own. I had just finished blowing off a request of his by shifting the topic to how I'd been "working my ass off on this book." He asked how many hours I'd put in that day, and I counted about seven. He then gently observed that sometimes I treat a full day's work—the same hours most people work—as something that deserves a medal. Ouch. His observation, hard as it was to hear, made me reflect on other times I used the "overworked" complaint as a way of getting the focus back on me when he asked something of me. I was channeling the martyr variant of the vulnerable bully—one that punishes through deep signs about how overworked and under-rewarded I am, or delivers slow and excruciating monologues about all I have done.

You will likely experience some wounds of realization as you read along. These narcissistic injuries are necessary to our growth and something we'll revisit in Part III. The good news is that the more open you are to looking at yourself realistically, the less likely you are to be a narcissist.

Adding to our own narcissistic vulnerabilities, the current political and social climate seems to be arousing the fragile bully in otherwise healthy people. We want to lash out with our opinions, but we don't want any backlash. We want to trim down our networks so only perfect mirrors remain. We trade real encounters for caricatures and rants. We may be caught up in the dehumanizing dance of narcissism without recognizing the steps. We'll look more closely at the steps in Part II, but first we'll explore the myth behind the fragile bully's partner, Echo.

6

ECHO, REVEALED

Ekho (Echo), the Nymphe of Kithairon (Cithaeron), returns
thy words, which resound beneath the dark vaults of the thick
foliage and in the midst of the rocks of the forest.

—ARISTOPHANES,
Thesmophoriazusae 970 (trans. O'Neill)

How do we talk about an echo? An echo is, by definition,
dependent on another's voice. A personified Echo can
only be the sidekick, the supporting actor. Yet, in Greek
mythology, Echo is well-known. She is the most famous of the
Oreiads, or mountain nymphs. She is Narcissus's counterpart
but makes regular appearances in other myths as well. As with
Narcissus's Echo, those who dance with today's fragile bullies
easily become invisible, but they are not just passive partners. If
we call Echo out of her cave, we can observe three qualities that
betrayed her: her helping nature, her mirroring voice, and her
need for a hero.

Echo's story starts before Narcissus's birth. The myth's most
famous author, Ovid, emphasizes this point: "Echo still had a
body then and was not merely a voice."[1] Like other nymphs,
she is a spirit of nature in the form of a beautiful woman. She

dwells among the mountains and personifies their essence. And though blessed with longevity, she is mortal. Echo loves to talk and enjoys the sound of her own voice. She shares gossip and likes to have the last word. In the beginning, Echo seems vibrant and full of life. More than anything, she wants to engage.

The Accomplice

Echo is a willing helper. As a nymph, she embodies both an idealized and limiting image of femininity: selfless, loyal, and protective. She frequently assists Zeus when he visits the mountain. When Zeus cavorts with nymphs on Mount Olympus, Echo distracts Zeus's lover, Hera, by trapping her in conversation until the nymphs escape. At this stage in the myth, it is hard to discern what Echo wants or needs from these relationships. She does not benefit directly: she is not Zeus's lover, and she does not seem to receive any kind of reward for the risks she takes. What we sense is that she is fiercely loyal. Helping is so much a part of her nature that she doesn't give thought to her own vulnerability. This quality is one that helps to distinguish what Malkin refers to as "echoism"—described by others as "inverted narcissism" or "codependency"—from vulnerable narcissism.[2] Echoists or codependents want to stay in the shadows and help while vulnerable narcissists use their fragility to attract help. Christina, whom we met in this book's introduction, was aware she was being hurt by the narcissist in her life but could not let go of her mission to help him. She described the values instilled in her: "We're not throw away people. If there's something broke, you fix it." Likewise, Echo does not question her commitment to helping. Not only is she more comfortable furthering the wishes of others than pursuing her own desires but, at this stage, she seems quite unaware that she *has* desires. According to another myth starring Echo, she flees sexual relationships with men and gods, treasuring her virginity.[3] For echoists, need is either taboo or dangerous. While echoism may be a radical expression of a helping nature, it can also be a clever way of masking one's need. By hiding behind the needs and wishes of others, the echoist avoids the risk of self-direction and self-expression. By staying in the caretaker role, the echoist avoids the risk of exposing need and being disappointed. Safer to live for the needs of others. Unfortunately for Echo, the helping role does not keep her safe. By offering help indiscriminately, she becomes an accomplice. And in the end, she is the one who is punished. This tragic outcome is one we observe with many who are attracted to the narcissistically impaired. Such a person may deny personal needs for fear of getting hurt only to suffer because their needs were denied.

The Voice, Appropriated

A quality of Echo's that seems out of character is that she loves her voice. She enjoys the sound of it and talks whenever possible. But from the beginning, she embodies a paradox. She has a passion for self-expression, but she borrows her material. She gossips, spreading stories started by others. And her choice to be Zeus's accomplice further limits her vocal repertoire. When Hera learns of the cover-up, she restricts Echo's ability to speak. Echo can no longer initiate speech, nor can she be silent after another has spoken.

It is interesting to observe that those hooked by the needs of others often become extreme talkers. They talk about the narcissist, complain about the narcissist, strategize about how to deal with the narcissist. In a conversation with an Echo, we do not hear her or see her. We see the narcissist. And this is the dynamic many are living out as they respond to the provocations of President Trump. Their discussions, their voices, have been commandeered. Looking at the proliferation of his statements on social media, Donald Trump's voice echoes over and over. As people repeat, react, and resist, they stop generating their own opinions. And they lose their own voices.[4]

In Search of a Hero

The song lyrics, "I'm looking out for a hero," have a different interpretation here. We want to warn Echo, "Look out! A hero is coming!" Narcissus is that hero—youthful, beautiful, seemingly perfect. He will make a good substitute for Echo's lost will, and that is why he is dangerous—and why she should look out. Julia Cameron, in her classic creativity manual, *The Artist's Way*, discusses the tendency for damaged artists to hide behind heroes—people, like Narcissus, who thrive in the limelight.[5] These artists participate in creativity vicariously. Safely. But the reality is, the hero doesn't always speak for his following. He may do so partially, as Donald Trump has for many of his followers. The sentiment for these followers may be, "I wouldn't talk the way he does, but he has the courage to speak."

My mother exemplified this aspect of Echo. A talented writer, she became Dad's anonymous editor, typing and advising him as he dictated his sermons. A talented musician, she sat behind the piano and watched for his cues as he directed the church choir. She repelled personal gain, refusing a salary for her administrative duties. She was harshly critical of women who sought the spotlight and told me in the midst of my graduate training that I could stop at my master's—no need to get a PhD. She also had Echo's beautiful nature. My early memories of her are tactile: her soft, cool skin, her enfolding body as she rocked me. She loved having babies—had ten of them and embraced the role of devoted wife and mother.

But her softest spot was for my dad. The daughter of a missionary serving in Madagascar, my mother saw her father choose the missions over the care of his wife, who needed to leave the island—bringing the children with her—due to health concerns. When my grandfather finally reunited with the family in the United States, he was no longer "right" due to the ravishes of malaria. I only have fleeting images of him, and they were frightening. After my grandmother's death, my grandfather married a nurse who had worked with him in the missions. He was not my mother's hero. But Dad was. He was tall, broad and handsome, eloquent and strong—a deep bass to her soprano in the college choir, fun loving, yet morally upright. A man who was raised with a stern, critical mother, my father was hungry for the warmth my mother offered. He was narcissistically hungry, and she needed her Narcissus. Their love story was so compelling that my cousins still talk about it. Dad was the hero she had been looking for, and Mom willingly became the supportive and loving sidekick. While Dad preached and composed music and designed and built pipe organs, Mom built up Dad. His desires became hers, and for me and my siblings, hers were barely visible. We sensed, for example, that Mom wasn't thrilled by Dad's dream of retiring on a small lake in the midst of Minnesota farm country. But they retired on that lake, and Mom smiled as they moved.

Even as echoists fan the desires of the hero, their own desires diminish. Like my mom in her youth, the early Echo is a passionate woman. Her voice may be limited, but her desires are alive and well. Ovid goes to lengths to describe the heat of the flame within her when she beholds Narcissus. She follows the young man in secret, longing to call to him, but remains trapped within her muted voice—until he speaks. When he calls out, she passionately echoes him. Reading the myth, you can imagine her mobilizing for action, unable to contain her enthusiasm. Finally, he invites her to meet him. Even as she sends the invitation back from the mountains—*Let us get together!*—she abandons her shelter in the woods and runs toward him. In her first act of self-assertion, she presents herself to Narcissus and throws her arms around his neck.

Tragically, for her, her presence is the very thing that offends the fragile bully. He doesn't want a person—he wants only the echo. Rejection greets her desire. Shame displaces her confidence. Narcissus's response reinforces her script: she exists to help, not to need. She retreats, but only partially. And this is a pattern we often observe in those who love fragile bullies. An Echo may even stay married to the fragile bully long after the desiring self has run for cover.

Loss of Body

Ovid tells us that Echo's love endures after her retreat, "increased by the sadness of rejection," and "her sleepless thoughts waste her sad form."[6] The longer she obsesses over the absent bully, the more she neglects the needs of her body. Though Echo's obsession takes the form of longing, mental echoing can also manifest in preoccupations with how to "win over," appease, or even defeat the fragile bully. Even as the mind toils and denies its needs and limitations, the body— boundaried and limited—cannot lie. Ovid describes Echo's physical decline:[7]

> She frets and pines, becomes all gaunt and haggard,
> Her body dries and shrivels till voice only
> And bones remain, and then she is voice only
> For the bones are turned to stone.

Internalized feelings can contribute to somatic concerns. Depression, sometimes described as "anger turned inward," causes sleep and appetite disturbances and can slow one down physically and hinder concentration. Anxiety, the fretting and pining described by Ovid, can influence a number of organ systems, including respiration and heart function. Poor eating and exercise can result in problematic weight gain or loss. My mother's story has some eerie similarities to that of Echo. While my dad's physique retained its youth, my mother's body lost its beautiful form through inattention. Obesity, back problems, and, eventually, Parkinson's disease afflicted her. In a cruel twist, the disease stiffened her gait and froze her facial expressions—providing a too-similar image to Echo's stone-hardened body.

It is notable that during the 2016 election, when narcissistic proclamations and rage-filled retaliations entered our daily diet, the American people were feeling the physical side effects. A Pew research poll found that, by July, 60% of Americans reported that they were already "sick and tired" of the election.[8] Mental health professionals were reporting more visits, including many seeking help for election-related anxiety.[9] Women, re-traumatized by the publicly demeaning comments toward women by Donald Trump, were particularly vulnerable. The American Psychological Association intervened by issuing a list of tips for coping with the election.[10] One of the tips advised, "limit your media consumption." Donald Trump frequently used the word "Sick!" to describe those opposing him, which oddly dovetailed with what many opponents described feeling about Trump's election.[11]

Feeling "sick and tired" is a cue that it's time to stop echoing.

Tragic Figure or Heroine?

Though we can view echoism as the absence of healthy narcissism, Echo's limitation is also a gift. Her capacity to reflect without interference is the basis of mirroring, reflective listening, witnessing—capacities I work to instill in future therapists and physicians. Most of us are tempted to tell our own stories, to anchor another's disclosure in our own experience, or to fix things by jumping in with suggestions or advice. The ability to set oneself aside long enough to comprehend another person's experience is indeed a gift. The mountain nymph is there to both witness and support, to further the pursuits of those around her. Is this a bad thing? The myth shows the tragic potential of this "all about you" orientation, but, as with narcissism, there is a healthy side as well. My mother stayed true to a deep value of hers: to serve. When I challenged her choices as a young woman, she firmly stated that she loved taking care of her family. I was the ninth child and witnessing her deterioration. But there was another story told by a photo I relished: Mom at the family campsite wearing a dress and beads, cooking a full course breakfast on a camp stove, her dimpled smile revealing her joy. What happened between those early days of halcyon family life and what I observed?

Indulging Limitations

Unlike Echo, my mother found a committed life partner, one who loved her deeply. But to the extent that they filled each other's needs, they also indulged each other's limitations. When Dad flew into a narcissistic rage, Mom explained away his behaviors, smoothed things over, and worked with us, her children, to help us understand him. What we learned is that we had to be more adult than him. He could call us vile names and use his booming voice to belittle and shame us, and her soft voice followed, placating us. She made it easy for him to stay at his narcissistic pool. She remained by his side, even when being there meant turning against herself. This fed Dad's intolerance of honest interaction and ultimately left him more alone.

And Dad indulged my mother's fear of responsibility for her own care. He became her project, her world, and gave her purpose. He made it easy for her own will to wither away. As for Mom's giving nature, her tired body and capacity for attention ran out. What I experienced in my teens was a mother who, while never unkind, was less and less available. We teased her about being "spaced out," her mind somewhere else. My little sister, across the table from my mom, tested this by saying, "My head just fell off and rolled across the table." Mom replied absentmindedly, "That's nice, honey." I think, in those absent stretches, she was Echo in her cave pining for something lost.

We know that a one-sided "all about me" orientation is problematic; however, those who echo reveal the problems with an "all about you" orientation. First, an Echo, when paired with a Narcissus, becomes consumed and less available to others who rely on her. We see this too often in unions in which Narcissus becomes the designated recipient of care, and children are asked to be co-parents. Second, if the Echo doesn't apply her nurturing capacities toward her own care, both her giving nature and her availability as a person will wither along with her preoccupied mind and neglected body. What gets missed in the "all about you" approach to relationships is that others need an individual to connect to, and even children need real human role models—not only mirrors—to show them how to be in the world. Finally, an "all about you" orientation is unsustainable. In an attempt at justice, Echo's body will cry for the help she fails to seek. As Parkinson's robbed my mother of mobility, she became quite demanding—even as she apologized for the demands. Her body seemed to seek the balance she refused to pursue, and Dad willingly cared for her. But as her body failed and her focus turned inward, she gradually left us. Heartbroken after her death, Dad was left, with us, to mourn the person lost along the way.

Introversion and Echoism

As I've written elsewhere, introversion is simply an internal orientation, the counterpart to externally oriented extraversion.[12] This means introverts prefer to process information internally and privately, and they require and enjoy solitary reflection. There is also evidence that, in contrast to extraverts, the brains of introverts are more sensitive to external input. The combination of constantly absorbing more, while also attending more intently to what they are processing, explains why large crowds, excessive noise, and fast-paced conversation leave introverts overstimulated and drained. By contrast, extraverts process information relationally—through conversation and trial-and-error—and generally seek, rather than limit, external stimulation.

Extraverts can be echoists for fragile bullies, as in the case of more combative echoists who react, proliferate the drama, and yet keep the focus on the fragile bully. And, as we've discussed, introverts may be fragile bullies themselves. However, some introvert characteristics are well suited to the Echo role. Introverts are absorbent; we take in what others say and think about it. An extraverted, grandiose narcissist can take advantage of that tendency and hijack our thinking.[13] Deprived of the space to think our own thoughts, we instead give our focus to the needy bully. In addition, even when we are thinking are own thoughts, a narcissist may interpret the quiet as an invitation to share his or her vast accomplishments and important worldview. And because introverts tend to be conflict-averse, interjecting oneself and challenging the narcissist may feel like too much work.

As much as my mother stood by her choices, she did admit to feeling alone in a culture that was telling her to be more assertive and independent. I was part of that culture and, with it, devalued her path. It was not until I started understanding my own introversion that I recognized what that devaluation felt like. We have a bias toward extraversion in our society, just as we have a bias toward self-preservation over service. Shifting the Echo-Narcissus power dynamic requires us to look not only at the roles each partner plays but the role of society in determining what, and whom, we value.

PART
II

7

VICIOUS CIRCLE DANCES

The stupid thing about anger is how people hurt you and then you let them keep hurting you by being angry about how they originally hurt you. It's a vicious cycle.

–SUSANE COLASANTI

As a graduate student and clinical psychology trainee in 1985, I remember my first reaction to my assignment to explore the writings of an innovative theorist named Paul L. Wachtel. I couldn't have been less receptive. My colleagues and I were up to our ears in reading, clinical work, and papers when a new professor had the gall to assign two hundred-some pages of Wachtel's *Psychoanalysis and Behavior Therapy*[1]—to be read by our next meeting. Not happy, we muffled our protests and dug in.

That burden was a disguised gift. My colleagues and I had become accustomed to a sort of "musical chairs" approach to therapy training. We changed supervisors each semester, even if our caseload remained the same. So one semester, I might be helping a client draft a behavior-monitoring plan, and the next semester, we would set aside the plan and explore the influence of old, internalized conflicts on current problems. Each approach held promise—and had strong advocates—and my colleagues and I struggled to choose our theoretical loyalties. Wachtel's model bridged the theoretical divide in my profession and within me. Up until then, when I heard "psychoanalysis" and "behavior therapy" in the same conversation, proponents of one were usually ridiculing the other. Viewed from the other side, behaviorists were the ones counting the times someone smiled in a therapy session, reducing life to the tidbits that were observable. And psychoanalysts, viewed from afar, only cared about the patient's infantile fantasies, while ignoring what was happening in the present.

Wachtel's comment in the introduction to his book could easily describe the political polarization we are witnessing today: "It is my experience that workers guided by either of these two broad frames of reference tend to have only a rather superficial knowledge (and sometimes not at all) of the important regularities observed by the other viewpoint."[2] Like the terms of today's political debates, asserting any loyalties came with pressure to reject everything identified with the opposition. Wachtel, trained psychoanalytically, had felt this pressure as well but decided to learn from—rather than reject—the other viewpoint.

Thinking Outside the Bubble

Paul L. Wachtel, who grew up in a lower middle-class neighborhood—as he put it, "in the shadow of Yankee Stadium"—was raised to be content with the givens of his environment. But he was too intellectually restless for that. He poured himself into academic studies, obtained his doctorate from Yale, and went on to pursue psychoanalytic training at New York University's postdoctoral program. Even as he resonated with much of psychoanalytic theory, and was excited about the way in which the discipline was evolving, he continued to explore divergent points of view—including *the* divergent view offered by behavior therapy. He later reflected on what it meant to incorporate this perspective into his thinking:

> I had learned little about behavior therapy in my training up till then, but I had learned one crucial point: it was not worth learning more. Behavior therapy, I had picked up, was superficial, manipulative, insensitive to human complexity. It was technocratic, pseudoscientific, and incapable of leading to genuinely profound or durable changes.[3]

As much as Wachtel appreciated the richness of psychoanalytic theory, he observed that proponents too often accepted what he called the "woolly mammoth model" of personality—the idea that crucial early experiences were preserved in their original form, frozen in the unconscious and inaccessible to learning. While this model disregarded the impact of learning, behavior therapy tended to disregard the impact of childhood. Young professionals like me were forced to choose what mattered most: childhood influences or current learning.

The third possibility Wachtel developed was that childhood experiences stay potent to the extent that current relationships recreate and reinforce those experiences. Even longstanding problems like personality disorders rely on current relationships for sustenance. This, to me, was the very reason psychoanalytic work was so powerful. The analyst, through intensive training and ongoing self-awareness, could engage in a different dance with the patient. But Wachtel also went beyond the interpersonal to the sociocultural, addressing issues like the often-futile discourse on race and helping us understand how such vicious circles actively perpetuate social problems.[4] Wachtel describes the values underpinning his perspective:

As I have reflected on the progress of my thinking…this theme of reclaiming—and, importantly, reintegrating or giving a place to—the disavowed or cast aside echoed in my thinking again and again. And in a different way, it defines as well my vision of the good society and my interest in applying psychoanalytic and psychological insights to the task of social renewal; that vision centers on reintegrating into the social mainstream those who have been disregarded and creating the conditions in which they, in turn, can reappropriate their own rights and potentials.[5]

A Voice for Our Time

Though I have been strongly influenced by Wachtel and other integrative thinkers throughout my career, I hadn't felt compelled to delve back into his theory until I started witnessing the destructive feedback loops popping up everywhere, from combative threads on Facebook to installments in the hostile but mutually reinforcing battle between Donald Trump and the media. In my social media circle, I saw conversations quickly escalate to either accusations and name-calling or "unfriending" and blocking—often between family members. As I read some of the longer, more heated threads, I noted a common progression. This fictional thread captures some of the general sentiments and types of comments I encountered:

"Trump is dangerous."

"Hillary is worse."

"How can you be defending a racist? You must be a racist."

"Poor little snowflakes. He's just talking truth."

"I can't believe you would stand for this. Time to put on our protest shoes, folks."

"You are technically organizing a protest during a time of war! You could be shot by firing squad."

"Are you retarded?"

"You elitists just protest. We work."

"Idiot. We care."

"Keep those protest shoes in your closet and go die."

What struck me is how these encounters left both sides in a weaker position, enacting the roles and stereotypes suggested by the opponent. For example, in the sample of responses I collected, members of the pro-Trump side used increasingly violent language, aligning with a stereotyped image of Trump followers. At the same time, the tone of condescension and superiority on the anti-Trump side gave weight to the suggestion that Trump opponents are elitists. This progression also reflects the operation of the "self-fulfilling prophecy," or the tendency for people to become what is expected of them. While those making the vilest comments—this sample excludes the worst—represent only a subset of participants, I was struck by the fact that more reasonable participants did little to quell their zeal. If anything, there seemed to be a cathartic element to watching the show.

This tendency to elicit the very responses that feed the problem is what Wachtel referred to as the "ironic heart of psychopathology." It seemed to me that this psychopathology had reached the heart of our political discourse. Revisiting cyclical psychodynamics has helped me make sense of the many ways pathological narcissism has come to define our current sociopolitical environment. The Facebook feeds, name-calling, media commentary, parodies, and insults flooding my world were more than a reaction to psychopathology—they were also its life force.

The Vicious Circle

According to Wachtel's theory of "cyclical psychodynamics," early relationships set in motion feedback loops, or vicious circles, which people carry forward and enact in new relationships. Cyclical psychodynamics addresses what Freud called "repetition compulsion," the tendency to repeat old patterns even when they are destructive. The work of behavior therapists helps explain this odd behavior. We don't repeat destructive patterns because we are masochists; we repeat them because we do what we know and others cue and reinforce those behaviors. What I didn't include in my Facebook feed example was the "cheerleading"—likes and comments applauding or supporting statements on either side. While these are positive reinforcers, getting a negative reaction can also be reinforcing—it's a reaction, after all—and can serve as a cue for a comeback. Looking at behavioral sequences can help explain why exchanges like this can be satisfying even as people feel enraged, hurt, or fearful.

Thankfully, other people are not only potential *reinforcers* of problematic behaviors; they can also have a role in *extinguishing* those behaviors. Culture can have a similar influence, for better and for worse. By including such behavioral concepts of associational learning and reinforcement, we can better explain how someone with a horrid childhood might, with new kinds of associations and reinforcements, break out of old patterns and live a healthy life.

Though psychoanalytic therapists would not likely talk about extinction of old learning, other terms like "corrective emotional experience" have a similar connotation.[6] For example, psychoanalysts, in unearthing and exposing childhood trauma and associated anxiety, essentially perform what behaviorists call *exposure therapy*. We know from work with phobias that the best way to overcome fear is to expose oneself to what is feared until the anxiety diminishes and loses its power. Regression to childhood trauma allows this exposure. By bringing together the clarity of terminology and scientific findings of behaviorism with the rich theoretical resources and fine-tuned interpersonal techniques of psychoanalysis, we have access to a broader range of resources for addressing problematic behaviors. To better understand the vicious circle at the core of this integration, let's look at a familiar example.

"I Drink Because You Nag"

Though cyclical psychodynamics holds the promise that new responses can interrupt vicious circles and extinguish problematic behaviors, Wachtel makes it clear that this is not an easy task: "We are often unfortunately and unwittingly experts in turning other people into accomplices in our neuroses."[7]

Wachtel illustrates this with a well-known scenario. One member of a couple says, "I drink because you nag," and the other argues, "I nag because you drink."[8] These responses to each other are self-perpetuating. While the specific partners vary, the dance is familiar. In fact, many of us have probably participated in some variation of the drink-nag dance. How does the cycle start, and how does it become so vicious? To understand that, we need a closer look.

Let's peek in on the dance between drinker, Tom, and complainer, Jane. If we look to Tom's childhood, we can see the roots of his self-numbing behavior. Tom's parents had very poor boundaries, and he was frequently the target of their unjustified, in-your-face confrontations. He longed to disappear and, as a teen, discovered that alcohol helped him do just that. When he drank, he felt calm and could detach from the intensity of his parents' projections. We can imagine that his drinking, while soothing him, likely justified his parents' accusations and actually strengthened this early vicious circle. And, where drinking is involved, the body responds with a vicious circle of its own, delegating to alcohol the role of activating calming neurotransmitters. The body signals the craving for this replenishment, and the more Tom drinks, the more alcohol his body needs to do the job.

Tom meets Jane. Jane knows Tom had a rough childhood, and her compassion for him deepens her attachment to him. Tom sees her as someone who "gets" him and provides the solace so lacking in his former life. Wachtel's theory allows that, even if one of the participants is the primary instigator of the dynamic, the dance pulls the partner in and both become complicit in the vicious circle. So, while Jane probably has her own Echo-like motives in the dance, we'll focus on Tom as instigator. Tom drinks. He does so secretly at first, and then, more and more, in her presence. He brings with him anxieties that Jane is not as trustworthy a supporter as she seems, along with some guilt and shame about his drinking. Jane, the helper, notices the drinking but does not want to become his abusive parents. Still, helpers help, and, more than that, Jane feels lonely. She longs for the earlier conversations with Tom when they shared their vulnerabilities.

So Jane eventually says something, trying to be supportive and loving. Tom, his fears affirmed, snaps at her. She might retreat for a bit, but now she's irked herself. She has refrained from criticizing him, and when she says one thing—*in a loving tone*—he responds rudely.[9]

Triggered by Jane's comment, Tom is flooded with fears that his parents' criticisms of him were justified. They—and she—need to be the problem, not him. So he pulls out the "nag" word. "Nag" conjures Jane's worst fears, and she further defends her intentions. The vicious circle takes hold. In addition to the reinforcement of getting his attention, Jane likely receives intermittent reinforcement for her efforts when Tom is more accessible or temporarily cleans up his act. She carries memories of Tom's warm and positive interactions, and she keeps trying to restore that intimacy. It is also possible that Jane is carrying forward a vicious circle based in her own past efforts to engage emotionally inaccessible parents. Psychologist Lindsay Gibson describes children trained on this intermittent reward schedule:

> Getting a reward for your efforts is possible but completely unpredictable. This creates a tenacious resolve to keep trying to get a reward, because once in a while these efforts do pay off. In this way, parental inconsistency can be the quality that binds children most closely to their parent, as they keep hoping to get that infrequent and elusive positive response.[10]

So Jane picks up the former role of Tom's parents, trying to break through the wall created by the drinking and focusing on his increasingly troubling behaviors. As these efforts evolve toward "nagging," Tom's self-numbing indulgence continues to escalate, as does the need to nag, and so on.

This example shows how both childhood patterns and present-day cues and reinforcers factor into the destructive dance. Rather than choose between a psychoanalytic or behavioral explanation, we can see how both apply. The role of alcohol in Tom's life has all kinds of meanings tied to potent childhood experiences. Accessing these may be crucial, even from a behavioral perspective, because exposing anxiety is the key to extinguishing it. However, as long as he's drinking, he will keep that anxiety at bay. So what needs to happen is a radical interruption *in the present*. He cannot truly heal until he gets rid of his liquid medicine. Jane, on the other hand, needs to relinquish her role as accomplice and stop trying to "help." These radical interruptions of the vicious circle are counterintuitive and may even seem cruel. Meanwhile, the dance beckons, offering its well-rehearsed steps.

The role of alcohol, of course, complicates the above scenario, but narcissistic disorders share qualities with addictions. Narcissus, so caught up with his reflection, stopped eating and caring for his body. Echo, so caught up with Narcissus, also wasted away. Without an internalized self, the narcissist needs to create mirrors everywhere. He's hooked on himself.

Dancing with Narcissus

Wachtel's model is very useful in understanding the subtle but powerful mechanisms that feed narcissism. We can see how fragile bullies thrive online, how we get hooked into giving our best mental resources to people who perplex us, and even how the fragile bully dynamic gained enough steam to pull a nation into its spin.

Viewing the narcissist as a solo actor is like seeing the alcoholic separate from the alcohol. The fragile bully continually reaches for a partner—not to interact with but to reflect and fill in something missing. And partners reach back. The vicious circle of narcissism functions like a dance, in which the fragile bully may take the lead, but the partner's steps fuel the momentum. Sometimes it is not so clear who is leading.

The Dances of Narcissism

In this section, we'll discuss six common vicious circles that feed narcissism. Here's a preview:

We participate in the *Join the Aggressor* dance when we secretly enjoy and identify with narcissistic aggression. Identifying with a fragile bully can be a way of taking power without taking responsibility.

One of the fragile bully's many paradoxes is that she hungers for reassurance and praise, but because she demands it, she distrusts its authenticity. Cue the *Reassurance Dance.* Offering the required praise and reassurance is a no-win solution that keeps the cycle in motion. As with alcohol, the narcissist needs more and more as the power of the buzz diminishes.

We see the *Provoke and React* in full force in the exchanges between Trump and the media. Counter-aggressive responses feed and justify the aggression of the fragile bully, and the dance goes on.

The Solo Dance reenacts the Narcissus-Echo dynamic. This vicious circle is at work whenever one partner owns and internalizes the pain that originates in the relationship. We also see this dance in our society when the more sensitive members withdraw themselves from public discourse and give over power to the needy bullies.

The Superior Dance occurs when the outrageous behaviors of a fragile bully allow his or her partner to feel psychologically superior. This can also explain the satisfaction opponents feel when Trump engages in the very behavior they bemoan.

The *Edit Me* promotes unhealthy narcissism by rewarding increasingly shallow and dehumanized identities. Narcissists often edit out the parts of themselves most in need of response, such as their vulnerable and imperfect qualities, and find the responses to their superficial qualities to be less and less satisfying.

As we explore each of these dances we'll observe how these vicious circles keep the fragile bully alive and unwell. We'll also look at how we can change up the steps and interrupt these destructive patterns.

8

JOIN THE AGGRESSOR

Aggression only moves in one direction—it creates
more aggression.
–MARGARET J. WHEATLEY

B arb moved through life as though she had paparazzi always in her wake. She had a way of being noticed, with her big smile and confident stride. Barb coached a women's gymnastics team, and she was tough. She used some controversial tactics, and it was important to her that her team demonstrate loyalty. She could be charming and entertaining, but if one of the gymnasts questioned her methods or complained about muscle strain, Barb mockingly imitated her voice and gestures. Coaching sessions often became venting sessions as Barb complained about how hard everyone was making things for her. She also nurtured an inner circle of top athletes and engaged them in gossip about the more awkward members of the team. When another coach confronted Barb about her favoritism, Barb tearfully complained to the team about how the other coaches hated her. The women were furious with these critics and responded by writing heartfelt letters in support of their coach. Even those Barb had treated most harshly felt sorry for their coach and penned their support.

Why are such overtly aggressive fragile bullies so often revered, even when their interactions border on or cross over into abuse? Why does it seem sometimes that the aggression itself is part of what binds the person to an authority figure?

Identifying with the Aggressor

Many of us refer to defense mechanisms when trying to understand some of the strange and seemingly contradictory behaviors employed by humans. Though Sigmund Freud typically gets credit for identifying the list of defenses we use today, another Freud deserves this distinction—his daughter, Anna. Her straightforward and groundbreaking manual, *The Ego and the Mechanisms of Defence,* stimulated a shift in the field to understanding and categorizing the creative ways people ward off anxiety and conflict.[1]

Anna Freud, a psychoanalyst who began her career as a schoolteacher, found that engaging children in play helped them to express and work through fears and difficulties in their lives. It was through these play sessions that she noticed the defense of "identification with the aggressor" at work. In her work, Freud discussed a play session she had with a boy the day after he ran headlong into the threatening fist of his teacher. The boy had transformed his tearstained countenance of the previous day and came to her "very erect and dressed in full armor," complete with toy sword and pistol. She observed, "By impersonating the aggressor, assuming his attributes or imitating his aggression, the child transforms himself from the person threatened into the person who makes the threat."[2] This simple example hints at why a leader who yells at or terrorizes others can become popular. By aligning oneself with the aggressor, perhaps even becoming a "groupie," we put ourselves in a safer position—on the side of power. According to Anna Freud, this defense is "one of the ego's most potent weapons in its dealings with external objects which arouse its anxiety."[3]

Freud published her analysis just two years before the threat of Nazism forced her, with her eighty-two-year-old father and family, to flee their home in Vienna. Jewish psychoanalysts had a painful front seat to the defensive management of victimhood. Psychoanalyst Bruno Bettelheim, imprisoned in a concentration camp, observed the ways that some Jewish prisoners identified with the Nazi guards. For example, he noticed that if an ornament or button fell off a guard's uniform, these targeted prisoners would wear or hold the item in a pocket—eager to share in a piece of the power. Some prisoners also became informants, or even executioners, on behalf of the Nazis.[4]

While there is a wide chasm between a verbally or emotionally abusive coach and a Nazi guard, both hold power and both arouse anxiety in those they lead. In the extreme, betraying oneself may seem the only way to save one's own life. In both cases, standing by that authority allows the threatened individual to move away from anxiety and toward the source of power.

Preserving the Bond

Anna Freud's theory accounts for the self-protective function of siding with the bully. Better to be the aggressor than the victim. But does this explanation account for the deep love and devotion Barb's players felt toward her? A similar question wracked the brain of the analyst who, before Anna Freud, coined the term "identification with the aggressor." Hungarian psychoanalyst and close friend of the senior Freud, Sándor

Ferenczi, had a dilemma. He was puzzled by the tendency of certain traumatized patients to become especially compliant at the very time their symptoms worsened—at times he expected disappointment and criticism. These patients had been, as he put it, "misused children"—children whose affections and innocence had been exploited by parents or other trusted adults. The love the children felt for these adults was real, which is what made the abuse so difficult to process. Ferenczi wrote eloquently of the dilemma of the child in this situation:

> Their personalities are not sufficiently consolidated in order to be able to protest, even if only in thought, for the overpowering force and authority of the adult makes them dumb...The same anxiety, however, if it reaches a certain maximum, compels them to subordinate themselves like automata to the will of the aggressor, to divine each one of his desires and to gratify these; completely oblivious of themselves they identify themselves with the aggressor.[5]

Ferenczi explained that assuming the will of the aggressor was a part of the "traumatic trance" that allowed the child to preserve the feelings of tenderness that preceded the trauma and had been misused by the adult. He labeled this phenomenon the "confusion of tongues" between the adult and the child.[6] This, he concluded, is why the most traumatized of his patients exhibited this puzzling tendency to be compliant at the very times he expected them to be disappointed or critical. He noted that, at the times these patients felt most threatened, they worked harder to "read" and comply and identify with him. But the key to Ferenczi's discovery was that the identification was so strong and unconscious that they did not know their own minds. This concerned Ferenczi because he saw the potential for him to accept their compliance and neglect further exploration.

We see in my example of coach Barb how the gymnasts not only defended a coach who bullied them but were also furious on her behalf. They saw a coach who worked hard, cared, and was committed to the team. They saw this, in part, because she regularly told them of her heroism, but she backed her words with action. If enduring her "misuse" of them meant getting to stand in her reflected glow, to be an insider, to share in her love of the sport, and even to feel that love from her, this was worth it.

Cyclical psychodynamics takes into account the behavioral side of this phenomenon. Coach Barb offered a number of perks to those who identified with her and made her look good: she confided in them, made them feel special, and gave them an elevated status. And, in turn, they defended her methods. Fragile bullies often nurture "insiders," doling out benefits in exchange for unquestioning loyalty.

Protecting the Bully

Coach Barb was not only an aggressor. She was easily hurt and regarded herself as a victim. Her vulnerability further confused the picture for her players and pulled them in when they might have protested. This provides a kind of compromised intimacy to her players: "If she won't care for me, at least I can take care of her."

The times they received the most care were the times she was also misusing them—venting about how burdened she was when she was supposed to be coaching them, asking them to betray teammates, expecting them to advocate for her at their own expense. Suddenly, the aggressor needed their support, and that felt good.

While it lures with the prospect of closeness, the bully's fragility also inspires forgetting. Like the misdirection used by magicians, fragility turns our focus away from what is happening to us and fixates us on the needs of the bully. This shift is so subtle that it can look like care. Consider the dramatic expressions of guilt and remorse a serial abuser expresses following the abuse. These expressions move the victim to protect the abuser from pain by minimizing the abuse, agreeing not to tell, or impulsively offering forgiveness. At worst, the misdirection is so complete that the victim feels like the aggressor, whose truth is an unwanted weapon. Successful misdirection and forgetting keeps the abuse cycle in motion.

The fragile bully's rage can even inspire protectiveness. It took me years to recognize this shift in the dance with my father. Even as he was ranting against liberals, I sensed that they must be more powerful than him to be so threatening. Here he was doing the bullying, and I wanted to protect him from the evil conspirators he seemed to fear. So my hidden protective impulse distracted me from his aggression. Identification with the aggressor and protection of the victim work together to reinforce the fragile bully's antagonism, and the dance goes on.

Though misdirection has the effect of a deftly performed magic trick, someone in the grip of narcissism has little awareness of the performance. Directing the focus back to oneself is a narcissistic reflex. The fragile bully's vulnerability is both a reality and a convenient tool. Barb, like Narcissus, couldn't bear to part with her own reflection, and her team became another way for her to affirm her fleeting sense of self. The team, in a sense, *became* her. This is why her dedication and commitment got so easily mixed up with bullying and control. Anything that shifted focus away from her was a problem needing swift correction.

Delegating Aggression

In addition to moving us closer to power and rewards, identification with the aggressor allows us to relinquish responsibility for our own aggression. Aligning with the bully comes
with its own form of misdirection: we can disavow our own
violent feelings while secretly appreciating that someone else
has expressed them.

For women, who face social constraints on aggression and
still have limited access to power, this identification may indi-
rectly empower them. The woman who marries a strong "bad
boy" may be considered weak, when she is actually—though
perhaps unconsciously—being strategic.

I recall my little sister and me tagging along with my dad
on his clergy visits to the elderly. My sister lacked my shyness
about asking for what she wanted, and at each stop blurted
out, "Do you have any candy?" I loved this, because when they
offered her candy, I got some, too. I even took to whispering
a prompt to my sister to remind her to make the requests. I
could remain sweet and quiet, and she was small enough to get
by with her less refined manners.

Though this is a benign example of delegating aggression,
it illustrates the reason why we may empower people we would
not want to emulate. An aggressive partner may embarrass or
appall us even as he or she gets us the candy—or much more
valuable benefits. The family or workplace troublemaker who
picks every battle often has quiet supporters who only express
their support in secret.

This secret support explains, at least in part, how polls and
proclamations were unable to predict the numbers of voters
who would endorse Donald Trump as their choice for U.S.
president. There certainly were vocal supporters, many of
whom were angry and wanted a president who heard them

and was willing to be angry on their behalf. But it was the quiet supporters who moved him from outlier to center stage. Many disavowed Trump's crass statements while finding it refreshing that he was not politically correct and spoke his mind. They wanted to look away but also wanted to peek and watch him do what, while they might like to, they wouldn't dare to do.

The Destructive Dance

Join the Aggressor

The figure shows how the fragile bully dynamic plays out in the Join the Aggressor dance. On the surface, we see an angry aggressor hurling insults, blaming, threatening. Those who identify with him join the throng and feel empowered. Their support, in turn, feeds the bully's fire, and aggression begets more aggression.

But, as we've discussed, the bully is also communicating fragility. This is not someone who is just picking on people—he's been harmed, she's reacting to a threat, he needs allies. For Donald Trump, the threat justifying his aggression was the media with its "fake news." For Barb, it was the hateful coaches. For my dad, it was the liberals who made him lose control with rage. This "victim card" further justifies aggression and supports the vicious circle.

To get a more intimate feel for this dance, let's look at the interactions between Coach Barb and one of her gymnasts. Nanci has Olympic-sized dreams and never complains about the long training hours. But Coach Barb seems to always find a way to pick on her, and Nanci is always on edge during practice. Today during training, Trudy, a less experienced gymnast, asks a naïve question. The coach sighs and rolls her eyes, looking over at Nanci with a sly smile before proceeding to mimic Trudy. Though Nanci has been in Trudy's place and wants to feel empathy, what she feels instead is joy. With that look, Coach Barb includes her, makes her an ally. Nanci starts to look for opportunities to expose the weaknesses of teammates, studying and mimicking the coach's treatment of them. Barb, in response, shows her more warmth and engages her in more conspiratorial looks and gestures. When Barb opens up to Nanci about an unfair confrontation by another, "horrible," coach, Nanci again feels the relief of being safe from Barb's wrath. But, more than that, Nanci feels a welcomed tenderness toward her coach. She wants to take care of her and promises to do whatever she can to advocate for her. Nanci shares tears and gratitude. In contrast to the terror Nanci felt at practices before, it feels so good to be Barb's ally and to want to support her. She does not fully trust this feeling—she knows Barb is likely to turn on her—but Nanci will do everything in her power to keep this alliance.

When someone who has been mistreating us is finally nice, the contrast can be mesmerizing. In a way, the fear of aggression empowers aggression. Nanci wanted more than ever to *just be safe*. The Join the Aggressor dance gave her that feeling—while only empowering Barb's aggression that much more. A vicious circle.

But Not ME

It is easy to observe scenarios like this and deny that we would align with a bully to this degree. Yet, history attests to the allure of siding with the aggressor as a way to access benefits. In today's hostile political atmosphere, we may cling to the side of power even when the person wielding it defies our values. And this can happen in very subtle ways. Consider your social media behaviors. Do you readily "hide" or unfollow offensive posts from the other side of the political spectrum while smiling to yourself as you read vile posts from your own side? Are you less critical of aggressors who are "cool," socially influential, or nice to you? Do you tolerate name-calling, violent images, and humiliation when directed toward a mutual target? Do you hide reasonable contrary points of view only because they might be unpopular with aggressive allies? Do you fuel a bully's fire by contributing evidence to support his or her rants? Do you support the bully in secret, through a private message or nod, while frowning more publicly? Do you nominate the aggressor to do your dirty work?

These behaviors can seem benign in isolation but have the cumulative effect of creating social media echo chambers that, unchecked by rational and diverse voices, proliferate hatred and aggression.

The Subtle Art of Managing Aggression

Stepping back from the Join the Aggressor dance does not mean denying aggression, as this denial is usually one of the steps. Freeing oneself may start with some uncomfortable realizations. Let's look at these realities and how they can help free you from the destructive dance.

It would be much easier if this were not true, but love and abuse can coexist. If you are in an abusive cycle, recognizing that what you love also hurts you is hard to accept. So when the bully goes fragile, his misdirection may be a welcome respite from that reality. The victim can ignore her hurt and focus on the bully's pain. In her harrowing account, *Silent No More*, domestic abuse survivor Krista Fink shows how writing down her reality was part of her salvation.[7] We see her start with lists of pros and cons of the relationship, along with the risks and losses that might come with changing its terms or, riskier yet, leaving. The lists evolve into starkly honest journal entries, poems, and letters to her husband. In the safety of this private space, Fink begins the long and rocky process of freeing her mind and escaping her imprisonment inside the dangerous dance of abuse. She explains that the outsider's view often assumes that an abuser has no redeeming qualities, that wanting to leave is a no-brainer. "Wrong." she writes. "The woman cannot simply give up on the radiance and beauty of the man she once knew."[8] The need for us to hold apart the meanness of the bully from his tenderness helps to trap abusers in vicious circles. While some observers don't "get" why someone stays, others don't see a problem. These outsiders choose to see the funny, charismatic, even self-deprecating charmer and wonder why his partner is so hard on him. They, too, want to hold onto his radiance and beauty. Exiting this dance requires the hard and often lonely work of becoming conscious of these incongruous realities. Documenting abuse serves the dual purpose of keeping yourself conscious of it and of—eventually—making it real for others you will need for your protection. Connecting with others who have lived the journey also provides the accurate mirroring you need.

Be prepared that, when you exit the dance, there will be grief. The grief of giving up, the grief of accepting what you've lost, the grief of seeing how you've been hurt, the grief of separating from someone who still holds beauty—however fleeting, the grief of giving up on that person, the grief that you are getting nothing back from your investment. As unfair as it is, the path may involve relinquishing a job, financial assets, or social status. You may have to break up a home. When a friend of mine finally decided to divorce the husband who had repeatedly betrayed her, she sat down with her children and told them honestly, "This is necessary for me, but it is not good for you, and I am incredibly sad about that." Allowing her own grief gave her the strength to let her children grieve too. Grief, as hard as it is to bear, is the first indication that you are letting go. Allow the grief to accompany you, to befriend you as you do this brave and devastating thing. In Chapter 14, we'll look more closely at how to manage these feelings with compassion.

Freeing yourself from another's aggression may also mean reconciling with the aggressor in you. This doesn't mean lashing out at someone in a rage. Not only is that dangerous, but it can also provoke more aggression—cue the Provoke and React in Chapter 10. But it is important to look honestly at how another's aggression might serve you. Is he or she fighting your battles for you? Are you working so hard to be good and pure that you refuse to defend yourself? Are you standing behind a bully who takes on someone you dislike? Even the subtle act of laughing at a joke can be a way of releasing something we'd rather not own. It is very hard to see that some of the qualities in an aggressor may also rest within us, especially if that aggression has become twisted and ugly. For someone alienated from her own aggression, even asserting and enforcing boundaries, refusing to indulge an abuser's convenient fragility, or deciding to ignore a provocative text message may feel too aggressive and hurtful. There will always be those forces—often within— telling you that aggression negates your own goodness. Anger is a clarifying emotion and helps us to take responsibility for our own care. Healthy aggression does not have to negate your tender qualities but can in fact protect them.

Freeing yourself means using your own words. I recall a conversation that woke me up to the risks of passive assent. Years ago, a reporter was interviewing me for a story about a cooking course I was taking. He was curious about the appeal of cooking for me, a busy psychologist. He had his own theory about this, something to do with how the tangible results of a cooked meal contrasted with the work of changing people. I understood his assumption, and I nodded that understanding. But I did not agree. My appreciation of cooking had much more to do with the process—the sensory experience of creating a meal—than it had to do with the quick and tangible results. As I politely listened, smiled, and nodded, he dominated the conversation with his views. By the time I shared my own perspective, he seemed ready to wrap up the interview. I quickly interjected some of my own thoughts and trusted he would capture my experience in his story. To my surprise and dismay, the article quoted me as saying the very thing I disagreed with—using *his* words! For him, my nods and smiles meant I agreed and apparently emboldened him to think he could safely attribute the thoughts to me. It was a minor story, but it left a major impression. He brazenly attached his ideas to my credentials—and I had let him. After fuming about it, I saw that a part of me was comfortable with him taking the floor, and that it was often easier for me to let others speak than to venture forth with my own words. The media interview is actually a great example of the art of managing aggression. Through interviews that have followed, I have learned to actively disagree and correct reporter's words that might be imputed to me, to interject key points not volunteered by the reporter, and to follow up if I think a point has been misinterpreted. My interviews are better, and reporters often come back to me to comment on subsequent stories. If we stop nodding and smiling at the aggressors on social media and in our lives—if we use our own words—new and more interesting conversations will emerge.

9

THE REASSURANCE DANCE

In most of our human relationships, we spend much
of our time reassuring one another that our
costumes of identity are on straight.

–RAM DASS

M y father was an excellent orator. His approach to
speaking was textbook: introduction, three main
points, each supported with evidence and brought
to life with colorful stories, then pulled together in a powerful conclusion. Though he indulged a rich vocabulary and
well-reasoned arguments, I remember him sharing with me
how important it was to appeal to the child in his listeners.
His stories, in fact, often featured children. He always arrived
at the pulpit prepared and confident, sermon text written out
and punctuated with underlines and red ink. When he delivered a sermon, his melodic bass voice filled the sanctuary.

So, after church, Dad's query, "What did you think?" was
always a bit puzzling to me. Wasn't he there? It was great! But
the question came, every week, loaded with expectation. This
was our cue to engage in the Reassurance Dance.

The Steps

Only the naïve would think that Dad was asking for an honest critique. He wanted reassurance, and not just reassurance that his sermon was good. He wanted—*needed*, it seemed—assurance that it was exceptional, flawless, life changing. But I'm not even sure those adjectives would have satisfied him. The Reassurance Dance (see Figure 3) exposes the paradox of narcissism: When a fragile bully effectively pressures a partner to affirm her specialness or superiority, the reassurance feels empty. The dance begins with its predictable steps:

1. **The preemptive demand.** A hallmark of problematic narcissism is the need to control the responses of others, and to use these responses to feed the grandiose self. Dad had a brood of children—ten of us, and we were easy targets for this control. Far from proper critics, we were cast in that role nonetheless. What frustrated me even more than this unwanted role was that Dad's question ignored or preempted any spontaneous expressions of my feelings about his message. He had already shaken hands with a long row of parishioners who provided their spontaneous praise. But spontaneity was too risky: he might not receive praise, and even if he did, it might not match his lofty expectations. As I look back, the fact that his children even listened and retained the messages in his sermon—*and we did*—was remarkable. But he couldn't take that in because anything below the bar enforced by the grandiose self was as good as nothing. This is the sad trick of narcissism: the responder's true feelings may be positive, but the solicited response robs the feedback of its authenticity. I longed for that real engagement with my dad and would sometimes pose theological questions that troubled me. More often than not,

he saw these questions as a threat. Maybe the question would expose the limits of his understanding or doubts of his own. Maybe, in those moments, he felt less like an authority and more like a fellow searcher. Truthful discourse means relinquishing authority and control, and that just feels too dangerous. Better stick to the script. So, he would laugh at me—sometimes raucously—and then make a comment along the lines of, "Isn't that cute?" Supporting the grandiose self means relinquishing real engagement—including the real rewards that come with it.

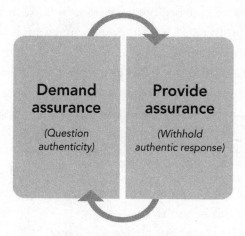

The Reassurance Dance

2. **The reluctant response.** When a request for feedback is loaded with the demand for praise, the stench of manipulation and control taints our reasons for responding. The response is no longer a gift, but a duty, and an impossible one at that. So the responder often walks a thin line between pleasing the requester and withholding. What often comes out is a dutiful, bland, and reluctant response. This isn't always the case; at times, we may gush because we really want to assure the requestor of his value.

But as the cycle continues, as it did with my dad, the dance becomes boring, and it gets harder to muster up the same enthusiasm. As I look back, I see that I withheld responses as much as I forced them. Years later, in graduate school, I saw this dynamic from the perspective of the fragile bully. I met weekly with a colleague and our supervisor to review our therapy sessions. I was irked that my colleague seemed to get a lot more support and validation from the supervisor, even though he was frequently late and didn't seem as invested as I was. After working together for several weeks, my supervisor admitted, "I find myself reluctant to give you positive feedback because you seem to expect so much of it." His comment stung, but I got it. I knew too well the oppression that comes with the demand for praise. But he was also identifying a problem: he had been withholding feedback on what I was doing right, and this was as important as his critical feedback. And, until he stepped back and observed what was happening, he was a full participant in the dance. His withholding had left me hungry and expectant, contributing to my neediness, which deepened his resistance, which heightened my neediness—and so on.

3. **Pushing for more.** Even when the fragile bully receives the solicited reassurance, he or she is skeptical: "This doesn't sound convincing," or "She said it just to make me feel better." And when reluctance gives way to withholding or weak responses, the requester undertandably wants something better. So he pushes: "C'mon, tell me the truth," or, like my dad, "So it was really bad, then?" This is an interesting step in the dance because while it feels like a plea for honesty, the responder knows that honesty will evoke a crisis. The paradox for the fragile bully is that he does hunger for a real response but just as desperately wants the right response. Few of us are exempt from this paradoxical

wish: tell me the truth and tell me how great I am. We laugh at the familiar, "Does this dress make me look fat?" because we know that anything but a quick and emphatic "No" is dangerous. For the fragile bully, however, there is much more at stake than the choice of the evening's outfit. The fragile bully needs a *self*. Since he can't accept the real one he lives in, he'll need others to reflect something better. He needs—or thinks he needs—responses that assure him he is safe and untouchable, above reproach, admired, and oh so loved. So with the request for more comes the unspoken instruction: "Tell me what I want to hear; just be more convincing this time." This phase of the dance may escalate in intensity, the bully becoming angry and belittling the reluctant responder, who in turn expresses anger about being controlled and insulted. This, at least temporarily, shifts the steps to the "provoke and react" pattern we'll discuss in Chapter 10. Though the steps have changed, the entrapping nature of the dance remains. Sometimes the new steps take over, and at other times, the dance circles back to the reassurance theme.

4. **Giving in.** In an effort to get out of the dance, the responder often—eventually—provides what he or she thinks will satisfy the fragile bully: "Of course you are (fill in the blank)." When the fragile bully calms and becomes personable, the responder may feel a sense of control. True, she is calming the bully, but the bully is also doling out rewards. Through the often-confusing process of negative reinforcement, he is rewarding her with the *removal* of the oppressive stimulus— his need-laden demands. Just as the child, by ending her tantrum, teaches her parents to produce the unearned privilege or toy, the indulged fragile bully teaches the responder to produce the inauthentic reassurance. In addition, the fragile bully may offer positive reinforcement—being more pleasant and engaging—after getting the desired feedback.

The hallmark of a vicious circle is that our very efforts to stop it actually keep it going. The reprieve is temporary; the lesson lasts.

5. **The next demand.** The next cycle begins when the fragile bully needs another positive spin. Cue the music.

Variations on the Theme

In the example above, the requester's vulnerability and neediness is quite apparent. A fragile bully on the grandiose end of the continuum is more likely to simply "take" affirmation and mirroring from those around her. Those caught in the mirror may feel nods and utterances of praise pulled from their bodies. Like a process called "entrainment" in which a strong musical rhythm generates responses of foot tapping or head bobbing, a narcissist's stories of her amazing accomplishments generate a rhythm of their own. Boldly delivered gestures, smiles, and affirmative nods come off as instructions to listeners, and we find ourselves nodding along whether we are impressed or not. In a group setting, other enthralled responders also entrain us. Just as the emperor's pride in his nonexistent clothes had his subjects doubting their vision, we may feel out of synch if we don't join the dance.

The Dance, in Reverse

So far, we've looked at the ways the fragile bully's demands fuel the sequence of events comprising the Reassurance Dance. What is going on with the partner?

Sometimes the partner is more of a trainee, a subordinate. This was the case for me as a young girl learning the steps from my father. And a powerful leader needing reassurance can simply hire partners to engage in the dance. Not all leaders do this. For example, Winston Churchill purposely appointed staff who would challenge him.[1] But too often, reassurance is part of the job description. Many wonder what compelled press secretary Sean Spicer to falsely claim, on newly elected President Trump's behalf, "This was the largest *audience* to ever witness an *inauguration*—period—both in person and around the globe."[2] Spicer later expressed regrets over the statement and even parodied this exaggerated claim.[3] An authority-subordinate relationship complicates the Reassurance Dance.

The partner may also reassure out of fear. A fragile bully prone to narcissistic rage may rant, despair, ridicule, or argue— or worse if the appropriate response is not provided. Feeding the beast will at least keep her from biting you.

Even in these cases, a partner caught up in the Reassurance Dance may identify with the fragile bully's insecurity and feel she is helping him by building him up. I certainly felt this pull as a child, thinking: "I wish Dad knew how talented he is! I want to make him feel okay." (Anything less than outstanding was not okay.) This is a common, and commonly unhelpful, response of family members to someone with an anxiety disorder. The plea is: "I'm anxious. Reassure me."[4] We want to help, and it seems easy enough to give what is asked. Sometimes we reassure because we're uncomfortable with the requester's vulnerability and want to do away with it. A part of the treatment of anxiety disorders is to train family members to withold reassurance. Narcissism, like anxiety, always demands more reassurance, feeding apprehensions about the unknown. The reality is, no one can reassure away the variability and uncertainty of life. To some extent, reassurance is always false. In small doses, it is a balm that smoothes the rough edges of life. As a steady diet, it is heroin without the high.

Sometimes the partner is the one leading the dance, and here's where the location of narcissism can get tricky. These partners, like Echo, are eager to offer a response. They quickly nod, validate, send a smiley face, voice their agreement—even when not particularly enthused and even when such reassurance is not requested. They may also be too ready with an "it's okay!" or "no worries" when the partner retracts an offensive comment. For these responders, the prospect of having a separate experience may be frightening. Focusing on and caring for the feelings of others at least puts the dancers in synch. A responder who withholds her independent response or offers empty praise may actually frustrate a partner looking for something more authentic. Over time, eager reassurers may train others to expect reassurance. My father, who grew up deprived of reassurance and praise, vowed to offer it freely to us. The problem was, my siblings and I became praise junkies while also learning to mistrust such easily earned recognition. He unknowingly made us needy by attempting to do the opposite.

The partner's contribution may also reflect a desire for reciprocity. We often give the very thing we crave hoping the partner will respond in kind: "I build you up, you build me up." This approach feels safer for people who don't want to come off as needy or egotistical. Let's look at an example of this and how it backfires for Colleague B, the one covertly seeking attention. The two colleagues are debriefing after they each advocated for a similar issue at a meeting:

Colleague A: I think my comment opened up a can of worms.

Colleague B: I'm so glad you spoke to that. Everyone needed to know what was happening.

Colleague A: Yes, I think…[elaborates on why she raised it, tells a story, etc.]

Colleague B: I really appreciated your advocacy. [Thinking: "Enough already. What about my comments? I raised the issue we agreed was central."]

Colleague A: I wanted to get the concern out there…[elaborates at length]

In this example, we have no indication that Colleague B has any need for attention or reassurance. Even at the first opening in the conversation, when B could have shifted attention to herself, she offers up another reassuring statement. For B, this is one last deposit toward the expected return. For Colleague A, however, this is great! More affirmation! Another cue to remain in the spotlight and elaborate on her contribution! The closer A is to the extreme end of the narcissism spectrum, the more B's reassurance will whet, rather than satiate, A's appetite.

But in this example, the location of narcissism is a bit harder to pinpoint. Colleague B does not want to ask for, much less compete for, the desired reassurance. She wants A to feel satiated and to willingly move over and hand the mic to B. Colleague B wants the same kind of rapt attention that she is providing, and her affirmation of A may be more concerned with this end than with a desire to offer genuine support. Rather than stooping to A's level and hogging the spotlight, B wants to set things up so she can remain humble *and* get what A is getting. If she's dealing with a fragile bully, her plan will be foiled. She may need to settle for feeling superior—see Chapter 12—and cue the Superior Dance.

B's role reflects a much subtler form of narcissism but shares its controlling nature. And, though A looks more like a narcissist, it is hard to know how much she would have dominated the conversation if B had interjected herself. In a true vicious circle, it is impossible to know where the problem originates.

Loving Reassurance, Accurate Praise

We all crave reassurance from time to time. Like the child frightened by a skinned knee, there are times when we need to know we are okay—that our fears are unfounded. An adoring look from a loved one can work like a superpower when we are about to face a challenge. Even the occasional white lie about the bad haircut, as transparent as it may be, can soften the sting of reality. And as excessive as my dad's applause might have been, I would never have traded it for the silence he received from his mother.

What distinguishes healthy reassurance from its destructive counterpart? I go back to the old wisdom, "The proof is in the pudding." Healthy reassurance promotes health. It provides a needed boost that sends the loved one on his way. It softens, but does not obscure, reality. It is freely offered. And it is enough. Destructive reassurance weakens the recipient and promotes detachment from reality.

When discussing the fragile bully, I often use the terms "praise" and "reassurance" interchangeably. Where an anxiety-plagued individual wants reassurance that everything is always okay, the narcissist seeks reassurance that he or she is always outstanding. Is the quest for praise always a bad thing?

Parenting expert Vicki Hoefle notes that praise puts the locus of control outside of the individual.[5] The praised child is relying on the parents' evaluation of her performance. Hoefle suggests using encouragement instead—asking the child about her experience, what worked, what didn't, what she liked, and what she learned. This approach equips the child to assess her own choices while identifying what is important to her.

While this is sound advice, does it mean that parents and loved ones should omit their own subjectivity from the interactions? Few of us are satisfied with the response to a new haircut, "How do *you* like it?" We do crave input from the world around us because that input is evidence that we have been seen, recognized. Feminist theorist and psychoanalyst Jessica Benjamin notes that *recognition* requires more than mirroring:

> Self psychology is misleading when it understands the mother's recognition of the child's feelings and accomplishments as maternal mirroring. The mother cannot (and should not) be a mirror; she must not merely reflect back what the child asserts; she must embody something of the not-me; she must be an independent other who responds in her different way.[6]

Genuine responses may indeed communicate enthusiastic approval. Sadly, the word "praise" often conjures something cheap and empty. I recall a comedian lamenting the fact that "hilarious" is used so liberally that it no longer distinguishes comic genius. Add overused responses like "awesome" and "amazing" and it becomes apparent how devoid of meaning praise has become. A recent longitudinal study of parent-child interactions found that when parents responded to their children's performance with inflated vocabulary, the kids ended up feeling worse about themselves than they had before the praise. What is notable about this study is that, overall, the children receiving the inflated praise had lower self-esteem at the start of the study and actively elicited praise from their parents.[7] Cue the Reassurance Dance.

The authors noted one exception: when parents directed inflated praise toward children with high self-esteem, the kids reported increased feelings of superiority, entitlement, and hunger for admiration—in other words, increased grandiosity.

Together, these results suggest that when it comes to praise, bigger is not better. The authors advise parents to use indirect ways of raising children's self-esteem—by showing them interest, warmth, and acceptance.

The Genius of Mister Rogers

In 1963, a man named Fred Rogers set out to make a difference in the lives of children. He wanted to connect with their "inner drama" rather than stimulating them with the imposed drama offered by cartoons and slapstick television programming. He built his show, *Mister Rogers' Neighborhood,* around this message.[8] He repeated at the end of each episode, "You've made this day a special day, by just your being you. There's no person in the whole world like you, and I like you just the way you are." Though loved by children and parents alike, critics later blamed him for the rise in narcissism among our youth and for the damage inflicted by giving children the idea that they are special. I think this critique is an apt example of the oversimplification of the self-esteem debate. A more intimate understanding of Mister Rogers's mission reveals how he worked to ameliorate, not empower, narcissistic impairment.[9] He saw how children were abandoning their inner experience and substituting grandiose fantasies supplied by the new medium of television. In his testimony before the Senate Subcommittee on Communications, he commented:

> We don't have to bop somebody over the head to make drama on the screen. We deal with such things as getting a haircut, or the feelings about brothers and sisters, and the kind of anger that arises in simple family situations... If we...can only make it clear that feelings are mentionable and manageable, we will have done a great service for

mental health...I think that it's much more dramatic that two men could be working out their feelings of anger— much more dramatic than showing something of gunfire... This is what I give every day—an expression of care.[10]

When Fred Rogers engages someone, we can often observe a palpable shift in the other person's demeanor. Rogers looks at individuals, children and adults alike, in a way that makes room for them. The recipient of his attention no longer needs to defend his identity and at once becomes more open. In the Senate testimony, Senator John Pastore, who starts out rather gruff and impatient, says to Rogers later in the exchange, "I'm supposed to be a pretty tough guy, and this is the first time I've had goosebumps."

There is a difference between telling a child that she is above humanity and telling the child that she is valued *in* her humanity. The former sets up a constant striving and precarious basis for self-acceptance. The latter serves as an invitation to be present, "just the way you are." And when there is room for us to be present, there is also room for us to experiment, to fail and to feel, and to grow.

Just as false or inflated praise can backfire, so can the squelched and austere responses of earlier parenting trends. Rogers showed genuine delight in the children he encountered, and this was not an evaluation of the child but rather a feeling of his own. If we enliven our vocabularies with words like "awe" and "delight," we can see the beauty of genuine praise. It is a moment where two subjectivities meet. I express me, and you feel a sense of awe and delight in what you see. The moment is so powerful because a wide range of responses, including very negative ones, are possible. I don't force your response, nor do you force my performance. What performer would feel fine looking out at a bored and dissatisfied audience? And what lover would be happy with a neutral response to a kiss?

Caring for the self of another requires both neutral curiosity about the other's experience and real, subjective responding. The latter is fraught with uncertainty, and the former helps us build the inner strength to face it.

New Moves

The Reassurance Dance, like any vicious circle, bars spontaneous responding. My husband can likely testify that he has faced the same landmine with me as I did with my dad. My "What do you think?" typically came with the message, "Assure me that I am special." Fortunately for both of us—though not always easy for me—he is the worst person in the world to provide false reassurance. And, because of this, he is also the best, most credible person I know to provide authentic praise. I joke that he is like Mikey on the old Life cereal commercial: the kid who hates everything. When Mikey first gingerly tastes, then aggressively digs into the Life cereal, the other kids know it is good. My Mikey readily praises me but only when he believes it. And he'll as readily say, "not your best work," if that is what he thinks.

Over our thirty-five years of marriage, we have worked out some new moves, ones that take us somewhere new rather than keeping us in the vicious circle. As well as I knew the Reassurance Dance, my partner just couldn't learn the steps. For that, I am grateful.

When I deconstruct what helped open me to a different and more flexible dance, I don't see heroic efforts. My hunger for something different was there in my attempts to engage my dad and probably in my pursuit of psychology as a career path. But I encountered a lot of life, loving helpers, and plenty of stuck points along the way. For example, as if to keep the familiar dance close by, I managed to find a series of bosses who cast me back in the dance with my father. I not only played Echo to their Narcissus but I found other places to forge mirrors of my own. I loved the stage and the podium but faced a familiar terror afterwards when I worried about parting with that positive focus. I recall a woman in a therapy group with me who called me on my needy, mirror-hungry presentation and said, "I think you are much stronger than you let on." I hated her at the moment, and later loved her, for saying that. But the most gentle and healing process for me came through my own psychoanalysis, in which I grieved the neglect I had experienced, indulged my need for mirroring, and eventually saw and accepted the shameful parts of me the Reassurance Dance worked to evade.

I still consider my relationship with my husband a sort of miracle. He did not follow my rules, nor was I particularly responsive to his anxieties. But we were mad about each other, and I think admired each other for the very qualities that perplexed us. We at times needed a translator and found a couple's counselor before we walked down the aisle. After playing both parts in the Reassurance Dance, here's what I've learned about freeing yourself from its grip:

1. **Establish safety.** The relationships that helped me the most, and that I was most able to impact, were ones that offered safety. If you are worried about abusive retaliation, you may be wise to play along until you can get out safely. If your boss is the one demanding that you play—or even compensating you for it—you'll need to look closely at what leverage you have to make changes, as well as possible consequences for trying alternate responses. An alternative job may start to look more inviting.

2. **Exchange false positives for real ones.** Freeing yourself from the Reassurance Dance does not mean depriving yourself or your partner of positive input, nor does it mean shoving bad

reviews down that partner's throat. In a classic longitudinal study of relationships, researchers John Gottman and Robert Levenson were able to predict, with 90% accuracy, which couples would stay together and which would divorce.[11] Their observations revealed something they called the "magic relationship ratio." They found that for every one negative interaction, healthy couples exchange five positive interactions. This did *not* mean they avoided conflict, but that they were able to interject affection, humor, and caring into their disagreements, and to make repairs where needed. This formula doesn't work if you're the only one providing the positives. And the more you feel manipulated and bullied, the more the positives will ring false anyway. What you can communicate in these situations is that your partner matters, that you care about the relationship, and that you need your partner, too. If you sense that the two of you are about to repeat old, destructive patterns, say so. Express your desire for it to go better this time and for both of you to end up with more. In his book, *Rethinking Narcissism*, Craig Malkin cites extensive research demonstrating that narcissists can become more nurturing and empathic when others support and encourage these qualities in them.[12] And even though narcissists push for reassurance of their competence, what deepens their commitment is assurance that they are loved and cared about.[13] By refusing to participate in something destructive to you, you are protecting your ability to remain loving. And by including your own feelings in the conversation, you are providing your partner an opportunity to practice empathy.

3. **Allow your partner his own experience.** What I learned from my husband is that staying free to respond authentically requires a certain amount of insensitivity. By this, I do not mean coldness or cruelty but rather resistance to the pull of another's emotions. The paradoxical gift of

this reduced sensitivity is that it allows the other person to have a separate experience. The fact that my husband didn't respond to the pull to rescue me from my discomfort was maddening at times, and terrifying at my most vulnerable points. He let me have my anxiety, and I learned that it didn't kill me. I'll note that this was not always a strength on his part—he acknowledges he would have made a horrible therapist. But even as he frustrated me, I filled those gaps with my own unrecognized strength. For highly sensitive people like myself, allowing others to feel discomfort can be challenging. Their discomfort becomes ours, and we rescue, in large part, to rid ourselves of those feelings—"Sure, everything's great. Now feel better so I can too." If we placate a fragile bully, are we responding to our own discomfort with the uncertainties of reality? Are we trying to be the same in order to avoid being alone? As a lawyer, my husband is comfortable with opposing views and even sees opposition as an avenue to truth. This trust in difference is a helpful perspective to adopt and one that I have come to appreciate as a therapist. I cannot truly see and empathize with my clients unless I allow them to experience their own feelings. Paradoxically, I cannot truly be with another unless I remain separate. And a partner cannot be with me unless I show myself.

4. **Acknowledge the limitations of your opinion.** When I asked my husband if he noticed the new layers in my hair after a cut, he said, "Yeah, I don't notice those things. For me, you either have hair or you don't, and it looks good or it doesn't. It looks good." I had to laugh because it was clear he was not the one to appreciate the subtlety of my long layers. I cared more about style than he did, and friends who cared might give me better input on the quality of the cut. But this could have also been an opportunity for my husband to learn more about what I was going for and

whether the haircut met my expectations. Hoefle's suggestion that we inquire about the other person's experience not only helps firm up the other person's sense of self, but it fills in the gaps in our understanding.

Let's see how these suggestions might help in a situation like the one I encountered with my dad. To remove the power differential, I am reimagining an interaction between my father and mother starting with his infamous post-sermon interrogative:

"So what did you think?"

"I think we've had this conversation before, and it doesn't go well. Can we talk about this in a different way?" (Caring for the relationship.)

"So it was lousy, huh?"

"Honey, I care about what you feel, and when you say something like that, I feel bad, like I'm just making you feel worse." (Sharing her valuing of him, sharing her feelings.)

"Well, I do feel worse."

"Tell me what you're feeling, honey. I feel like we don't talk about that." (Expressing interest, listening.)

"Oh, I don't know. I'm just not sure I did that great of a job."

"Sounds like it's hard when you're not certain." (Letting him have his own experience, offering empathy.)

"Of course it is! For all I know, they are going home talking about what a lousy job I did."

"What do you think about the job you did?" (Filling in gaps in her understanding, bringing her closer to his experience.)

"How does that matter?"

"What you feel matters a lot to me. It's hard for me when you put it all in my hands." (Expressing caring, sharing feelings.)

"Well, I liked the illustration I used. And people said good things about it afterwards. I enjoyed making them laugh."

"I enjoy hearing you relive that. Maybe we can do that more often."

Though these alternative steps would not come as easy as this scenario suggests, they show how new responses can shift the conversation. The takeaway from the new conversation is not whether Dad did a good job on his sermon. This conversation has a different outcome: two people sitting together with the scary uncertainty of life, seeing each other a little better, and sharing something real.

10

PROVOKE AND REACT

Each episode vilifies one single person specifically and he ends up getting killed off. You enjoy seeing them get screwed although it's totally wrong and sick. You enjoy seeing them screwing others, getting screwed themselves, playing dirty, getting it back, escaping and finally getting kicked out.

–review of *The Apprentice*,
posted by y_turks on imdb.com.

The Provoke and React dance gets ratings, and it launches careers. After presiding over biting feuds on his reality TV show, *The Apprentice*, Donald Trump became the captivating antihero in his own presidential contest. He took center stage in the 2016 Republican primary, as his insults and unfiltered declarations inspired a backlash of vitriol. His war with the media fed on itself, assuring his place in the spotlight and guaranteeing ratings for participating news outlets. By the time the dance reached debates between Trump and Clinton, the verbal combat became so biting that parents questioned whether to allow their children to watch. The dance reverberated through Twitter wars and Facebook arguments while our much-manipulated "reality" TV dramas continued to bank on the same formula: captivate the mind with the very provocations we find repellant.

Reality TV started to capture the public's attention just as Christopher Lasch launched his book *The Culture of Narcissism.* Critics of the genre have noted that the first attempt at reality television failed. Too boring. So producers decided to make things interesting—put Paris Hilton in overalls and have her try "The Simple Life," cram strangers together, give them a few lines, stir up some conflict. What resulted is what television critic Marvin Kitman called "enhanced reality."[1]

How better to enhance reality than to recruit someone whose personality is defined by enhancement? No need to prompt a narcissist to put more emphasis on "Huge!," to syrup up the syrupy voice, or to alienate others by acting superior. And how better to engage viewers than to provoke them?

The viewer at the beginning of this chapter noted the paradoxical appeal of this reality TV device on *The Apprentice.* The featured villain, filled with narcissistic prowess, ridicules others, takes advantage, and elbows her way to the top. Then, predictably, new alliances form, victims retaliate, and she "gets screwed," humiliated, brought down to size. The lower the better. She deserves punishment equal to what she's been dishing out. Though some reality shows "kill off" the villain at this point, others allow the dance to circle back. The barrage of hateful responses to the villain transform her to victim. She is disgusted with the way others have treated her—how low *they* have stooped. She may even become a sympathetic character. Her aggression is now justified.

The viewer gets to enjoy another round.

The Joy of Hating

Rather than hiding behind and joining the aggressor, this vicious cycle involves reacting to and opposing the aggressor.

If the quest for love empowers the Join the Aggressor, what is it about hate that keeps us engaged?

Washington Post pop culture reporter Hannah Jewell was curious about what was happening in her brain as she sat mesmerized by TV's *The Bachelor.* Scientists at Indiana University in Bloomington agreed to take a look.[2] Using fMRI technology, they observed activity in her brain as she observed provocative scenes and contrasted this with her responses to neutral scenes on the same show.[3] The most interesting pattern they observed was that, every time the show's villain, Krystal, appeared on the screen, Jewell's brain appeared to be on fire. Oxygenated blood flooded the amygdala, a center that stays alert to disturbing emotions like intense dislike and anger. At the same time, brain regions responsible for regulating emotions lit up. And, finally, the striatum, implicated in drug addiction and craving, showed enhanced activity. Jewell's brain, on Krystal, was at once fuming, working to manage her intense feelings, and craving another Krystal fix.

Though this experiment didn't pretend to approach scientific rigor, researchers at the University of Kentucky found that when reacting to provocation, vengeance is sweet indeed. They observed brain activity during a competition. When provoked by particularly loud noise blasts from an opponent, retaliating was associated with increased activity in the nucleus accumbens, a region that is stimulated during rewarding and pleasurable experiences. In their 2016 research report entitled, "The Pleasure of Revenge," the authors noted aggression generated pleasure only when it was inspired by provocation.[4] Revenge cravings are a call to engage in the Provoke and React.

Could this association explain why it is so hard for us to let go of people who enrage us? Could it explain how the very reactions aimed toward defeating Donald Trump actually kept people involved with him?

What few seemed to anticipate is the way in which the hatred of Trump would engage the press, the public, and the addict within all of us. One Trump adversary I spoke with acknowledged that he was obsessed with the man he hated. He shared, "I want to see him get slapped this time. I just want to see him go down. I'm addicted to him. Why can't we get more dirt on him? Wasn't his association with Russia enough? I'm in battle with this guy. Why is it so personal?" Like the *Bachelor*-obsessed reporter, he wondered why he kept looking for more of the very thing that disturbed him.

Fragile bullies have a way of infiltrating our brains, even when—perhaps *especially* when—they enrage us. And this is why reality TV recruits—and creates—narcissistically vulnerable characters to play out the villain role. We'll look at this selection process more closely in Chapter 13.

The Steps

1. **The Provoke.** A fragile bully does not usually regard his aggression as an act of provocation. He or she sees it as self-defense. The hurled insult, belittling comment, and/or

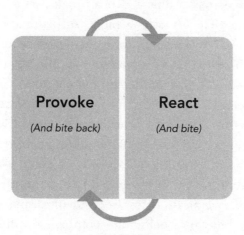

Provoke and React

exploitive behavior issue from a need to regain control by diminishing the other and expanding the self. These very efforts are the kind that get under the skin of the person targeted, and this may reinforce the bully's feeling of control. A fragile bully can also provoke simply through an attitude that is hard for others to stomach. One of the maddening qualities of narcissists—especially the grandiose type drawn to the spotlight—is their unwavering certainty regarding their superior giftedness and desirability even in the face of evidence to the contrary. They may take credit for ideas or products generated by others. They may simply fail to acknowledge the contributions—or existence—of others as they flaunt their self-made success. Whether this grandiosity is organic or prompted by a director, reality TV villains are skilled in this craft. One reality TV star, who ranks on more than one "best villain" lists—and who served a short stint on the Trump administration—stated without a trace of doubt, "I'm exceptional in everything that I do and aspire to do."[5] *The Bachelor's* Krystal Nielson concluded that she was "flawless," even as viewers cringed at the breathy, exaggerated voice delivering such assertions. Donald Trump's string of "nobody better" claims covers a broad range of expertise including, "There's nobody bigger or better at the military than I am."[6] When such words are paired with his casual, almost bored vocal tone—a male version of "mean girls" speak—visceral reactions begin to foment.

2. **The hook.** Whether the fragile bully's provocation comes in the form of a verbal attack or a posture of superiority, the effect on us is one of obliteration. Perhaps it registers with us as an annoying feeling of being left out—or identifying with others who have been left out, too (e.g., all the top military experts Trump's statement dismissed). When a fragile bully uses belittling—emphasis on the *little*—the experience we have of being obliterated is more palpable.

My dad's laugh when I asked a serious question had this effect. Trump's degrading statements toward women and immigrants have this effect. Though rage and hatred may swell in these moments, feelings of helplessness and panic surface as well. The very experience the fragile bully is trying to escape—obliteration, invisibility—is now thrust upon the recipient.

When I taught a course on "unhooking" for divorcing adults, the question on the table was, "What hooks you into staying engaged?" For those with narcissistically impaired partners, they desperately wanted to correct the ex, to interject their own reality, to set the record straight. They wanted to be seen by the ex even though the whole relationship had proven that impossible. Beyond that, there was an impulse to cut the ex down to size, to diminish the arrogance, to essentially obliterate his or her presence. The reality was that the attempts to obliterate only kept the ex close at hand.

A colleague of mine described an interaction he observed in a couple's session featuring a fragile bully: "They had this trigger issue about what to do about this parcel of land they had. Whenever the conversation drifted away from him, he would raise the issue. She fell for it every time, shifting her focus back to him, arguing the opposite of whatever he said. It always erupted into a battle. The weird thing is, they both seemed to enjoy it. And I realized at some point that they seemed to be performing for *me*. What I had to offer seemed of little consequence."

Online forums seem particularly conducive to the hooks of the Provoke and React, especially for people who do not dare to wield such aggression in face-to-face interactions. In fact, a recent study reported in the *Journal of Interpersonal Violence* reveals that only *covert* narcissism predicted both cyberbullying perpetration and victimization.[7] In other words, while the cyberbullying can seem grandiose and direct, the online bully is more likely to use indirect strategies in real life. The other interesting finding of this study is that covert narcissism also increases one's vulnerability to becoming a *victim* of cyberbullying. There are certainly victims who are just at the wrong place at that wrong time; the ones who stay engaged and justify bullying back are the ones more likely expressing covert narcissism.

Those who indulge in reality TV also appear to have a higher loading of narcissism, though it is unclear what causes what. People who are more narcissistic may be drawn to reality TV, reality TV might reinforce narcissism in its viewers, or there may be a mystery factor that influences both.[8]

3. **The React.** Once hooked, the imperative to respond follows. And as we noted earlier, responding may come with a rush of pleasure. After the ex sends a text chewing you out for a random behavior, you feel great as you tap out a top-notch defense and lay into him or her for sending the text in the first place. You temporarily feel victorious—until the next text pops up. Your dance steps are falling in line with the Provoke and React.

When provocations are televised, we cannot directly engage the opponent—but we can tweet, rant on Facebook, complain to those around us, and/or post humiliating memes. Deceived by the pleasure of these retaliations, we breed more of the very thing we are trying to eliminate. We find ourselves getting sick on the candy.

Attempts to obliterate the aggressor have become a national pastime. The extremes to which some have gone to belittle are notable in their absurdity and viciousness. Many enjoyed photographing the grotesque statue of an obese and naked Trump, sans testicles, installed as a protest in cities around the country. The same group that commissioned the statue, created by a horror artist, also painted the message, "Rape Trump," on a fence at the U.S.-Mexico border.[9] The vicarious thrill in seeing such humiliating images of Trump is evident in the more than 134 million Twitter likes for Jim Carrey's "official portrait" of Donald Trump gorging himself on ice cream in a sexualized manner.[10]

Perhaps you are thinking, "Isn't this kind of reaction justified by Trump's repellant behaviors?" I say you are asking the wrong question. A better question may be: "Does my reaction help my cause?" If we, as a people, start getting a charge out of the very strategies—dehumanization, objectification, humiliation—that we seek to diminish, these injuries, justified or not, will multiply. We end up doing exactly what fragile bullies do: we use righteous entitlement to justify amping up the aggression, and humiliation becomes a form of entertainment. What struck me the most about the response to the naked Trump statues were the reports of how much fun people had snapping photos and sharing them.

Meanwhile, *these reactions insure that the focus remains on the fragile bully.* Negative press is still press.

Finally, as the cyberbullying study reveals, provocations can be a used as an unhealthy, if convenient, justification for violent expressions of our own. Remember D, the YouTube host I discussed in Chapter 5? A rival host of a popular "content cop" video series took on the media villain. The challenger's video starts with funny footage and a step-by-step deconstruction of D's tactics—for example, the way D uses his support of less-known YouTubers to keep them loyal. And though this exposé is laced with offensive language itself, it doesn't devolve to D's revolting level until the end. The punchline to the video is, "This will be the first time I actually say unironically and mean it, 'kill yourself.'" The "content cop" response to D was sobering to me, as was the chorus of D's followers who echoed the invitation for him to kill himself. These findings place a new lens on the "react" side of the fragile bully dynamic. In addition to justifying aggressive responding, there seems to be some kind of payoff in being appalled, horrified, and indignant to the point of abuse. After all, D's appalled fans could have just unfollowed him rather than posting their horrified and counter-abusive comments in the feed. At what point, as we dance with the bully, do we become him?

4. **Bully becomes victim.** When retaliatory blows go low enough, the bully can justifiably claim victim status and lash out some more. Now, in addition to keeping the bully in the spotlight, he becomes an empathic figure—and the provoked party becomes the bully. Even after openly insulting and belittling someone, the fragile bully is shocked and hurt when others respond in kind. The brittleness of the bully takes center stage, and he now is only retaliating. He bites back, and the circle is complete.

Even when the retaliation is more benign—an expression of concern or questioning of reported facts, for example—the fragile bully may take great offense. Some of the most abusive bullies are also the most sensitive to slights, and here's where the dance gets trickier. The focus shifts to the bully's fragility, and there is something both pathetic and compelling about such distortions.

I know these feelings well. I remember the day I took my dad and his grandson—my three-year-old—to the Minneapolis Institute of Art. We enjoyed the museum and the time together. Everything was fine until I left my son with grandpa while I went to fetch the car. When I returned, they were not where I left them, and, after a brief search, I found my son alone with no idea where grandpa went. I was freaked out and furious. Dad nonchalantly came out of the bathroom, and when I confronted him, he made excuses talking about not feeling well. I had a bad feeling in the pit of my stomach as I fought the pull to see Dad as the victim. The pull was strong. What started as a simple need to use the bathroom became an impassioned plea to prioritize his vulnerability. Nothing about his behavior had suggested he was sick or distressed. And nowhere in his defense was there mention of the three-year-old child wandering around in a huge museum. If anything, Dad was mad at me for being so hard on him. My simple confrontation of the fact of his neglect was an affront to him. The angrier I became, the more he could justify his victimization.

Shifting the Focus

Tarana Burke, senior director for Brooklyn-based Girls for Gender Equity, saw her own limitations in responding to a girl desperate to tell her story of sexual abuse. Though Burke directed the girl to a counselor, she wished she had said two simple words: "me too." In discussing the words that became a movement, Burke later shared: "As a community, we create a lot of space for fighting and pushing back, but not enough for connecting and healing."[11]

The spirit of the #MeToo movement was not about retaliation, and that may be the secret to its power. On October 15, 2017, in the wake of allegations of sexual misconduct by Hollywood producer Harvey Weinstein, actress Alyssa Milano tweeted an invitation to women everywhere who had experienced sexual harassment or assault: "Write 'Me Too' as a reply to this tweet."[12] Within twenty minutes, she received 10,000 replies, and a hashtag was born. The *Telegraph* reported that, by early November, #MeToo had been tweeted 2.3 million times from eighty-five different countries.[13] Burke's two words allowed the world to see the vast numbers of women who share a history of sexual abuse. Those two words breathed life back into those dehumanized.

This movement followed a simple communication rule used by couples' therapists: Use I (or me) statements. Fragile bullies absorb the focus even when the focus ends up dehumanizing them. By staying inside your own experience, you do not bite on the hook. You might see the futility in responding to that text and instead share your feelings with someone who understands. You might have the courage to tell your story to help someone else who feels alone. And in some cases, you might successfully invite the bully to set aside his fragility and to see you. Doing so with my father meant withstanding the anxiety that he would either fall apart or take me apart. Here's the rest of that story:

I was stuck at first, fuming with anger but also emotionally captive to his vulnerability. Anything I said provoked a response that kept the focus on him. So I internalized my dilemma even as I was tortured by it—cue the Solo Dance of Chapter 11. But, in a later phone conversation with Dad, I returned to the issue. I tried to impress upon him how scared I was when I couldn't find my son, when I recognized that he was lost and alone. Dad then shifted from focusing on his own ill feelings to calling me repeatedly, morosely guilt-ridden and apologetic, and pressuring me to reassure him and say it was okay. The focus remained on him. But I didn't feel like reassuring him this time. I persisted in asking him to look at me and at the fear and trauma I had endured during those minutes when I looked for my son, as well as the immense frustration I experienced when Dad played the victim. I stayed the course, not hurling accusations, not protecting him from responsibility. Finally, something changed. Something changed in me. I stopped seeing him as fragile. In a way, it was the first time

I treated him with full respect and humanity. And, finally, he stopped acting fragile. He said, "You're right," and he apologized. Sincerely. Without drama.

It takes great self-discipline to resist the pulls of the Provoke and React. As with addiction, we need to recognize the rush or relief we get from indulging the dance. Not engaging or engaging differently may be a more boring and temporarily more painful path.

For me, walking that path for the first time was harrowing. And it made all the difference.

Tic-Tac-Toe

Though I was able to change the dance steps with my dad, some vicious circles do not allow that option. What do we do when every move we make seems to signal retaliation?

In the 1983 movie *WarGames*, a teenager, played by Matthew Broderick, unknowingly hacks into a military computer to play a game called *Global Thermonuclear War*.[14] The problem is that the game simulates a real attack. As Broderick innocently taps at the keyboard, big screens in the U.S. strategic command bunker display incoming Russian missiles. In the famous climax, after the military escalates its preparedness and the nations are poised to destroy each other, Broderick asks the operating system, Joshua, to play a game of tic-tac-toe. Joshua obliges. Programmed to win, Joshua repeats trial after trial at increasing speeds and extrapolates the game to a missile exchange. Finally, the program arrives at a crucial insight—one to keep in mind when Provoke and React beckons:

"Strange game. The only winning move is not to play."

11

BANISHMENT
AND THE SOLO DANCE

Away with these encircling hands! May I die
before what's mine is yours.

–NARCISSUS to ECHO, Ovid, Book III

s we recall from the myth, Narcissus wants to be loved without being touched. He is happy with his faithful band of followers, groupies who dote on him without expecting anything back. When separated from them one day, he recognizes his loneliness and calls out, "Is anyone here?" Echo responds, "Here." Narcissus wants to see her and becomes increasingly insistent: "Come to me!" "Why do you run from me?" "Here, let us meet together." With joy, she responds, "Together," and emerges from the woods, arms open. Then, a twist. Rather than accepting her embrace, Narcissus runs. His last words to Echo are harsh and final: he will die before sharing himself with her.

Spinning Away

Anyone who has been abruptly "dumped," "ghosted," or otherwise cut off from a relationship that seemed to be going well knows the hell of banishment. You want to ask why; you want to talk about it; you want to recover even a portion of the power taken from you. The word "hell" derives from the idea of separation. Its Old Norse origins refer to a "concealed place" such as a cave or cavern.[1] If this hell is not enough, add the torture of betrayal when you are not only left but replaced by another. Even though Narcissus did not have a literal affair, he did take another lover: himself.

Banishment takes on a broader meaning in the fragile bully dance. The fragile bully may remain physically present, even committed to the relationship, while unable to make room for another set of needs. Those have to go. So, if you had a lousy day and want to talk about it, the fragile bully predictably had a worse day and has a more pressing need to talk about it. Banished. You can't wait to share your excitement about the promotion you just received, and the fragile bully becomes sullen and withdrawn as soon as you mention it. Banished. The fragile bully begs you to attend a work party to show your support then fails to introduce you to anyone and shuts you out of conversations. Banished. You reach out to express your affection, and the fragile bully turns away. Banished.

Echo responds to her banishment by hiding out, internalizing her pain and longing. She continues to focus on Narcissus to the exclusion of everything else. Her isolation protects her from further rejection but also cuts her off from sources of nourishment and stimulation.

When I envision the banishment as a physical dance, I see the fragile bully in the center of the floor inviting the partner to mirror his moves while both enjoy what seems like mutuality. As she adds a flourish, or tires and lags, he begins to swirl and twirl her, asserting his control. He may teach her to flex better in response to him. If her nudges toward independence frustrate him, he eventually spins her away—too hard, too fast. Rather than bringing her back to him, he moves on looking for a new partner. The fragile bully's dance remains the same.

If she remains in the dance with him, her own will shrinks, pushed to the recesses of her consciousness. Even when freed from the dance, the partner continues to spin. Like Echo, she symbolically takes Narcissus with her into the cave of her thoughts and remains involved with him. Analysts call this process incorporation—the counterpart of projection. It is a psychological consumption of the other person, rendering him safer and easier to engage. I recall a moment at a women's spirituality conference when the presenter mentioned the vows, "and the two shall become one." Without a beat, the woman next to me whispered, "and we know which one they'll become." Though she was speaking to the problems of patriarchy, she could have been talking about narcissism. In a partnership with a fragile bully, the two may become him—or at least the grandiose fantasy of what he is.

The dance of banishment and incorporation comes in many varieties. We'll explore literal banishment, including the extramarital affair, as well as the in-house banishment that occurs when threatening aspects of the partner are shunned or undermined via gaslighting. We'll also investigate the spin-off dance, the destructive engagement that occurs in isolation. Finally, drawing on the theme of malnourishment and starvation associated with the myth, we'll explore how affected individuals can reconnect with sources of real support and nourishment.

Another Love

Fragile bullies at the extreme end of the narcissism spectrum often leave a trail of extramarital affairs or serial relationships. The affair functions like a scripted defense mechanism, insuring fresh mirrors for the grandiose self. Charm a lover, overwhelm her with attention, flattery, and expensive gifts and dinners. Feel the glow of your reflection, the idealized nothingness of it all. Be convinced this is love, and indulge in the fire of the mutual attention, the sexual lust. Make promises, share intimate secrets, maybe even get married. Be everything to her. Then open your eyes. Notice that she is awkward sometimes, and she has bad moods. Feel annoyed when she disagrees with you, when that sparkling smile gives way to narrowed eyes and a furrowed brow. Worry when she outperforms you. See that she is more complicated than you would like her to be. Wish for the days when she gave you the attention and admiration you deserve. And then notice the younger woman at work who laughs at all your jokes and always smells good. Feel better when you're with her. Invest in this relationship and get a better payoff than you do at home. Complain about your demanding wife and bond through your pain. Have great sex. Feel alive. Be assured that this new woman is committed to you, then tell your wife it's over. Commit again. Appreciate this newer, better mirror. Be convinced she is the one you've been looking for.

Then open your eyes. Notice that she is awkward sometimes...

The affair cycle is obvious to everyone except the ones caught up in it. There is an element of identification with the aggressor in the attachment to a philanderer. He or she gives you the opportunity to be the hero rather than the discarded one, as if these were the only choices. For an Echo, someone with the soul of a helper, getting to save the bully from his critical, unempathic partner may feel like a calling. Fragility plays into the seduction right alongside grandiosity—the narcissist dazzles you while also dubbing you his savior, the only one with the power to make things right.

The memory of these feelings of power and specialness make the later banishment all the more devastating. Once the answer to everything, you are now the problem, the burden. Once the recipient of exclusive attention and care, you've been tossed aside and replaced. You are left to witness someone else indulging in what was yours. Patricia aptly described her husband Tom's unapologetic disclosure of his new love interest: "He told me at dinner. He said she was everything to him, his best friend, his confidant. He gave her everything…I lost my value to him." She compared her status to one killed off after a hunt, "Once the hunt is over, you have something that's dead. It's always the hunting and getting. To fill a hole that will never be filled."

What is helpful to keep in mind, is that the other lover, for a true narcissist, will always be the person in the mirror.[2] Affairs are very much about preserving the mirror while pushing aside those who threaten the desired reflection. Those eliminated are often the very people who could help the fragile bully grow.

Banished at Home

The fragile bully has a problem with reality. The real self is too vulnerable, and real others may be unreliable, exploitive, or overly needy. He also has a problem with difference, seeking compliance and admiration rather than honest and spontaneous input. Preserving his idealized image provides him a sense of safety and control. Disagree on an issue, and the issue is soon forgotten while concerns about image, being right, looking good, even being loved, come to the fore.

Though my dad was deeply loyal to my mom and to his family, he effectively banished expressions of difference. We joked that I had made a scandalous choice when I decided to attend a Swedish Lutheran college rather than the Norwegian

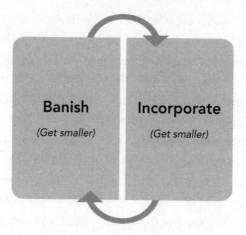

Banishment and the Solo Dance

Lutheran option. But this levity was a pleasant exception. I recall Dad having rageful reactions if someone simply defended a different preference in music or art. We were made to feel disloyal, even abusive, if we did not support his views—even in the private space of our home.

For a fragile bully, what's at stake is not just being either right or wrong. What is at stake is being either right or humiliated. To shift sexes for a bit, let's look at Jean's reaction to her husband John. The two are also professional colleagues, both well respected in their practice. At a meeting, John asks questions about an idea that his wife had just dismissed. After the meeting, Jean is enraged. She privately chastises John for voicing interest in the proposal:

Jean: What was THAT?

John: I thought the idea Bob raised was at least worth considering.

Jean: That has nothing to do with it. I am your spouse, and I am entitled to your unconditional support.

To say her partner's views "have nothing to do with it" is a form of banishment. For Jean, providing "unconditional support" means John must suppress his own thoughts and views, keeping the mirror clear to reflect her unassailed rightness.

Jean's statement shined a light on the one-sided contract John had inadvertently signed off on. He had repeatedly agreed to play small so that she could stand out. The unconditional support his wife demanded came with the fine print requirement, "don't disagree," or more simply, "don't be."

Tom, whom we discussed earlier, had a similar expectation for Patricia. She commented: "His biggest problem with our marriage was that I was independent and had my own thoughts. He could not tolerate an opinion. He needs someone with him all the time to agree and treat him like a king. He tells me that's the reason why he loves our dog better than anyone. Unconditional love."

I once told a client, to his horror, that unconditional love has no place in adult relationships. To expect that a partner offer love and support without sustenance or reciprocity is the definition of narcissism. And yet this is the very burden we often place on our partners: give me what I didn't get from my parents/exes, focus on me, fill me up, make me whole. One good argument for psychotherapy is that it protects our primary relationships from the burden of this need. Psychotherapy, by definition, is a one-way relationship, a sanctioned space to receive exclusive focus and the tolerant help needed for healing.

Tom's expectation of unconditional love and exclusive support was so absolute that he could not tolerate the competition offered by his own children. According to Patricia, "He left all his wives (note plural) once they had children. Children threatened him. He felt pushed aside, and then it was 'I'm out of here.' I was lucky—my son was not his. He has no contact with his six children except for maybe a Christmas card." This is an extreme case and tragic: Tom banished his own children and the richness of those relationships in exchange for his precious reflection.

Dimming the Gaslight

In the harrowing 1944 film, *Gaslight,* starring Charles Boyer and Ingrid Bergman, we observe the maneuvers of a husband set on making his wife believe she is insane.[3] The husband, Gregory, starts with subtle undermining, noting how forgetful Paula has been and how she imagines things. To add substance to his concern, he misplaces things for her—the brooch they agreed to store safely in her purse is not there when he asks about it later in the day. But the most frightening maneuvers are imposed hallucinations: his footsteps in the boarded-off attic, and his temporary dimming of the gaslights in her room. This iconic movie provided a term—gaslighting—for the psychological manipulation that causes another to question his or her sanity.

Gaslighting is a particularly cruel form of banishment. Rather than suffering rejection, the victim succumbs to pressure to reject herself—her judgment, her perception of reality. In the film, Paula makes multiple attempts to escape the captivity of her home. Every morning, she dresses for a walk and steps out on the stoop ready to meet the day. But as soon as the maid asks her what to tell the "master," she runs back in and up the stairs. The thought of him reminds her that she is not to be trusted. She longs for fresh air and freedom, but venturing out on her own has become too risky. Instead, she stays in her bedroom tormented by internalized messages from her husband and by her efforts to scrutinize her own mind.

Negation is a much more common form of gaslighting. Suddenly, what you experienced no longer exists. Your partner didn't say that. He wasn't mad (though he was throwing things). He looks at you innocently, even with an expression of concern, and says, "I don't know what you're talking about." The term "crazymaker" is used colloquially to describe someone who denies a reality that is painfully apparent to another: the alcoholic mother who returns home after a bender and chats with the family as if nothing happened, the boss who announces a pay cut and then asks employees to share what they value about the organization. These maneuvers can cause recipients to question their own reality and to participate in banishing their awareness of what is real. The child of the alcoholic thinks, "No big deal. Mom's fine now. I don't know what I was worried about." The employee wants to scream at the absurdity of the request but stifles this awareness as others share testimonies about the organization's merits.

Children who are trained to question their own senses and feelings will be particularly vulnerable to the effects of gaslighting as adults.

The Two Shall Become Small

In the myth, a curse accompanies Echo as she encounters Narcissus. She may only repeat the words of others. She is primed to reduce herself. Partners of fragile bullies may have endured a similar priming as children, learning, as psychologist Lindsay Gibson put it, "to put other people's needs first as the price of admission to a relationship."[4] This is a vicious circle carried forward: be small to get in and get smaller to stay connected. The ground rules for connection paradoxically assure emotional abandonment.

In the myth, the banished Echo hides, and "her sleepless thoughts waste her sad form." Echo's illness is a combination of obsession and isolation. Whether she retreats into her head or moves across the country, the effect is similar.

Though Dad was indeed demanding, Mom was accustomed to privatizing her needs, pulling them inward and managing them on her own. For my mother, poor health and disability created a demandingness she was never able to pull off on her own. With Parkinson's disease, her body made external care a necessity. Even as she apologized for bothering us, she frequently requested that someone move this or clean up that. I sensed that she was finally able to be liberal in her demands toward Dad, a hard-won gift of her illness.

Echo, rejected by Narcissus, becomes an archetype of somatization. Banished, her self-care lags, and the stress takes its toll. She ignores everyone else in her life, caught up in the futility of trying to resolve a relational problem all by herself. This is the starvation that occurs with obsession. And though Echo's spinning takes the form of pining and longing, obsession can take on a malevolent quality—fuming, plotting, or engaging in fantasies of revenge. Swallowed poison.

While banishment seems to be a one-sided affair—at times literally—the story of Echo and Narcissus reveals how both partners have a similar experience. Both suffer a lack of nourishment. Both eventually waste away. Echo and Narcissus invest their life energy on something inaccessible. By dismissing anyone who challenges him, the fragile bully cuts himself off from opportunities for growth. As he constructs a world in his image, he finds himself more and more alone. Echo, by agreeing to his unwritten contract—diminish yourself to make me feel better—becomes smaller even as she feels heroic. The two live a sort of parallel deprivation—one inflated and isolated, the other devalued and isolated. They both, in their own ways, starve as they succumb to the ravages of narcissism.

Searching for Jewels

In one of the closing scenes of *Gaslight,* husband Gregory's diabolical plan is finally exposed: he had been working to render Paula insane, ship her to an asylum, and then rob her of her inherited jewels. Now detained and tied to a chair, he tries to engage Paula in freeing him. She deftly lavishes him with the fruits of his efforts: she acts helpless and insane. As the police officer finally escorts him out, he looks to Paula and confesses: "I don't ask you to understand me. Between us all the time were those jewels. Like a fire—a fire in my brain that separated us—those jewels which I wanted all my life. I don't know why."

His final sentence, "I don't know why," haunted me long after the credits rolled. The jewels, like the promise of the grandiose self, seduced him into destroying life and the potential for love. But Gregory was not the only one distracted by the jewels. Paula abandoned her musical pursuits to relish the intoxicating attention Gregory offered. She welcomed him when he intruded on her private retreat, happily relieved of her ambivalence about committing to him. She gave up her dream of living in Paris, returning to a home she had associated with horror, because Gregory wished it.

Narcissistic hunger is bigger than any individual caught in its clutches. It seeks only what is inaccessible and unassailable— the perfect jewels, the perfect life, riches forged by someone else and gained without toil or conflict. At each step along the way, this hunger passes by or destroys what is life-giving and nourishing, searching for those unattainable jewels. By the time Paula recognizes this deprivation, she has become an unwitting accomplice in her own banishment.

Returning to Life

The banishment dance casts a wide net. Even partners in an otherwise healthy relationship can suppress certain needs and conflicts. On the other extreme, abusers enforce banishment through emotional and physical control. An "echoist" may banish her own needs as an assumed prerequisite for relationships. What these examples share is a theme of deprivation and emotional malnourishment. How can one break open the circle of banishment enough to let in light, fresh air, and food for growth? Let's look at some starting points:

1. **Recognize your limitations.** A colleague of mine often reminded her clients: "You are not an artificial plant. You require care." Those accustomed to managing their needs privately may regard unmet needs, even those arising from a neglectful or abusive relationship, as a sign of personal failure. Maybe you learned early on to manage without help, or to keep your emotional needs to yourself. You may have very particular blind spots around seeking care. Once ridiculed by my father for asking questions, I resolved to answer questions on my own. If I had a question, I would go to books and journals, but rarely to people. I somehow made it through college and graduate school with this aversion to help even when asking a simple question might have saved me hours of work. I was a young professional before I appreciated the time and toil I could save by asking someone to provide the piece of information I was missing or to explain a concept that confused me. I learned, to my surprise, that people didn't insult me for asking for information but were usually eager to help. I also realized that I could do more in less time when I opened myself to the minds of others. I wasn't a failure. Others made me smarter.

In fact, the rewards of this engagement were so abundant that I initially feasted on it like a two-year-old eagerly asking "why?" Once a banished little girl with a question, I had been welcomed back into the conversation.

If you are a victim of gaslighting, you are going to need help recovering your reality and detaching from the crazy-maker. Paula had a witness—someone who could validate what she was seeing and help her escape her entrapment. I recall working with Tracy, a woman whose mother, an untreated schizophrenic, had tried to kill Tracy and her sister when they were young children. Tracy had internalized the guilt and shame imposed on her by her mother. Though she impressed me as kind and insightful, Tracy carried a belief that there was something wrong with her that had made her unacceptable to her family. She asked me to evaluate her. After giving her a psychological assessment, I said to her, "You aren't mentally ill. Your life just sucks." I was rarely so blunt, but the words just came out. Tracy released a hearty and grateful laugh and, along with it, the burden of what she was carrying on her mother's behalf.

Breaking the bondage of self-containment starts with acknowledging our need and hunger for new sources of sustenance. This is hard to do when we have no assurance the need will be filled. Some of the loneliest people have a partner across the table they do not dare to engage. But, as experts on loneliness have noted, listening to our own emotional yearning is the very thing that leads us to seek connection.[5] The simple exercise of listing the kinds of responses you desire from another person can start you on the journey to getting what you need. That other person may be the one across from you, a therapist who can help you heal, or someone you need to prepare yourself to meet. By acknowledging your need for emotional connection, you are befriending it rather than joining others in banishing it.

2. **Listen to your body.** When we stop listening to our emotions, physical symptoms may pick up the slack. You may feel sick to your stomach because you sense there is something wrong. Listen. You may be having trouble sleeping or suffering from headaches or muscle tension. Listen. In our culture, we have done a better job of legitimizing the physical than we have the emotional, and you may not feel worthy of attention until your body hurts. Emerging research is revealing that the pain of banishment—"social rejection, exclusion or loss"—invokes the same neurobiological regions as physical pain.[6] If you hurt physically, your body may be validating what you cannot. Take your body's cues as reminders that you are indeed not an artificial plant. You are vulnerable and limited and require ongoing maintenance. Good self-care builds your resistance to unhealthy influences.

3. **Find healthy mirrors.** While the fragile bully demands constant mirroring, the echoing partner finds few surfaces to reflect what is inside her. Healthy mirrors provide both recognition and an outside perspective that allows us to see ourselves more fully. A healthy mirror also delivers input through the eyes of love, not in an effort to humiliate or invoke shame. An unhealthy mirror may limit feedback to nodding and agreeing while indulging your suspicions and anxieties. Therapeutic mirroring is one of the most difficult skills to teach and one of the most powerful to experience. This is because mirroring is too often seen through the lens of narcissism: as a way to appease rather than reveal. This kind of mirroring can actually widen the rift between the ideal self and the real self. Therapeutic mirroring helps a person both see herself more clearly *and* to better tolerate and accept that reality. Think of the child who falls and

skins her knee. She pauses for a moment, looking to the parent to see how she should respond. If the parent freaks out, she freaks out and learns to fear her pain. If the parent scoffs and tells her to buck up, she learns to deny her pain. And if the parent acknowledges the hurt while remaining calm, the child learns that she is hurt a little, that it's okay to feel the hurt, and that she will be okay. Therapeutic mirroring helps clients better tolerate the awareness that helps them grow. Couples can learn to provide this type of mirroring for each other, but this is difficult to do until they have received the benefits of such responding.

During my graduate training, I witnessed intense debates on which therapy techniques were best. Since that time, meta-analyses of outcome studies have concluded that (1) therapy works, and (2) all approaches are helpful.[7] Specific techniques do not make that much difference, but shared elements do. One of these shared elements is simply having a trustworthy relationship with someone who is able to witness and empathize with your experience and to explore what matters to you. This may be a first for someone who has spent a lifetime accommodating the needs of others.

Notice what kind of mirroring you receive from the people in your life. Friends can be helpful mirrors, and they can also help you stay stuck. My sister still talks about feedback I provided her that helped her finally leave a destructive relationship. She had been complaining about her husband, as she typically did, and rather than validating her feelings, as I typically did, I said, "Frankly, this is beginning to bore me. I am just much more interested in what you're going to do about it." I was rarely that direct, but I was mirroring the lack of vitality I saw in her. I was also showing her something of me. I wanted my sister back. Though my feedback was hard to hear, she now tells me that my comment helped her realize how comfortable she had become with the victim role. She did take action, and our conversations got much more interesting. Now in a healthy marriage, she talks about her life in a much richer way.

4. **Remember what you love.** Cameron notes that crazy-makers can provide us a convenient excuse to relinquish our creative pursuits.[8] Has the vicious circle helped you avoid a creative project you've been afraid to begin? What could you do with all the energy you've been investing in the dance? In the movie *Gaslight*, Paula's abandonment of music sets the stage for her captivity, and her memory of this love is part of her recovery. Paula's love of music is tied up with much of what feeds her—close family friendships, the pleasure of indulging in a shared interest, delight in the music itself, and the freedom of self-expression. Patricia, a victim of gaslighting we met in Chapter 11, had sacrificed to Tom her enjoyment of the ceramic arts. Now healing emotionally through therapy and strengthened physically through running, she has regained her vitality and playfulness through her return to ceramics.

Like any vicious circle, the Solo Dance narrows our focus. Sometimes quiet rumination can help us work through major life difficulties. However, we too often cut ourselves off from pursuits we love in order to preserve our resources. Using a beloved activity as therapy can be a way to reinvigorate ourselves while also working through difficulties. Painting the pain, kneading bread dough, or venting on a manuscript page engages us in life-giving pursuits rather than dead-end rumination.

12

THE SUPERIOR DANCE

Scandal is great entertainment because it allows people
to feel contempt, a moral emotion that gives feelings of
moral superiority while asking nothing in return.

–JONATHAN HAIDT

In the late 1980s, comedian Dana Carvey gained fame for
his depiction of the "church lady," a judgmental host of her
own talk show, "Church Chat." Her show was a forum for
exposing the sins of the guest and ended with the church lady's
haughty performance of her hip-gyrating "superior dance."
Carvey's character took particular delight in her accusations
and clearly got many of her own narcissistic needs met as she
ripped on the excesses and scandals of her high-profile guests.

This parody exposes a much subtler dynamic in relationships featuring a fragile bully. The narcissist's partner may
enjoy the benefit of moral superiority even as the narcissist
offends her moral sensibility. Only the methods are different:
the partner does not chastise the fragile bully nor strut superiority but stays above the interaction by remaining tolerant, for-
giving, and self-sacrificing. Harboring feelings of superiority
may be the only reward for managing an extremely difficult

relationship. Where the Provoke and React goes low and the Solo Dance makes one small, the partner in the Superior Dance always goes higher.

Angel to the Buffoon; Hero to the Helpless

For their longsuffering patience and tolerance, partners of fragile bullies seem to take on divine attributes. We were all convinced that my mother was an angel. Others are saints. These partners seem able to tolerate the provocations of the fragile bully without getting riled. Not only are they calm and understanding but they may be calm and understanding in an unsettling sort of way—in a way that accentuates not only the narcissist's weakness but also our own. Next to this divine figure, the fragile bully appears especially petty, self-indulgent, and immature.

Christina, whom we met in the Introduction, seemed superhuman in another way. She was tough as steel, witty, and articulate, and these qualities were especially evident when she talked about Jim, the man she now identified as a narcissist. As she recounted conversations with him, she impressed me with her ability to convey the dialogue word for word. And her responses consistently reflected her superior wit and intelligence. Though these accounts came after the relationship had deteriorated, she recalled what attracted her initially: "I was hooked by how kind he was. He told me horror stories about his exes. And when one of them bombarded me in an email, I believed him...I thought, 'People take advantage of him'...He said that, all his life, women had been hurting him and using him. So I took on this large project." This project put her in danger from the start, but this seemed to only add to her heroism. She shared, "His mother threatened to kill me, she sent mass emails defaming me to everyone she knew."

For those who invest in the project of rescuing a fragile bully, the Superior Dance is an insidious vicious circle. These rescuers do not typically strut their superiority, and, in fact, often fight feelings of guilt. They may believe they can never be good enough, so a grand project like Christina's promises redemption. The Superior Dance allows the partner to feel separate from and above the selfishness of the narcissist. The fragile bully plays on this need, undermining the partner's efforts to be good, which only increases the partner's need to defend her elevated virtue.

In contrast with the rescuing angel is the ridiculing critic. We see the latter in opponents' reactions to Donald Trump. Pointing and laughing at his buffoonery places critics above him even as he makes his way to the White House. The devaluation creates the illusion of power. As long as the bully is the buffoon, there is no need to take him seriously or hold him accountable. He then has free reign to misuse his authority.

The Superior Dance plays on the need to be good. Let's look at the steps that keep it in motion.

Drunk on Idealization

Christina's story is a familiar one. She is drawn to the generous, wounded soul who had been so injured by other women. For many of us, the prospect of being the one who can help where others failed—*the answer*—is an intoxicating one.[1] Add to this the singular admiring attention of the fragile bully, and the hook sets in hard. These seductions shut down rational scrutiny. Otherwise discerning women overlook histories involving multiple marriages and enraged exes and conclude that the string of women left behind are uniformly crazy. Competitive feelings—the desire to out-love the bad lovers or to out-mother the bad mother—also play in. My mother was the kind and warm counterpart to Dad's strict and withholding mother. Patricia was the attentive alternative to Tom's emotionally distant and rejecting mother. Christina hated Jim's mother for keeping him from growing up. She told me, "At age forty-three, he had never written a check, couldn't cook—she controlled his every move." Also critical of Jim's exes, Christina later found camaraderie in one of them. The same hook had caught them both.

Compassion clearly factors into these attachments, but so does the promise of specialness and superiority. Narcissists defensively use idealization and devaluation and can trigger our own vulnerability to sorting the world into angels and demons. And, let's face it, being idealized feels good. Christina recalled, "He always told me how beautiful, sexy, perfect I was. He was totally enamored with me."

Christina's description reminds me of what I learned about the idealized woman in my home. My dad would refer to these women as "knockouts"—beauty pageant looks, always pleasant, always available and helpful. If one of us misbehaved, my sister and I would deepen our voices and parody, "You're not being a knockout." As far as we have come as women, these mantras still run in the background. As one feminist critic put it, these standards end up "reducing our wild human existence to certain mythological standards that are not meant to ever be achieved."[2] For women whose real, "wild human" self remains unmirrored, these mythological standards offer a blueprint for the grandiose alternative. As Elizabeth Waites put it, "Women who rely on the idealization provided by a partner as the major source of their self-esteem are sometimes willing to accept pathological features of a partnership rather than give up this narcissistic support."[3]

Though women are the more visible dancers in this dynamic, men take on relationship projects as well. For men, internalized social pressures to be the hero may prime them for relationships with fragile bullies on the vulnerable end of the spectrum. These narcissists are perpetually needy, and the heroism of the partner enables the continued neediness. Craig was attracted to Denise's liveliness but hooked by the way others continually failed her. He doted on her, championed her causes, and committed himself to being the hero who would make things right. Her fragility and hunger for mirroring helped him feel important. She frequently told others how perfect he was, inspiring envy in her friends. He brought her coffee in the morning, sent flowers when she was down, and readily got angry on her behalf. He relished being perfect in her eyes, and had to—he received little else from the relationship.

High Road to Your Low Road

Inevitably, the fragile bully's idealization of you gives way to some sort of injury, which triggers their narcissistic rage. You didn't defend him when someone questioned his story. You hogged the attention when you were both exhibiting your work. Once enamored with you, he starts to act like a jerk. He insults you, invents paranoid explanations for your behavior, pouts, stonewalls. You stand in disbelief, stung.

Then you regroup. You tell yourself it's okay, you can work with this. You remind yourself that you are better than the others. Then you respond lovingly. You gently deny the villainous intentions he projects onto you. You reassure him. You speak softly. Though he hasn't asked for it, you forgive him. He's been through a lot.

Your goddess-like forbearance may pay off. He may calm down, even become nice again. Or not. He may punish you further—keeping up the quiet treatment, rejecting your entreaties, challenging you to prove your love. You tell yourself you've got this. You remind yourself that you are better than the others.

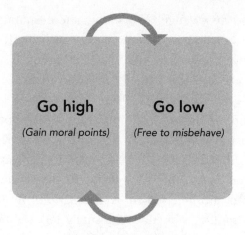

The Superior Dance

In this scenario, your need to stay in the idealized position becomes a trap. As long as he is dissatisfied, you will keep trying. He may even throw you a reward from time to time. Intermittent doses of idealization are compelling because they keep you busy trying to crack the code to make it happen again. In the meantime, the two of you will move further and further away from any awareness of what you need.

Perhaps your approach is not quite so goddess-like. You are appalled he would accuse you of such things, and you respond by defending your virtue. No, you didn't hog the attention at the exhibit—you told everyone you could about how great his work was. How could he suggest such a thing? Christina had an experience like this. She had gone to great lengths to obtain a special entry pass for Jim at an event, and he told everyone that a dignitary had given it to him while accusing her of being jealous of him. Christina angrily reminded him that she was the one who had gotten him the pass, and, far from being jealous, she was who had supported him the most. He responded, "You hate me, don't you?" Refusing to be the villain, she back-tracked clarifying that his *behavior* was what she disliked. He frequently turned things around this way, effectively inhibiting her expressions of anger. Years later, she desperately wanted him out of her home where he had been living free without contributing to expenses. But her attachment to being good was so strong that she barred him only after he voluntarily packed up and left.

In addition to the hook of moral superiority, a partner may indulge in the psychological superiority he or she feels in relation to the fragile bully. Projective identification, often used by narcissists, allows a person to insert unacceptable feelings into another person. A colleague of mine referred to this as "getting slimed." We usually talk about the ways narcissists effectively manipulate others to feel their rage or humiliation, but the same can happen in reverse. Because fragile bullies are so easily provoked, they can be ready recipients for our own discarded feelings. Consider this scenario: Fragile bully insults you. Rather than stooping to anger, you respond with a pitying look or smug smile. Blurt a laugh. He becomes enraged, blushing with humiliation, and you relax. He's doing you for you.

This may be a dangerous game to play with the bully, so you might take it on the road, sharing stories of the fragile bully's buffoonery with anyone who will listen. In these cases, the satisfaction may come more from other's validation of your superiority. This is a common reaction people have to their feelings of outrage toward Donald Trump. Focus on his entertaining reactions to provocation, share them on social media, create clever memes, smile, and relax. Rather than feeling the pain of the bully's treatment of you, you can revel in your psychological superiority. The lower he goes, the higher the high. But as with any addiction, the high is part of the sickness.

Low Road to Your High Road

The fragile bully may be more than happy to indulge your need to be good. In fact, he or she likely feels entitled to your goodness. The bully can also use your need to remain innocent as ammunition, charging you with sins and challenging you to prove your virtue. The higher you go, the freer the bully is to go low, demanding attention, complaining over slights, indulging rants and accusations. If you pass his tests while he continues to fail you, the roster of material to support your superiority grows, but where does that get you? Therapists and healing professionals are vulnerable to this trap in their own personal lives. One therapist I know reflected on her romances with men who turned out to be narcissists: "I wanted a relationship, but I was like the therapist. I felt like I knew all the answers. I was smarter, and this person just wouldn't wise up. For me, empathy has been a problem. It became an excuse. They don't ask for it, don't apologize. It's all my fault anyway."

While relationships can be therapeutic, one partner cannot be the other's therapist. The work of setting oneself aside and attending fully to another person's experience, especially when that person may be dumping the worst of what they've got into your fifty-minute hour, is extremely demanding. Imagine granting this kind of service 24/7 without the benefit of a fee. Then imagine offering this full-time, focused attention without the help of proper training, and without any indication that the client is interested in change—in fact, knowing that the client is likely to be hostile to change. The only payoff for the helper is getting to feel extremely virtuous. Absurd? Maybe. But once the perks of the new relationship wear off, this is what the Superior Dance looks like.

Though psychotherapy is structured as a one-way relationship, the patient is still accountable to compensate the therapist, to respect the parameters of the relationship, and to work with the therapist to achieve change. Therapy breaks down when these boundaries break down. Psychological resources, when misused, only enable regression and bad behavior.

Being Less Good

When I left my work at a psychiatric clinic to open my own practice, clients no longer paid for sessions at the front desk. They paid me, and if I didn't get paid, there was no corporate umbrella to cover my salary. I had good coaching on the business side of practice and learned to establish clear parameters about payment from the beginning. But I was devastated one day when a client quit on me and sent me a scathing letter about how I seemed more interested in getting my fee than in helping her. Her letter played on my every worry about whether I was really a good person, whether my motives were indeed selfish. I asked an experienced colleague what he did when clients complained about his fee. He said, "I tell them I like money." He wasn't being cheeky. He was being sincere. He went on to share that to deny his interest in being paid would be dishonest and unhelpful. He said, "Of course I explore with them what it means for them to pay me and the associated feelings, but the reality is, my fee is part of what makes me enjoy my work." I reflected on this for a long time. To admit I liked the money meant relinquishing my superiority. The client needed something; I needed something. I wasn't above her; I was across from her. My desire for money was not opposed to my desire to help her but an integral part of it. And if we both got what we needed, we would both be happier to be there.

The way out of the Superior Dance is to allow yourself to be less good. By "less good" I mean less selfless, less controlled, and less removed from human needs, desires, and impulses. So the fragile bully accuses you of hogging all the attention at the exhibit. Instead of denying this possibility and defending your virtue, try, "Yeah, I like attention, too." If the fragile bully accuses you of not defending him at a meeting, you might admit that your needs were in conflict with his at that moment. These responses don't have to be flippant or insensitive, and in fact can come hand-in-hand with expressions of empathy. Meanwhile, they keep the reality of your humanity in the conversation.

Another way out is to change your definition of what it means to be good. If making your needs and desires accessible allows you to be more present in the relationship, that is good. If getting your needs met reduces your resentment and enhances your loving feelings, that is good. And if you see yourself as an equal rather than morally or psychologically superior, that is good.

When Relationships Heal

Like an alcoholic, a fragile bully may indeed want to change, but his system is hooked on something more powerful. Within the fragile bully is a vicious circle of its own—a vulnerability to shame and humiliation answered by grandiose overcompensation and interpersonal manipulation. Over and over. As we've discussed in these chapters, people play into this dynamic in any number of ways. When can a relationship reach beyond these vicious circles and promote healing rather than hurt? This, of course, is what therapy aspires to do. But can relationships in the world help our narcissistically impaired loved ones? And, perhaps the more important question: can this be done without endangering the partners in those relationships?

First, it is helpful to remember that narcissism exists on a spectrum. Those on the extreme end of the spectrum—those who exhibit features of sociopathy, such as the absence of a social conscious and comfort with lying and exploitation—are not good candidates for therapy, much less the healing influence of love relationships. They are far too comfortable. Anyone who resorts to physical abuse and intimidation tactics has already demonstrated his danger to a relationship. Even these individuals may arouse empathy—they often have suffered abuse themselves—but as long as they are unable to inhibit their destructive impulses, they are not capable of a healthy relationship.

But when we look to the more moderate region of the spectrum, we see evidence that relationships can help move a fragile bully in the direction of health.[4] We all have some degree of narcissism within us, and, as we've discussed, there is a healthy side to feeling special. So how do you know when a relationship with a narcissistic spin has potential?

Paul Links and Michelle Stockwell outlined indications for the use of couple's therapy in the treatment of Narcissistic Personality Disorder.[5] These indicators are useful in considering a partner's potential for change. One caution here: this is not an argument to go into a relationship with the desire to change your partner. That is almost certainly a formula for failure. But you may be in love with someone on the spectrum and wonder if there is hope. Consider the following:

1. **Is your partner able to curtail acting out?** *Acting out* is a primitive defense mechanism in which the person expresses impulses through action rather than bearing or managing those impulses. Most of us are able to feel angry without slugging someone and to experience sexual attraction without demanding immediate sexual gratification. When

someone discharges anxiety via acting out, there is no incentive to work within the parameters of the relationship. Though affairs and direct expressions of rage are the most common examples, other forms of acting out can undercut such processing. Links and Stockwell use the example of a narcissist who acted out his anger by impulsively purchasing a second home thus sending the couple into bankruptcy.

If you cannot trust that your partner will contain impulses enough to assure the safety and fidelity of the relationship, you have nothing to work with.

2. **What is your partner's level of defensiveness?** Defensiveness is a frequent visitor to marital conflict but not necessarily a deal-breaker. Even healthy individuals cringe a bit when a partner points out an offense, but they usually take in the feedback and consider it, returning to the conversation with more openness. Partners need to have some capacity to trust and open themselves to outside input, or there will be no real communication. When stuck in a vicious circle, such as the Provoke and React, both members of the couple may need to learn how to deliver feedback more productively. However, if one reacts with disdain, paranoia, and/or counterattack to any kind of input, the walls are too high.

3. **Does the relationship feed you both?** Links and Stockwell call this "complementarity of narcissistic gratification," meaning both partners feed the other's desire for mirroring and idealization. I found this criterion interesting because we often assume that narcissistic gratification is a bad thing. But the reality is, mutual idealization is almost always present in love relationships, and when complemented by mutual respect, can offer sustaining gratification for the couple. Links and Stockwell note

that even in relationships in which one partner is comfortable in a more nurturing role, while the more narcissistic partner brings worldly status to the relationship, that complementarity can be present. John Gottman's seminal research found that couples offering each other regular hits of good feeling was a measurable predictor of relationship success, and if positive communications didn't outweigh the negative ones, the couple would likely divorce.[6] This criterion can be tricky to assess when a narcissistic disorder is involved. A fragile bully may "love bomb" someone more as an effort at possession and control than as an expression of true desire. And if desires are based on a projected image rather than a person's real qualities, a fragile bully's "love bombing" may also be a sign of manipulation.

The key here is "complementarity." "Love bombing," though seemingly generous, is one-sided.[7] One test for this is to ask yourself, "Do I truly admire the person across the table, or do I only enjoy how much he seems to admire me?" If, on the other hand, you are the one doing all the work and getting few perks, this is another kind of imbalance. Finally, the presence of contempt by either or both partners is a fatal sign. In these cases, idealization may be a thin veil covering envy and devaluation. I often find it helpful to ask partners, "You tell me you love each other. Tell me this: Do you like each other?" The answer to the second question may say more about how much gratification and pleasure the relationship provides.

4. **How invested are you both?** Warren Buffett uses the phrase "skin in the game" to refer to having incurred risk by investing personal resources. If executives have "skin in the game," they are more likely to commit themselves to the success of the company. Investing in a relationship

means being willing to be vulnerable enough to grow, being committed enough to prioritize the health of the relationship, and being strong enough to endure through challenges. I felt safe enough to challenge my dad in his later years because I knew, deep down, that as much as his narcissistic needs factored in, our relationship mattered to him more. And it probably helped that I wasn't living with him and could engage over time by phone. That is not to say that he made it easy for me. I endured his efforts at manipulation and a prolonged and painful conflict. And he endured relinquishing dearly held defenses in order to access empathy for my situation. As painful as it was for both of us, we kept picking up the phone and trying again. We weren't willing to let the investment go bad.

13

EDIT ME

Don't come. I don't want you here. I don't know
what is up with you, but I cannot have a 2.6 at my wedding.

–NAOMI to LACIE, *Black Mirror* episode, "Nosedive"

lack Mirror, the British sci-fi series and Netflix hit, imagines sinister and disturbing consequences of our new technology. In the episode, "Nosedive,"[1] Lacie tries to navigate a world in which everyone rates everyone else all the time. She picks up a latte, and the barista rates her as she smiles and rates him. She passes a neighbor on the street, and her smartphone immediately informs her of the person's composite rating on a zero-to-five scale. Lacie spends much of her waking life attending to her rating. The perfectly swirled foam atop her latte sustains her more as a photo op than as an enjoyable beverage. She painstakingly prepares a pâté just so she can photograph and post it for ratings. She practices her smile, wears a sweet, pastel, perfectly pressed dress, and even seeks a consultant to help her improve her rating. In this world, good ratings translate to material benefits—better services, better hotel and transportation options, access to better real estate. If vulnerability or unpleasant emotions bleed through the pleasant façade, others quickly register negative ratings. In her rush to get to an event that will enhance her rating, she causes a passerby to spill her coffee. The subsequent ratings set off a vicious downward spiral for Lacie. Her rating drops too low for her to qualify for a seat on an airline, her subsequent outburst at the reservations counter gets her a full-point penalty, and, from there, she continues to nosedive into oblivion. What remains? Plastic-looking people living artificial lives.

Though science fiction, we see signs of Lacie's world in our midst. The young woman at the coffee shop photographs her steaming latte, then smiles at her own camera, posing and snapping selfies for her Instagram feed. She'll post these as artifacts of the pleasant afternoon she had photographing her pleasant afternoon. We are free to indulge in our social media reflections anytime and everywhere, heads staring down into the mirror, reminiscent of Narcissus by the pool. Lacie's hypervigilance seems familiar when we observe our own resistance to putting down the electronic mirror. The hunger for likes, worries about one's "ratings," and desire to impress people we don't even know can sweep us into another dance with narcissism—one I call the "Edit Me."

Though this dance is not exclusive to narcissists, it plays on and exploits our narcissistic needs. And while there is nothing new about posturing and posing, public stages for the indulgence are now freely available. Social media and reality TV extend to all what was once the purview of celebrities—an audience. We even have our own followers.

The Edit Me is a feedback loop that constructs and maintains the false or grandiose self. We have discussed how this happens in childhood, but vicious circles have a way of playing out in new forums and even gaining steam. Celebrities, for example, have to work very hard to resist the siren song of grandiosity even when they start with a well-rounded sense of self. In the Edit Me, we present to the world an edited version of ourselves, others selectively reinforce and further distort this edited identity, and we become more and more alienated from our real selves.

This Is Me

There are few pleasures that compete with the joy of self-expression. Studies demonstrate that talking about ourselves releases the feel-good neurotransmitter dopamine, and is so rewarding that, in an experimental setting, people will forego a monetary reward for the opportunity to self-disclose.[2] Add the presence of an audience, and the dopamine charge increases. One of the challenges of face-to-face communication is accommodating others who want the same dopamine fix. The average person consumes about 30–40% of a conversation with expression of their own views and experiences.[3] Get online and that percentage can escalate as high as 80%.[4] This is great for people who were unable to get a word in during those live conversations—aka, introverts—and those who want to share important views and values early in a romantic relationship.[5] The freedom to create a profile and to openly share views seems like, and can be, an opportunity for authentic expression. But, with everyone expressing and few people paying attention, how does the online economy really work?

The online economy works, for a hungry user, very much like a self-absorbed parent. She'll pay attention when you're bad or when you're very good. Or when you give her attention. But she'll probably ignore your more commonplace needs and reflections. Still, she'll give you just enough to keep you invested. And when she responds, it feels so good that you want more. So you figure out how to make her respond again. A little editing will do the trick.

This Is (Edited) Me

Psychologist B.F. Skinner first demonstrated the power of operant conditioning by teaching rats and pigeons to press certain buttons in exchange for food. In his essay, "Skinner Marketing: We're the Rats, and Facebook Likes Are the Reward," *The Atlantic*'s Bill Davidow noted how "internet handlers" use our hunger for rewards to keep us engaged with their services and products. The parallel to Skinner's rats and pigeons is eerily apt: "His pigeons pecked at buttons in search of food. We peck at keys in search of virtual rewards—good news arriving in an email, a retweet, a thumbs-up on a blog post."[6] Facebook feeds you more of what you like; Reddit lets you earn "karma" for getting "up votes" from individuals who share your interests; and YouTube feeds you more and more extremist content because its algorithm says that's what people like.[7] And, on social media, we live with the same intermittent reinforcement schedule offered by unpredictable parents. You don't earn a treat every time, which actually assures that you stay in the game and work harder to get the goodies.

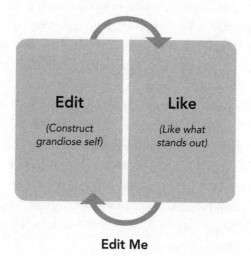

Edit

(Construct grandiose self)

Like

(Like what stands out)

Edit Me

We talk frequently about the manipulative tactics used by narcissists. But it is as important to look at how our cultural institutions manipulate and exploit the narcissistically hungry. Edit yourself further—emphasize your grandiose, victimized, or extremist self—and you'll get more attention and more mirrors. The edited self shows itself in our social media personas, but there is no better example of this phenomenon than in the world of reality TV.

While my son was studying at West Virginia University, he and a group of friends were solicited by an MTV casting crew looking for participants in an upcoming reality TV series called *Buckwild*. The setup was to place a group of young women and men in a house in rural West Virginia and encourage them to go "buck wild"—playing, as it turned out, on every stereotype of what it means to be a West Virginian. The recruiters said they wanted a representative group, and they were looking to fill the college student demographic. My son's good friend, Katie, saw the role as an answer to her anxieties about paying for school. She also enjoyed a good time and thought the experience might be fun. Though her exposure was limited due to the series cancellation after the first twelve-episode season,[8] she said it changed her: "I went from being a normal person to getting all this attention, BIG attention, like a billboard in Times Square. Then you get used to it, and you want more of it. It's a validating feeling. You want to continue—you want people looking at you." What seemed to captivate Katie most was the intimate attention she received from fans. She said, "It's a high. They (viewers) would remember things. I had a bio on my Twitter. People would read it and bring it up. Their comments were really detail-oriented. To have people THAT interested in my life. I wasn't even a central character. Some had people proposing to them. Being on TV makes people really, really interested in you." To me, Katie said, "There's an obvious connection between TV—especially reality TV—and a level of narcissism."

Though she enjoyed the high, it came at a cost. Katie assured me that the characters we saw on the screen had little resemblance to the real participants. She said, "You have no idea how you're going to be edited. They can butcher your words in such a way that they make it into an insult. They edited me to be prudish, bitchy. One episode: the guys were rowdy, one was driving. I said, 'I'm really uncomfortable.' The car was going too fast. The producers and the guys said, 'It's fine,' but it was scaring me. They made me look like a brat. Everything can be twisted, and you're an 'instajerk.'" Another tactic Katie described was to keep them on set until they did something interesting. She said, "Nobody wanted to see what we were doing organically. Drinking wine and talking—nobody wanted to see that." Katie recalled, "One day it was 3:00 a.m., and I decided, 'I will do anything so you'll let me go home'…I finally just threw a literal fit and was really dramatic about it. It made it on the episode. It was just me screaming."

Years after her stint with *Buckwild,* Katie reflected, "Once you've been on TV, that's who you are and how people perceive you for a long time. Even a lifetime. No one is ever going to say, 'She used to be a ballerina,' or 'He scored really high on the SAT.' It's always going to come first that you were on TV because that's what people think is the most interesting thing…That's why so many people who have been on TV become crazy."

Reality TV and social media play on the narcissistic temptation to accept cheap and immediate attention in place of more meaningful rewards. Compared to nonviewers, people who watch reality TV are more motivated by feelings of self-importance and vengeance and less by desires for morality and honor.[9] Increased levels of narcissism are associated with increased TV viewing, a preference for reality TV and political talk shows, time spent on Facebook, and social media addiction.[10] Because most of these studies only establish correlation, it is impossible to know to what extent narcissism drives participation and to what extent participation feeds narcissism, but the two appear to be dance partners. On social media, someone looking for attention selectively presents aspects of the self and then eagerly waits for the likes and comments. The responses reinforce that the user must keep editing the self to keep the attention coming. Meanwhile, as with other narcissistic exchanges, the real self gets little attention or nourishment. Paradoxically, even as narcissism increases along with social media use, a number of studies show a parallel decline in self-esteem.[11] Could enhancing your self-presentation leave you feeling worse about yourself?

Not all studies show this decline in self-esteem. But even studies demonstrating self-esteem enhancement or other benefits of social media may offer insights into the problem of favoring the idealized self. For example, an experimental study found that subjects who viewed only their own Facebook profile subsequently reported higher self-esteem than those who also viewed other profiles.[12] The study also found that self-esteem was higher for subjects who had just edited their profiles during the study than for those who did not. These study authors hypothesized that by allowing constant editing of one's self-presentation, Facebook promotes awareness of one's "optimal" self. This may be liberating for those who have little opportunity to explore and express their personal preferences and aspirations. But what happens when others are also expressing their optimal selves?

It seems that bringing others into the mix messes with this pleasurable self-focus. According to social comparison theory, we measure our own worth based on how well we stack up in relation to others, and places like Facebook give us a steady stream of people to compare ourselves to. A 2017 study of a large college-aged sample links Facebook use to increases in both self-objectification and social comparison, which, in turn, correlates with reduced self-esteem, poorer mental health, and greater body shame.[13] If others are posting only their exotic vacations and best poses, we'll feel worse about ourselves.

Even when others affirm our optimal selves through their "likes" and "loves," we may still feel bad but for a different reason. A longitudinal study of Facebook use found, to no one's surprise, that when people posted positive content, they received more positive responses than if they posted negative content.[14] But the researchers were surprised when they found that increased positive feedback was associated with reduced self-esteem.

Alienated Me

When social rewards are based on an edited self, we may have a hard time believing positive feedback. And even when posts are accurate, solicited "likes" and "loves" or predictable comments may feel empty. I recently noticed this pattern in my own Facebook posts. My husband and I love to travel, and most of my posts consist of the best moments of a recent trip. My friends, always supportive, comment about what adventurers we are. They are responding to a part of myself I value, but there is a certain emptiness to these interactions. I am getting back exactly what I elicit, as if saying, "Look at my adventures!" and getting the response, "Look at your adventures!" I am alone looking in the mirror. Missing is the fact that I didn't get to Europe until I was fifty, that I had suffered nightmares about dying before I got to see Japan, and that travel, for me, has been a hard-won joy. My photos show the conclusion, not the story. When I see someone else posting photos like mine, I see their conclusions, too, and I may even convince myself that they got the conclusions without the story, feeling envy and wondering why it was so hard for me. Photos and posts stripped of context can leave us feeling ashamed and anxious about the real lives we are living. We become alienated from ourselves. We suffer FOMO (Fear Of Missing Out) because we aren't having what they're having.[15] We carry this anxiety, this idea that we are behind, that we should be having more fun. We become alienated from others.

When we individually or collectively alienate parts of ourselves, those unintegrated parts can atrophy. Then, ashamed, we push those parts further into oblivion, and the vicious circle continues. This dynamic occurs offline as well. I think of a student of mine. When he walked into the classroom for the first time, my mind automatically registered "winner." He stood tall, smiling and engaging with his friends, and when he spoke in class, he exuded confidence and charm. He was an athlete and had aspirations to become a lawyer. I assumed he was extremely bright. Until I graded his first exam. I was confused, and after checking and rechecking the score, I asked myself, "How could this student have scored a D minus when all other indicators said he would ace it?" I got my answer later through a personality theory paper in which he identified his own struggle with narcissism. He shared in that paper that his parents had always thought he could do anything, so anything that didn't come easy, he saw as a deficiency. Rather than seeking help with areas in which he struggled, he distanced himself from his need. When I later asked him about his exam performance, which had become a chronic problem, he said:

I truly believed that I could walk into an exam and ace it regardless of whether I studied or not. My friend Jim always proclaimed that he could simply sit through lectures and then ace exams. I think I was trying to prove to myself that I could do it too. After all, the narcissism in me was practically screaming that I was capable of it. Plus, if I would do poorly, it was easier to say, "Oh, I didn't study," rather than admitting that I studied and still didn't comprehend the material... On a deeper note, admitting that I failed would be proving some deep-down feelings of inadequacy that helped form my narcissistic personality in the first place. If I admitted that I wasn't good enough, two things would happen: I would either A) enter a depressive episode after realizing that I may not be good enough for college and begin to reevaluate what I am doing with my life, or B) have to reassure myself that I am good enough, further cementing my narcissistic personality. In order to allow myself to go forward through college and not fail the aspirations that had been set for me, I essentially continued telling myself that "I am the greatest" and further bought into my narcissism.

This student's very need to "be the greatest" kept him far from that reality, at least academically. The two possibilities for him were either to wallow in shame or to deny inadequacies and attach to the grandiose self. The third option—to integrate and care for the part of him that didn't have the answers—was yet to be discovered.

Filling Out the Picture

This chapter has been a tough one for me. No, that's only part of the truth. They've all been tough. Embarrassingly tough. I can recall days where a single paragraph was all I had to show for my labors. I get stuck in loops, writing and erasing the same sentence multiple times. At the beginning of a new chapter, I am convinced I have nothing to say, and I'm pretty sure I don't know how to write. I'm frequently convinced that I don't *like* to write.

I started posting notes on these embarrassments on my social media because I want this part of the story—this part of me—included along with the one that has me finally holding my completed book. The responses I've received have been so much more meaningful than the love emoji for a perfectly framed vacation photo. From the "hang in there, honeys," to funny suggestions, to the commiserations of fellow writers, the post broke into a lonely place—for me, and perhaps for others—and offered company. On a larger scale, the internet can give voice to the disenfranchised. In the ten years since *Introvert Power* was published, those who felt "different" and "weird" found online communities; introverted bloggers and cartoonists made us visible; and an outcry of protests from mental health professionals kept introversion out of the diagnostic manual of mental disorders and placed it back where it belongs—right next to extraversion as a viable personality style. The #MeToo movement broke the isolation of those who had suffered sexual assault and harassment. This is the potential of social media. Just as use of these outlets can promote narcissism and alienation, they can also facilitate connection and integration. Social media use has the potential to enhance empathy and promote healing.[16] These contradictory findings reveal that we have a choice: feed the Edit Me dance or integrate and connect.

Here are some suggestions for resisting the hooks of the Edit Me:

1. **Recognize the price of quick rewards.** Look at how much time you are spending online, and then look at what you are doing with it. If you're like me, you may have a "circuit" you reflexively run through—like a trained rat: Facebook, Twitter, (insert other social media), email. Notice how you get pulled in and ask whether you really want to go there. How many times do you check for responses to posts? What rewards are keeping you hooked, and how satisfying are they? If you are engaged only in browsing other people's

posts and comments, something researchers call "social snacking," you may feel superficially engaged but subsequently more alienated.[17] If you're only working your own profile, you may enjoy the reflection while avoiding the real work of self-development.

2. **Change it up.** The myth of Narcissus shows us the ways in which narcissism starves the host even as it keeps him entranced. Pull away from the reflexive circuit and feed yourself. You can do this by engaging in the world beyond your phone, but you can also change up what you visit online. There's an app for everything, and you can find a poem, look at art, read classic literature, learn just about anything, or engage in a nonpartisan political discussion— yes, this exists.[18]

3. **Edit less.** The best kind of editing actually helps us communicate better by assisting us in saying what is difficult to say. But unless we're writing a blog or essay or book, we are likely engaging in self-presentation editing. Try filling in the picture of who you are rather than limiting it to your best side—or your angry side, or your victim side, or whatever persona you put out front. I appreciate whoever advised me not to limit photos of our children to times they were smiling. One of my favorite baby photos of our boys captured a huge pout, and even the ones showing them crying help us remember a broader range of experiences with them. Consider, in your offline as well as online life, what parts of yourself you keep isolated. Where can you begin to include those aspects of you? What learning are you closing off out of fear or shame?

4. **Go offline.** Solitude is essential for intimacy with the self, as are authentic, real-time connections. While social media can facilitate connection, its omnipresence can work like a drug: a too-easy and too-empty companion. Have a media-free time of day or day of the week—or take a leave

of absence. A Danish study demonstrated that subjects who took a week off Facebook experienced greater life satisfaction and more positive emotions compared to those who stayed connected.[19] Engage in the slower work of feeding real connection. Set up lunch with a friend. Write freely in a journal to make room for what you've left unexpressed. I recently had the opportunity to meet in person someone I have gotten to know online. Seeing each other in our unedited states has changed our online connection. We still communicate similarly, but we see humans where we once saw profiles, and that has made all the difference.

5. **Move outside yourself.** One of the best things we can do to relax the focus on our own image is to immerse ourselves in other stories. When medical students I work with get caught up in their performance, I remind them to shift their attention to the patient. What is he or she saying? What is it like to be in that person's shoes? This shift not only enhances empathy and diagnostic precision but it takes pressure off the performance. Similarly, research has found that reading literary fiction enhances empathy while travel improves perspective taking—both antidotes to excessive narcissism.[20] It is interesting to discover that looking outside ourselves not only improves empathy but can also be a source of enjoyment.

As it turns out, self-focus is a lot of work.

PART

III

14

DESTRUCTIVE DANCE DETOX

Dance, magic dance.

–DAVID BOWIE, *Labyrinth*

n the 1986 cult classic film, *Labyrinth*, David Bowie's Goblin King looks nothing like a goblin.[1] Lithe and striking, makeup accentuating his intense eyes and hair plumed like that of an exotic bird, he is even able to charm the baby he snatched from his crib. The baby's self-preoccupied babysitter and sister Sarah, played by a young Jennifer Connelly, first wishes to be free of the baby, and then, horrified by the actualization of her wish, sets off to rescue him. As she tries to navigate the huge labyrinth leading to his castle, the King uses every means of deception to keep her spinning in circles. After escaping several of his traps, he lures her with fruit that both erases her memory and draws her into a magical fantasy. They are together at a masquerade ball, and he pulls her into the dance. For a moment, they lock eyes, and she moves in step.

Sarah is successful, not because she avoids the dance but because she learns through each deception. As a psychotherapist, I have danced with many fragile bullies. I have had to guiltily admit to myself feelings a therapist is not "supposed to" have: contempt, a desire to please, a wish to win, an impulse to run. What I learned in my training, however, is that getting caught up in the dance is part of what helps us understand it. My own fallibility has been an important tool. I may be one step removed from the dance, but I'm also in it. The psychoanalytic relationship acts as a template. The patient does what he or she does in relationships (transference), and the analyst feels the elicited feelings and impulses (countertransference). The difference is, the analyst uses the countertransference thera-peutically rather than acting on it. But we do get pulled by the momentum, and it can be hard work to keep our footing.

When I talk to clients, friends, and family members who are trying to exit a destructive dance, two consistent themes emerge: feelings of failure for being unable to fix the fragile bully, and feelings of shame for staying in the dance. Even with an arsenal of tools and the convenience of professional dis-tance, I have had to terminate psychotherapy with certain nar-cissists who sought only to exploit the relationship, and who found the rewards of the narcissistic high to be more compel-ling than the prospect of change. Christina shared her distress over leaving her fragile bully after twelve years of hard work: "I've made such massive improvements with him—someone else is going to get all the sweet benefits."

Even while struggling to separate, those in relationships with narcissists get used to the question, "Why don't you just leave?" This question is problematic for a number of reasons, including the fact that it does not respect the way change works. But the question can also be unhelpful because it assumes that the relationship is a purely interpersonal one—leave the person and it's over. Anyone who knows the anguished thoughts, second-guessing, and internal dialogue that rises out of a breakup—or who has dated the same person over and over in different bodies—knows that it's not always over when it's over.

In reality, the dance takes up residence inside us as much as it does between us. Object relations theorists propose that every external relationship has a counterpart inside of us. We talk to the internal stand-ins for real people in our private ruminations. To complicate matters, those internal stands-in are not always fair representations of the real people in our lives. We have already discussed ways of shifting specific dance steps, and this can often shift the dance—internally and externally—in productive ways. Sometimes the partner's moves dominate, and efforts to change it up become wasted energy. Exiting the dance may or may not require leaving the relationship.

How do we leave behind our mastered steps, familiar patterns, enticing reinforcers, and—when necessary—people we truly love?

Like an addiction, a destructive dance with narcissism stands in as a substitute for real frustrations as well as real satisfactions. Let's look at how to build resilience to the rote steps of the dance.

Treat Yourself with Compassion

A common obstacle to change is that, for many of us, our recognizing that something is not working too easily translates to feelings of shame and judgments of ourselves as a failure. We may utter laments such as, "Why was I so stupid?" "How could I have let that happen?" Or we might shutter at the thought of having any responsibility at all. These feelings are not only unkind; they can kick us back in the dance. We may decide that it's better to keep at it than to admit failure.

Ironically, feelings of shame and judgments of failure often have a source in our own narcissism. They come with the assumption that we should be self-made people, invulnerable to the powerful relationships in our lives, unmoved by the rewards that keep vicious circles in motion. These feelings may also reflect a collective impatience about the learning process. Our "just do it" society neglects the reality that change happens over several repetitions and with contemplation and planning. When violence is involved, leaving the relationship abruptly may be dangerous. According to the National Domestic Violence Hotline, domestic violence victims leave an average of seven times before they stay away for good.[2]

James Prochaska knew intimately how difficult change could be. Alcoholism eventually killed his father despite the best efforts he and his family made to interrupt this very vicious circle. As a clinical psychologist, Prochaska, along with his colleague Carlo DiClemente, sought out smokers who had successfully quit on their own to better understand the mechanisms of change.[3] What they discovered is that successful change requires a fair amount of internal work before it manifests in action. People initially resist change, then start to weigh pros and cons in an extended contemplation phase, *then* start to plan for change and rehearse how it will go, and finally take action. But even when people implement changes, making them stick requires ongoing maintenance. Relapses happen, and these can spin us back into old patterns. But Prochaska and his colleagues noticed that relapse was also part of the change process, providing opportunities for further learning and the strengthening of intentions to change. Sometimes, we just need to get bored enough or mad enough or tired enough to stop and say, "Enough." Prochaska and DiClemente's "stages of change" model is an example of what Wachtel refers to as a "virtuous circle." Positive effort and experiences inspire more positive efforts and experiences, and even setbacks are used to promote learning and build strength. A new dance spirals upward into a healthier repertoire.

Figure 2 represents the stages of change described by Prochaska and DiClemente:

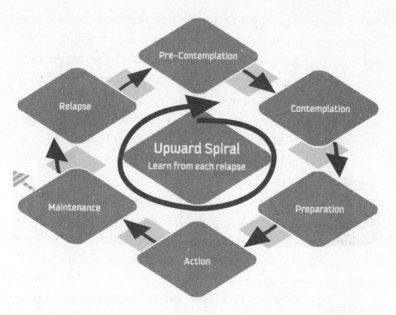

Figure 2

Both shame and grandiosity threaten the virtuous circle by distorting reality. Shame renders problems as unforgivable, and grandiosity denies that there ever was a problem. Compassion, toward ourselves as well as those we encounter, interferes with these narcissistic reactions and allows us to engage the wise counsel of reality.

Recognize the Cues and the Steps

Notice the statements, behaviors, or thoughts that cue you to engage in the destructive dance. As long as it's safe, just do what you do for a week and observe the triggers you encounter along the way. Also pay attention to the times you do *not* engage destructively as well as times you are able to engage productively. For example, anger channeled into an effective confrontation is an example of healthy engagement, not destructive reactivity.

Write down your triggers and notice any patterns. Do they happen at a certain time of day when you are tired and crabby? Are they tied to a particular issue or conflict? The fragile bully may not always be the instigator; a seething friend may rile you up to engage in the destructive dance. Once you identify what sets you off or pulls you down, note your feelings before and after the event. What thoughts flood your head?

Once you notice the cues and hooks, you can follow the sequence of interactions. So much of the work of exiting a destructive dance involves simply identifying the dance. In psychodynamic therapy training, I teach students to recognize the dynamics through their own moves as well as the client's. When we locate the problem, we feel less helpless about our ability to modify it. One caution here: trying to be your partner's therapist is a trap of its own. With awareness, help, and lots of practice, you can change your moves—sometimes the only way to do this is to move OUT—but trying to change the fragile bully is often part of the destructive dance, not an exit strategy.

Perhaps you can relate to all of the vicious circles we've discussed and even find yourself moving between them in the same relationship. Or maybe one of the dances, or a specific combination of dances, captures much of your experience. It is also possible that your experience doesn't quite fit any of the vicious circles listed in this book.

There is great power in knowing and naming the interactions that hold you captive to narcissism. You can customize this awareness by mapping out the sequence of steps in your problematic relationships then giving a name to that particular dance. For example, let's say you have the following interaction with your charming but exploitive boss:

1. Boss asks you to do something you don't feel comfortable doing.
2. You start to object.

3. Boss pours on the charm, telling you how skilled you are and how capable you are of doing the hard thing he just asked you to do.
4. You feel empowered, competent, and forget your objection.
5. You agree to do it.
6. The minute you walk out the door, you know you've been had.
7. You look back at him through the window, ready to return to Step 2.
8. He smiles and waves, clearly pleased with you. Move to Step 4.

Naming the dance allows you to externalize it and see it more clearly. Just as a child calms fears through stories, mindfulness and narrative therapy approaches help us externalize problems and gain perspective. Using playful names can help to detoxify and open space to view what's happening. In this case, you might use a name like "Flattened by Flattery" or "Objections Overruled." The point is to give your dance a name that exposes the repetitive circle. You can then fill in more detail, observing the sequence and noticing what hooks you—as in this journal recap of events with the boss:

1. Boss explains assignment. I nod and smile to be respectful, but I'm not comfortable with what he is asking me to do. He's so enthused; I want to let him down easy.
2. I start to express my hesitation, but he looks impatient. I pause. *Hook: impatient look.*
3. He says, "Don't worry. You've *got* this. I wouldn't ask just anyone to do this." He talks about how gifted I am, expresses his complete confidence in me. *Hook: flattery.*

4. It feels really good to hear these things—to get this kind of attention. I like that he believes in me, and I don't want him to lose faith in me. *Hook: attention, trust.*

5. I say, "You can count on me," and he's elated. *Hook: desire to please.*

6. I walk out the door and then realize that I just betrayed myself. I can't believe I've done it again! I ask myself, "How did I let that happen? How can I undo this?"

7. I look back at him through the window ready to knock on his door and try to get out of the assignment.

8. He smiles and gives me a thumbs-up. "Damn!" I think. "It's too late for me to back off." I smile and walk away, beating myself up. *Hook: commitment.*

As she navigates the labyrinth in the movie, Sarah encounters the goblin Hoggle, who is swatting delicate little fairies as they fly through the air. Disgusted by the goblin's behavior and charmed by the tiny fairies, Sarah offers her finger as a perch for one. The fairy bares teeth and bites her. Hoggle shares one of the important lessons to help her navigate the labyrinth: "Things are not always as they seem."

In vicious circles, things are often not as they seem.

In the above scenario, the source of the problem *seems to* rest with the employee. She has the burden of objecting to inappropriate assignments, and the boss has the luxury of appearing to be supportive and encouraging. She beats herself up for betraying herself without questioning why he has asked her to do so. His very request seems inappropriate, but he shifts the focus to the question of whether she is competent to perform the task. With this sleight of hand, he gets her to forget her original concern. At the same time, from an operant conditioning perspective, he selectively rewards her compliance while ignoring her or looking impatient when she objects. His bite is disguised behind his winning smile.

She is also making choices as she goes. Why is she so protective of his ego? There is a power differential—he's the boss, so that is a very real factor. But is she also bringing some old dance moves to the interaction? Did she learn early on that attention and support are in limited supply? Was she asked to betray herself in order to make a parent happy thus forging a link between self-betrayal and shared pleasure?

The more the employee can unpack what is really happening, the more power she will have to exit the dance. Recognizing the above, she might refrain from nodding and smiling when her boss talks about the assignment. She might even practice—with a friend or therapist, perhaps—remaining loyal to herself even as she notes what is positive about the interaction. For example, she might say, "Your opinion of me means a lot, and I appreciate your confidence in me. It's also important to me to know that you respect my concerns." In a situation like this, where there is a power differential, documenting all communications and/or involving an advocate may be necessary, but it is hard to know his capacity for responding if she has never asked him to do so.

Make Room for Observation

In the scenario above, the employee recognizes the dance only after she exits the room. The challenge of vicious circles is that they are harder to see when you are dancing within one. This is why abusive relationships and cults limit observational space, depriving participants of contact with outside parties. By reading this book, you have made a space for yourself to explore the vicious circles of narcissism. You can expand on this space in a number of ways. Therapy is a space designed for reflection with the advantage of providing you a trained observer to offer perspective and guidance.[4] The pages of a journal offer the freedom to say what you might not dare to utter out loud. Mindfulness meditation builds observational capacities, helping people watch events as they occur—even internal events such as thoughts and feelings.[5] Time away from the dance partner—whether he or she is on the news, at your workplace, or in your living room—is extremely important. I was only able to shift the dance with my father when I no longer lived with him *and* through the help and support of my psychoanalyst. While a move across the country may not be realistic right now, a long walk may be an option. Think of wedging open space for the virtuous circle of change.

Sometimes, we are the ones limiting our time alone. We get addicted to the drama, the conflict, the unsolvable problem. So expect that, when you take that walk by yourself or secure your quiet home for the evening, you might feel uncomfortable at first. You may also find yourself dwelling on the fragile bully or bullies in your life. This section includes tools, such as mindfulness practice, for detoxifying your solitude.

Practice a New Dance

Vicious circles gain power through repetition, but so do virtuous circles. Once you identify the dance steps in your vicious circle, you can practice new responses.

We've already discussed ways of countering the expected steps in the dances outlined in this book, but your own mapping of steps will help you arrive at customized alternatives. Sometimes the only alternative is to stay away.

To borrow the approach used by narrative therapists, start to track your alternative storyline. Note the times you do not engage in destructive sequences, map your journey along the stages of change, and mark the times when you shift the dance enough to make real contact. Applaud your courage to go just a bit longer without the drama of destructive patterns.

Find witnesses to this alternative reality. A therapist may serve this role, especially when new behaviors are fresh and you require guidance and support. The right friends can be excellent cheerleaders for your journey. As we've discussed, friends and family members may be tied into the dance, too, so be selective. Narrative therapy employs very concrete strategies that allow individuals to detach from destructive storylines, author new stories, and reinforce the new narrative. You may need to change how you talk to the people in your life. They'll need updates on how the story has changed. Writing the new narrative helps make it official. You can even write a letter to the old dance and inform it that you no longer have need of it.

And, if you'd like, borrow the words that Sarah spoke to the Goblin King:

"You have no power over me."

Make Room for Grief

Interactions with fragile bullies can be infuriating, and anger is the emotion most readily identified by those pulled into the dance. Anger can be both clarifying and empowering, and we'll discuss the importance of this emotion further in Chapter 15. The emotion often neglected—the one that takes many worn-out dancers by surprise—is grief. Grief is a close companion to change because all change involves loss.

Consider what you lose if you exit a destructive pattern with someone close to you, and be honest with yourself. You may lose pride, martyr status, or material rewards. If you leave the relationship and not just the dance, you may be relinquishing the hopes you had for the relationship and, often, access to a person you still, at some level, love. Even when there are no traces of love left, losing the villain in your life may leave you feeling empty—stuck with a dull script.

It seems counterintuitive to grieve something that has *caused* pain and suffering, but we do. In fact, it is often when we decide to let go of something hurtful that we can finally acknowledge and feel the hurt. In his classic paper, "Crying at the Happy Ending," analyst Joseph Weiss noted that we often discharge grief only after receiving assurance that the pain has ended.[6] This is why, he suggested, we cry after the resolution at the end of the film. Tearful reunions with loved ones, sobs of relief when the biopsy is negative—these resolutions allow us to acknowledge how scared we were or how much we missed that person now in front of us. I recall comforting my own husband, who had worked over five years in Afghanistan, when he was finally home and in a position to release and grieve the horrors of the war. Similarly, in leaving behind a destructive relationship pattern, we are allowing ourselves a view of the destruction.

Avoidance of grief is one of the reasons we tolerate hurtful interactions and bad relationships. "If I keep trying," the logic goes, "maybe all this effort will be worth something." What makes vicious circles vicious is that they are fueled by a passionate desire to fix things. In the Provoke and React, we react because we think that reaction will resolve the provoked feeling or teach the provocateur a lesson. In the Reassurance Dance, we reassure in order to heal the bully's fragility—and perhaps make him or her more available to the relationship. To admit that our efforts only fuel the circle is to admit loss. It takes courage to let go of a pattern you have mastered, an idea about yourself you have relied on, or a person you have loved.

Acceptance is a prerequisite for letting go. Carl Jung once wrote, "We cannot change anything unless we accept it. Condemnation does not liberate, it oppresses."[7] The paradox of grief is that when we hold it at a distance, other emotions such as anxiety and depression attach to it and make the feelings more threatening. Grief, when accepted and nurtured, has a lighter presence. Mindfulness exercises can help us tolerate the comings and goings of grief. When I feel the tug of grief, I regard it as a dear friend and invite it to sit next to me. This imagined interaction helps me allow grief to be present without overwhelming or consuming me. I can go about my work or play without abandoning the part of myself that is hurting.

Keep in mind that grief is different than an obsessive reliving of old scenarios. You will have these, too, but these fillers distract us from loss. Grief acknowledges loss and gives way to emptiness. The simple act of setting down the phone and parting with the endless chatter of social media may engender such feelings, but when allowed, they pass and make room for more satisfying experiences. Poets and therapists write of the potential in emptiness. Mary Oliver's poem, *The Journey*, uses the metaphor of a life-saving escape into darkness, and the founder of Gestalt psychotherapy, Fritz Perls, used the desert to represent what he called the "fertile void."[8] Perls wrote, "And we find when we accept and enter this nothingness, the void, then the desert starts to bloom. The empty void becomes alive, is being filled. The sterile void becomes the fertile void."[9]

We spoke in Chapter 4 of the narcissus flower that grows in the void where Narcissus once pined over his reflection. Sarah, once obsessed over the magical world of the Goblin King, ultimately relinquishes the dance to return to the ordinariness of her home—her own fertile void. But what was once empty becomes full. She tenderly attends her baby brother in his crib, lovingly appreciating what she almost lost. She then returns to her room alone. Looking in her own mirror, she now sees Hoggle and all the friends who had helped her along the way. Christina was only able to escape the dance with Jim by obtaining a Domestic Violence Protective Order, and she is still dealing with him via the courts. But she is recovering space. She told me recently, "I realize that I practically gave my true self away while with him. I am now trying to find her, so I can have her back…my friends miss her, too."

I asked her what she was finding in the space where her Narcissus once was.

"Peace," she responded. "Joy."

15

RULES OF ENGAGEMENT

Never go to bed mad. Stay up and fight.
–PHYLLIS DILLER

Narcissus is lonely. His followers have scattered, and he is alone in the woods. He cries out to see if anyone is there. Echo, who has been waiting for her opening, eagerly responds. Narcissus shouts, "Come to me!" and Echo runs with arms ready for the embrace.

As soon as Echo makes contact, Narcissus runs, too, but in the other direction.

Why the about-face? How did a meeting that seemed so promising end this badly? What does Narcissus want?

Narcissus wants company. He calls to Echo after his "faithful band of followers" has dispersed. He may even long for a companion, someone to love. But when she appears, he sees that she has needs, too, and this he cannot tolerate.

Narcissus wants to be alone.

The Conflict of Interests

Learning to negotiate the space between one's desire for independence and the need to connect with others represents a huge developmental challenge. Margaret Mahler used the term *rapprochement*—a French word meaning "approach, again"—to describe the focal point of this conflict.[1] According to Mahler, the "approach again" in development occurs after the peak of healthy narcissism when the confidently independent toddler bumps up against her limitations, feels her isolation, and rushes back to the open arms of mommy or daddy. As any parent observes, this return is not a one-time event but involves leaving and approaching again *and again.* Mahler noted that this extended phase is "characterized by a sometimes rapid alteration of the desire to reject mother, on the one hand, and to cling to her with coercive, determined tenacity in words and acts on the other hand."[2] The child is beginning to recognize her separateness, which is both exhilarating and terrifying. She is discovering that the world and its inhabitants no longer revolve around her. She is whole and separate (self-constancy), and others are also whole and separate (object constancy). She can approach and withdraw—and so can others. The child wants to be distant and then wants be close, and she plays with this tension over and over. Her back and forth ultimately results in the capacity for ambivalence— the simultaneous desire for separateness and connection.

This crisis of desires extends into adulthood as we continue to reconcile our wishes for independence with our need for company. Narcissus's extreme and contradictory responses to Echo demonstrate how far he is from striking this balance. The problem for the fragile bully is that he essentially wants to be alone *in the relationship*—to have the kind of company provided by a mirror. As discussed in Chapter 1, he lacks an internalized mirror and so continues to cast others in this role. Narcissus has this undemanding reflection from his "band of followers," but Echo wants more.

When Echo approaches, Narcissus sees two options: be alone—and keep searching for the perfect mirror—or disappear into Echo's needs. Allowing Echo's embrace threatens to annihilate his fragile sense of self. So he runs for his life.

The fragile bully splits his world in order to protect his precarious sense of self. The developmental literature refers to two kinds of divisions that must be resolved in rapprochement: independence versus relatedness, and good versus bad. Narcissus's flight not only represents a fear of losing his autonomy; it also reveals an abrupt shift in his perception of Echo. In their initial dialogue, she is an angel who saves him from isolation, and he wants to move toward her. When she comes to him, she becomes a devil who threatens his very existence, and he must run for his life. He has employed the narcissistic solution to relational uncertainty. He splits and separates everything "good" about himself and others—contents of the grandiose self and idealized other—from the "bad"—the shame-ridden self and belittled other. Destructive dances support this polarization. Partners run between extremes of engulfment and abandonment, between the joys of idealization and the hell of devaluation, never quite meeting in the middle where humans live and relationships thrive. The dances of narcissism allow partners to avoid the compromise of rapprochement and the vulnerability of bringing the whole self into contact with a wholly human other.

To understand this problem, it is helpful to explore the alternative—one that requires partners to negotiate the sticky territory between "I" and "we," and between perfection and worthlessness.

From Destructive Dancing
to Healthy Engagement

As we've seen, a destructive dance can involve plenty of fighting, but there's an automatic and passive quality to the exchange. We pick up the cue and respond with expected steps, and these steps polarize our sense of self and of the other. Narcissus jumped to the conclusion that Echo's desire was too much for him, and Echo accepted the cue, absenting herself and wasting away. They both had a range of responses available to them but went with the reflexive ones. Couple's therapist and researcher Judith Siegel has studied and quantified "dyadic splitting," or the shared tendency by members of a couple to ignore complexity and react on emotionally charged assumptions. She cites evidence that trauma, frequent in the histories of these partners, is associated with changes in right brain functions that compromise emotional processing. Siegel notes, "Couples defined by narcissistic vulnerability are highly reactive to disappointment and blaming."[3] This reactivity is evident in both those who lash out—the exploders— and those who pull in—the imploders.[4]

True engagement requires overriding splitting, and couples' therapists have developed approaches to facilitate this. Siegel starts by helping partners to identify what happens during this phenomenon. She uses the metaphor of a two-drawer file cabinet—one holding the "all good" emotions, memories, and associations, and the other holding the "all bad" relational experiences. When a trigger in the couple's interaction opens up one of the drawers, the other one remains locked. And when a partner is particularly anxious or hits on a potent trigger, he or she may pull open the "all bad" file drawer and become flooded as all of its contents tumble out. Siegel helps couples to identify the vulnerabilities and triggers that activate splitting and to work together to bring interactions back into the present. Rather than enacting vicious circles or "walking on eggshells," couples learn to collaborate in the face of conflict.[5] This engagement, by itself, interferes with the "all bad" polarity and promotes healing. To do this—to resist the destructive dance—requires leaving behind predictable steps and practiced outcomes. Engagement can be messy.

I came of age as a psychologist in the heyday of "couple's communication," the catchall phrase for couple's discussions, disputes, and verbal banter. "I" statements and reflective listening are now household tools for improving communication. As much as I resonate with and use this advice, I rarely see couples—even the happiest of them—"communicating" according to the recommended formulas. In fact, the couples who watch every word and preserve peace at all costs are often the ones who eventually take their desires elsewhere. After researcher John Gottman observed the spontaneous interactions of hundreds of couples, tracking their relationships for as long as twenty years, he concluded: "The notion that you can save your relationship just by learning to communicate more sensitively is probably the most widely held misconception about happy marriages."[6] He concluded that something more was needed—a true intimacy more similar to friendship than to our Hollywood images of romantic love.

Engagement, whether in an online dialogue or an intimate discussion, requires moving from a defensive position to one that makes room for our contradictory desires. Let's look at some ways couples can protect and promote healthy engagement.

Keep It Safe

Otto Kernberg, one of the pioneers in entering the psychological world of the narcissist, emphasized the importance of the therapeutic frame. That frame includes boundaries held by the analyst and expected of the patient—from establishment of a fee to agreements regarding containment of destructive impulses. Unlike rules to restrict or limit, the frame opens up space for free expression. The challenge of establishing rules of engagement is that what is safe for one person may not be safe for another. A highly sensitive person will more easily feel bullied than someone who enjoys aggressive banter. Safety also has many meanings. A violent, even destructive dance may feel safe in ways that honest engagement does not. That is because the dance is built on efforts to defend the self and does not require growth.

That said, there are a number of givens regarding safety. Partners need assurance that there is no threat of physical aggression. Blatant lying is a rule-out as it undermines trust and renders communication meaningless. The bottom line is that healthy engagement requires a balance of power that allows both partners to share what is truly important to them. Any one party's determination to undermine this balance, whether aggressive (name-calling, insulting, gaslighting, and emotional abuse) or passive-aggressive (self-harm, habitual stonewalling, suicidal threats), renders the interaction unsafe.

You may be thinking that a frame that excludes these behaviors, by definition, excludes anyone with narcissistic proclivities. This is likely true at the severe end of the narcissism spectrum, and even those in the moderate range may have a hard time pulling off such fair terms. If playing fair had worked for the narcissist in early life, he or she wouldn't be in this predicament in the first place. A fragile bully's incapacity does not justify waiving the rules of engagement—quite the contrary. Clear boundaries communicate that you will not engage in something that will harm you and do further damage to the relationship.

While the more obvious boundaries of safety and trust create hard lines around relationships, partners' subjective experience of safety is important as well. Nancy may feel bullied when Kathy raises her voice while Kathy feels bullied when Nancy gets quiet and weepy. The key here is that partners, at any point, have the power to negotiate the terms of interactions. Behaviors that feel threatening, for whatever reason, can be discussed and limited. For example, Nancy gets to say, "When you raise your voice like that I feel intimidated," and wait for Kathy to tone it down. Kathy gets to say, "When you get weepy, I feel guilty and unable to express myself." Gottman refers to efforts like this as "repair attempts" because they are geared toward deescalating tension and protecting the interaction.[7] If you've ever seen a flailing baby calm when wrapped tightly in a blanket, you know the power of containing reactivity. When a couple cannot provide each other this containment, this is a good indicator to seek therapy. The skilled therapist provides what D. W. Winnicott referred to as a "holding environment" for engagement.[8] Siegel aptly describes this function: "The therapist must supply soothing and/or structure to help spouses regain a more benign stance."[9] This "benign stance" helps them to be present for the interaction rather than reacting out of preconceived assumptions.

Working with your partner toward a balance of power often involves turning down intensity, but it can also call out feelings or desires that have been submerged. When your partner attacks your desire or disengages, try finding out what he or she wants. You cannot engage if your partner is not participating.

Fight "for"

This is a rule that may have changed the character of the 2016 presidential campaign. The fighting between candidates, and between their constituents, became a contest to see who could declare, in the loudest way possible, what was despicable about the opposition. If, as you read this, your next thought is to argue what was despicable about one or both candidates, you see how compelling the destructive dance is. When we get excited to witness and exploit the depravity of the opposition, something is wrong. This ugly side of politics is not particularly new, but the 2016 iteration was particularly vile and hate-filled, as were the spin-off conversations in our living rooms. We've already discussed the election-related stress felt around the country, and I think this stress, in part, has to do with the way in which all of our communications have been degraded.

Couples too often stop fighting for what they want because they are too busy fighting against what they fear. Even simple online exchanges can be improved if we keep the "fight for" rule in mind. I recently posted an image of an older woman smiling serenely and enjoying a concert as everyone around her focused on taking photos and recording the event. Though most of my followers appreciated the reminder to be present, one commenter expressed anger and disgust. While ridiculing the post and adorning her response with eye-rolling emojis, she mentioned that she would be one of the people recording the concert, so she could share it with her sister. Another commenter jumped on her for voicing intolerance even as she protested intolerance. Part of me appreciated the protective response and wanted to let the two of them go at it. But, standing back, I was able to see that behind the first commenter's disgust and ridicule was her intention to share a positive association with something I had used as a negative example. By validating her sentiment and sharing what the image meant to me, the collective conversation evolved. We talked about what it meant to be present, as well as the irony that this photo was taken by someone with a camera, and yet helped us to consider putting down the camera.

When we remove the dangerous associations to fighting, we can see its life-giving elements. Defensiveness is easy. Fighting involves energy, passion, desire, and commitment. Commitment? Think about it—do you bother to engage with people who are not important to you? We wrangle with people we value the most for what we value the most—and we should. To relinquish the fight can mean to reduce ourselves and our relationships.

Healthy engagement means pursuing two outcomes simultaneously: fighting for your self—your desires, needs, and values—and fighting for the relationship. In our culture, we often split these two goals. And in a relationship with a fragile bully, the partner is often working to preserve the relationship while the bully focuses on preserving the self. Craig Malkin's "empathy prompts" bridge this disparity. These two-part expressions communicate both a valuing of the other and a personal desire, need, or feeling. To say, "You are important to me," and "What you said hurt," or "I want something from you," is to put yourself in a vulnerable position, and this is exactly what softens the recipient of such a message. A message like this says to the inner Narcissus, "I see you and value you," *and* "I want you to see me, too. You needn't run to preserve yourself." Malkin notes that a narcissist who remains unresponsive to empathy prompts is not a good candidate for a relationship.

Holding the tension between individual and relational desires requires a shift in attitude—an unwillingness to relinquish one side of the paradox. It means bringing to each interaction the sentiment: "This is really important to me, *and* our relationship is really important to me." I'm amazed at the number of times I hear a client complain that she has to relinquish her dreams because her partner will not tolerate the change. Often, the two have not even discussed her aspirations because she has held them dearly, not wanting to expose them to the challenges imposed by the relationship. The two options she then considers are relinquishing her dream or relinquishing her partner. The alternative? Pursuing both.

Relinquish Entitlement

The tricky fact of intimate partnerships is that we load onto them all of our unmet longings for acceptance and support. As children, we looked to our parents to tune into, know, and even help *us* know our needs and desires. This is appropriate, and skillful parental mirroring helps us firm up a sense of self and the capacity for independence. But even if we've had that kind of mirroring and support, the demands of adult relationships can make us feel like Narcissus and want to run in the other direction. The fact that we need to communicate what we want in these relationships comes as a huge disappointment to most of us. I often hear the protest: "But having to ask her spoils it." I agree. The "it" that gets spoiled is the wish to be cared for without having to participate.

Consider the following complaints:

My wife never wants to go to the game with me.

My brother never asks me about my day.

I really could have used a hug after a day like that.

Wishes to be played with, hugged, or given attention don't end with childhood. These needs are healthy and getting them met is important. When we complain, however, we are often back in childhood when we expected our caregivers to be attuned to these needs and possibly even recognize them before we did. Adult relationships are more complicated. For example, when the man I reference in the example above was hoping for his wife to "want" to go to the game with him, maybe she was wanting him to go to a play with her. The one-way attention provided by parents is not realistic for adult partnerships. This doesn't mean the ball game can't be part of the picture. It does mean that the man needs to express his wish. And it may mean that the theatre will be on next week's agenda.

Lead with Desire; Expect Positive Outcomes

As we've discussed, that odd phenomenon called repetition compulsion means that, for a variety of reasons, we may be compelled to repeat the failures of early relationships. See if you can relate to the following scenario: You weakly express a desire, then withdraw as soon as your partner protests. Later, you feel rageful that you were cheated, that you weren't heard. So you express anger and bitterness to your partner, who appears clueless, which further enrages you. This kind of enactment is at the crux of vicious circles: you want one thing but facilitate something else. In this case, you want your desire to be satisfied but facilitate dissatisfaction and anger.

Let's look a little closer (and don't tell me you haven't done this!):

Sara: I saw this nice patio set that might look good on our deck, but I know you're concerned about the money.

Robert: Yeah, we need to watch our spending.

Sara: OK, just forget it.

Note that Sara not only expects resistance, she plants the resistance and then conforms to it. It is a powerful shift to expect that your desire will be met *and* that your relationship will improve. With this attitude, what happens next may be less clear. You may get no fight at all. Or, your desire may not be met in the precise way you present it. For example, Sara and Robert may decide to target a future date for purchasing the patio set, allowing them to save the money and reduce Robert's anxiety. Or Robert may disclose something he had his eye on, and the two of them will contend with how to meet both of their desires. Your partner's input will challenge you to distill what is most important, and you will provide the same challenge to your partner. The outcome is then a creative product of the interaction rather than a repetition of what is expected.

In the example of Sara and Robert, Sara's response is based on the expectation that Robert will deprive her. Let's say Robert does object and adds, "How can you expect to buy more furniture when we haven't put anything aside for our vacation?" Now Sara could respond, "I just want one nice set of furniture—everything we have is so ratty!" Notice that Robert and Sara have engaged around the issue of deprivation. Robert feels deprived, so he can't respond to Sara. Sara argues that she is more deprived. Stories of their impoverishment will probably continue to escalate.

We use deprivation to play on guilt and force a response. This approach is characteristic of vulnerable narcissism, in which fragility justifies entitlement. While extracting a response through guilt may appear temporarily effective, it ultimately shuts down engagement and drains satisfaction from the relationship.

Engagement becomes life-giving when we risk putting our desires forward simply and honestly. In our example, Robert might say, "I have really been wanting to put some money away for our vacation." Sara could offer, "I want to make our deck more inviting, so we can relax there in the evenings." The more the two of them can be curious about their own and each other's desires, the more they open themselves to the possibility of ending up with more—not less—than what each of them started with. The deprivation-oriented version would have cut short this kind of exploration.

Expect to Change—Slowly

To make the most of a therapy process, I often need to help clients shift from experiencing sessions as isolated events to experiencing them as an "ongoing conversation," as a colleague of mine put it. This shift allows them to use the between-session time to develop the session material and integrate change. It could be argued that it is in the between-session time where change happens. I believe that the same is true of conflict in an intimate partnership. When partners are interacting directly, they are limited in their capacity to take in each other's feedback. After the encounter, they have more room to toss around that feedback, struggle with it, integrate new learning, and arrive at new questions. Often the benefits of the struggle occur silently in changed behavior and new understanding. This contrasts with the "kiss and make up" format of conflict we have been taught to expect. This familiar format demands an unnatural, one-session emotional shift to harmonic feeling and sets us up for feelings of failure. Real conflicts evolve over time and pressure us to grow.

Real conflicts also rarely get resolved in one round. If it seems you and your partner keep having the same fight, you are not alone. Working the territory between each other's desires is challenging and, like most skills, takes time and practice. My husband and I reminisce about our twenty-five-year fight about the relative importance of money versus passion—a fight that evolved alongside time spent raising children and enjoying each other. Over time, the conflict evolved from a vicious circle to a committed effort to support each other's priorities to an expanded repertoire. The good news is that repeated mistakes, whether in the same relationship or multiple ones, help us to know the thing we need to relinquish. Consider this: you may be having the same fight repeatedly because the conflict is important to you. Real resolution takes time, persistent fighters last several rounds. And through healthy engagement, both the relationship and the individuals emerge stronger.

Turn Toward Each Other

Echo approaches; Narcissus turns away. If Gottman had observed this interaction in his lab, he would likely shake his head in recognition.

Through exhaustive observations of couples' interactions, Gottman's team noted that partners often made what he called "bids" for attention and affection. When one partner made a bid, the other partner either turned toward them or turned away. The gestures Gottman and his team observed were often small ones—volunteering to grab the item needed from the store, laughing at a joke, offering a shoulder rub. Gottman noted that these responses seemed to build the couple's store of good feeling that would then help them through challenges. His study revealed that the couples that stayed together had turned toward their partner's bids, on average, 86% of the time. By contrast, those who divorced only turned toward such bids an average of 33% of the time.[10]

If we transformed the Narcissus-Echo story into that of a sustainable and healthy relationship, the story might lose its dramatic appeal. Echo would approach more gently. Narcissus would be sort of a jerk, but Echo would hold her ground and also see his fear. They would both be closer to the middle of the narcissistic spectrum, so we would probably have to change their names. They would fight, but not to harm—only because relationships are hard, and they are learning.

They might even start to run, feeling that life is easier alone, with a band of admirers or in the safety of a cave.

But, each time, they approach again. And, in doing so, they learn to engage.

16

SPECIALNESS IN ITS PLACE

*But nothing disturbs the feeling of specialness like
the presence of other human beings feeling
identically special.*

–JONATHAN FRANZEN, *Freedom*

There are lines in certain books you remember forever.
One such passage came to me as I perused a book recommended by a graduate school professor. The line read,
"Perhaps the most difficult thing for a patient to accept is that
he is quite *ordinary.*" When I read these words, I'm pretty sure
I exclaimed out loud, "What?!" I tried to get my head around
this: "That's the punchline? I'm studying to be a therapist so
that I can show people that they are *ordinary*? And—wait—if
they're ordinary, that means I am too!"

The insight came from psychotherapist Sheldon Kopp,
via his book, *If You Meet the Buddha on the Road, Kill Him!*[1] His
words were at once devastating and liberating. As a fatigued
graduate student, I was comforted by the idea that perhaps I
didn't need to work so hard to stand out. I could work for what
I cared about and rest into the comforting awareness that I
had company in my ordinariness.

Still, I wrestled to reconcile this idea with childhood messages that I was special—the best, even—and could do anything. My nine siblings were also the best, which, if you do the math, makes no sense. I wanted to be the *most* special, as did my siblings, and the unspoken competition helped the ten of us make much of what we were given. The family resources were limited to a rural pastor's salary, but we all graduated from college, most of us went on to add graduate degrees, and our visible credits include a two-star general, a couple shelves of published books and academic articles by the family's authors, original musical compositions, and rooms of commissioned paintings. I'm not sure we would have done so well if Mom and Dad had told us we were ordinary. So what is the right place for narcissism in a healthy life?

Thirty years since this conundrum first entered my mind, with the help of other thinkers and mentors, my life experience and my clients, I have arrived at some answers. Healthy narcissism thrives when we use it more as a muse than a foundation—when we embrace the ordinary, and when we open ourselves to a variety of sources of input from others.

The Narcissistic Dream

My sister and I frequently touch base on our creative projects, and invariably, our childhood conditioning enters the conversation. She, also a therapist, is a singer-songwriter currently recording her second album. We both entered the world with big dreams, stoked by the encouragement of our father, and we both have fallen many, many times. She recalls producing her first album early in her artistic development, Grammy visions in her mind, and performing one CD release concert at an almost-empty venue. I cringe as I recall the modelling and talent search I entered years ago. Unlike my sister, I do not have a trained voice, and I took the stage to perform in front of an auditorium I now wish had *not* been full. I knew it was a bad sign when, as I received my critiques, a judge commented on how much she liked my shoes. I read comments about my gown and how poised I was. Of the little that was said about my voice, one word popped out—a word that strikes horror in anyone raised with musical appreciation. "Flat." At the end of the competition, I waited to find I had received no callbacks. As I looked around the lobby at prepubescent contestants talking with potential agents, I felt a wave of shame.

What was I thinking?

What was my sister thinking?

We were thinking we were special. And, as experts like Twenge and Campbell might have predicted, this belief set us both up for our subsequent falls.[2] The grandiose visions we had for our success could not pass the tests imposed by reality. As much as the two of us bemoan the burden of our inflated visions—my sister recently complained, "This follow your dreams shit is just too much work"—those visions have pushed us into worlds otherwise off-limits to two girls from rural Minnesota.

Narcissism is healthiest as a source of inspiration and unhealthiest as a dietary staple. The toddler rises up to walk, for the first time looking down on the world. In that moment, he can do anything. He has power, authority, and lives at the center of everything. This is the narcissistic dream, and it doesn't last long. Nor should it. The fall is as important as the rise. Soon the child learns to reconcile his vulnerability with his power—another *rapprochement*. But before we go there, let's set the pause button on that rise, that unsustainable high. This is the seed of vision, that lusty feeling of transcendence that tells the toddler anything is possible. Kohut emphasized the importance of mirroring these moments of power and prowess. Memories of these moments are precious fuel for enduring the knocks and skinned knees to come. As adults, we revive these moments when we identify with performers in a Broadway musical or athletes on ESPN or when a song makes us feel we can indeed live forever. My husband and I recently spent some time in New York City, and we felt like we were bathing in collective grandiosity. The lights of Times Square, ads as large as buildings featuring celebrities shining like gods, Tiffany windows showcasing the kind of jewels that inspire movies and fantasies—all beckoning us to dream bigger. Even though we knew we couldn't afford the necklace, that I'll never dance on Broadway, and that he'll never hit the winning run for the Cubs when they take on the Mets, we were buoyed by the views.

Vision does not emerge from the adult mind but out of our naïve, overblown dreams. Vision, by definition, is inflated. It comes fully formed, without toil or setbacks—success achieved, often with life-changing results. The product idea works and makes peoples' lives easier, the remodel makes your home the envy of your neighbors, the book is fully written and enlightens readers with the brilliant concept that just popped in your head. As someone well-schooled in pipe dreams (both metaphorical and literal—my Dad designed and built full-scale pipe organs as a hobby)—my youthful imaginings may have been particularly lofty. But I am writing this book because of them.

The Fall

Speaking of this book, here's a peek into my process: Something I have been observing and thinking about jells. I pitch the idea to my agent, Jessica.[3] Jessica hates most things I pitch to her—or at least that's how I translate her kind rejections, but she likes this idea. "Great!" I think, "She'll pitch this to publishers." Then she tells me to write a proposal. I reluctantly write a proposal. It's a pain, but it does help me flesh out the idea. Fifty pages later, I send her the proposal. She says she needs more. I hate her but get back to work. Seventy-five pages and I abandon shortcuts in favor of a well-researched and supported, solid proposal. She likes—no, loves—the proposal. I love her again. Fast forward through the roller coaster of matchmaking with an editor, and the trail of rejections along the way, and I have a book to write. And it is toil. I remember that every fully formed idea I brought to this project needs to be *communicated*. And some of my ideas don't hold. My research updates my thinking, and I have to, as the classic advice goes, "kill my darlings."[4] For every chapter I write, I have another file where I dump all my false starts. That file could comprise another book—not a good one, but a long one. When I complete a chapter, I thrill at the completed product, the hard-won victory of translating thought to words. Then I start all over again staring at the new blank page.

There is nothing unique or special about this process. Quotes abound to remind us of how far the realities of writing are from its romanticized counterpart. Here are a couple of them that have kept me company during my process:

Thomas Mann: A writer is someone for whom writing is more difficult than it is for other people.[5]

George Orwell: Writing a book is a horrible, exhausting struggle, like a long bout of some painful illness. One would never undertake such a thing if one were not driven on by some demon whom one can neither resist nor understand.[6]

The process of writing a book, like that of any challenging goal, is an exercise in falling, getting back up, and doing better—repeatedly. Though the toddler's fall from grace represents a fault line for narcissism, falls throughout life provide us opportunities to either retreat to our grandiose fantasies or contend with reality.

Narcissistic Injury

The problem for the fragile bully is that the high, the grandiose vision, is not treated as inspiration but as a source of daily sustenance. For the narcissist, the high becomes everything, and she becomes a bully willing to knock others down to get what she needs. Rather than becoming more, she becomes less—sharpening the skills that get her attention and neglecting the humanity that hones wisdom and connects her with others. Rather than walking on the ground, she envisions herself above all, and any reminder of the contrary is an offense, a source of injury requiring retaliation.

The kind of falls I discuss in the previous section are challenging, and those at the far end of the narcissism spectrum are masters at finding shortcuts and ways of fending off the awareness of limitations. As my student shared in Chapter 13, one method for doing so is to act like you are above the challenge. Don't study for the exam, fail, and blame circumstance. Another method is to let others do the work and then take the credit. But even the narcissistically impaired can work hard and accomplish goals. The kinds of falls that feed narcissism are the ones orchestrated by narcissism. The visions that precede these falls are not regarded as glimpses of what might be but as expectations, privilege one is entitled to. Distorted self-perceptions set up this kind of standard and unwillingness to entertain any deviation. Reviews will all be five-stars out of five. The grade will always be A with the plus. Devotion will be absolute.

If we can't integrate the falls into a richer understanding of who we are, we're in trouble. Our narcissism needs to get knocked around a little to transform it into a grounded self-image. Narcissistic injury, if we can stand it, is a gift. When I read Kopp's reminder of my ordinariness, my narcissism took a hit. Narcissistic injuries show us our limited selves, the self that is like everyone else, the self that needs to work and pay her dues. And that can be hard to take. Hard but essential to the creative challenge of living well.

When I emerged from that talent exposition with no callbacks, I was devastated and humiliated. The dark side of narcissistic shame took over. I wanted to hide, even to vacate myself from the planet. I felt a fool. This is the torture that can push the narcissist in a number of directions. I could have sought the mirroring I demanded, begging, borrowing, or stealing to get it. I did get plenty of "poor baby" and "what were they thinking?" from my family back home, but I didn't insist that the world was missing out on the next great talent. I could have complained to the organization, belittled the agents and called the whole thing a scam. I could have lashed out at those who got callbacks. I could have retreated into a fantasy that the world just wasn't good enough for me. I could have led with my vulnerability, sinking into a depression and asking the world to continue to reassure me that I was permitted to live in it.

While reveling in that shame, I felt the impulse to do all of the above. But I woke up, looked around, and made a different choice. The hotel lobby had a bar. Not a drinker, I rarely notice when there's a bar in a hotel I'm staying. But this time I thought, "There is one thing I can do that none of these underage lovelies can do." And I pulled up to the bar and ordered a shot of tequila. Like a grown up.

Though I don't advocate alcohol as a solution to pain, the shot was not about getting drunk. Besides, I had only one. Having the shot allowed me to laugh and to tell a different story about this experience. As I felt the warmth of the liquor go down, I looked at the small trophy in my hand. Masks symbolizing comedy and tragedy decorated the gold exterior, and the affixed plaque read, "First place, original monologue."

Delivering that monologue—a sixty-second fantasy portraying my liberation from an oppressive society—had been an isolated moment of pure joy. My focus on the big prize I had lost made me forget this one that ultimately held more meaning. That monologue, "The Retreat," later made its way into a dream that did find fulfilment—my book, *Introvert Power*.[7]

My sister and I have both come to terms with our falls and have discovered something our bold visions left out: the gift of simply getting to do what we enjoy doing. For her it's songwriting—those moments with her guitar and notepad when the perfect lyric to a musical phrase finally comes to her. She says that sometimes those creative moments feel so holy she is moved to tears. For me it's what I'm doing right now. The hard thing that allows me, once a quiet girl lost in a big family, to be part of the conversation.

Mirror, Mirror

We have discussed the kind of mirroring a child needs to emerge into the world with both vision and grounding. We continue to benefit from mirrors that show us who we are, that reflect our gifts as well as our limitations. Fragile bullies are selective about their mirrors and work hard to control the ones they use. Like Narcissus gazing in the pool, such mirroring keeps the fragile bully right where he is. So what kinds of mirrors do we need?

I think we benefit most when we avail ourselves of a variety of mirrors as well as people who pull us away from ourselves and stretch us. A good friend provides the validating reflection that helps us feel understood as well as the "on our side" loyalty that helps us bear difficulty. John Gottman talks about the importance of having this kind of mirroring from an intimate partner at the end of a hard day.[8] We also need mirrors that show us, in loving ways, where we need to grow. In Chapter 5, I shared how my husband's observation shined a light on something I didn't like hearing but knew to be true. My sister still thanks me for the hard reality I mirrored back to her when she was stuck in a bad marriage.

Do you engage with people who hold values and viewpoints that differ from yours? When we eliminate new perspectives and relationships, when we create echo chambers, we deprive ourselves of this varied input. Finally, though the world can be a tough place, we do best when we can tolerate and consider the unvarnished feedback of impersonal mirrors, like bosses, editors, and critics. To take an inventory of the input you are receiving, ask yourself the following:

- Do you have the friend who knows what to say when you need a lift?
- Do you have the intimate mirror who can help you see and tolerate the realities that make you cringe?
- Do you have people who see your gifts when they are invisible to you?
- Do you have people who are hard for you to understand and make you better for the challenge?
- Have you consulted someone outside your world, like a therapist, to be the mirror others are unable to provide? Therapy is valuable to the extent that it goes beyond what you want to hear to what you need to hear.

Climb the Mountain or Sit in the Shade?

In my twenty-five years of therapy practice, I have worked with many more people at the low end of the narcissism spectrum than those who would benefit from feeling a little less special.

Those lacking healthy narcissism have a hard time claiming a space in the world, and they have a hard time appreciating what they have to offer. But whether someone is grasping for something positive to say about themselves or they run out of session time listing their great qualities, they may be focusing on the same thing—the question of what gives them value. This, I believe, is one negative side effect of a culture that emphasizes what we can see, measure, and commodify. Part of the relief I felt in the message that I was ordinary came from the idea that I was part of a collective. I didn't have to stand out or define myself. With all the slogans telling us to climb the mountain and be our best, can we find value in resting into ordinary? Would doing so mean we sink into stasis and stop growing? For me, these questions point to a needed cultural *rapprochement:* one that allows us to hold the shared value of being human at the same time that we seek to participate in an individual way. We'll take a closer look at that vision in the next chapter.

17

MENDING
THE NARCISSISTIC DIVIDE

The greatness of America lies not in being more
enlightened than any other nation, but rather
in her ability to repair her faults.

–ALEXIS DE TOCQUEVILLE

America has historically felt pretty good about herself.
Others look up to her. She likes to tell other nations
what to do and usually thinks she has the right answer.
She looks great—purple mountains, amber waves of grain.
Though she's seen some wear, her national parks still show off
her best side. Her people make her extremely interesting and
complex. And she has a very strong foundation.

But lately she's not feeling so well. She's harboring a lot of
internal conflict, and she is really touchy these days. And it's
not helping that she spends so much time on Twitter. She's
mad half the time and makes decisions before she counts to
ten. You'd think, at the age of 242, that she would know better.

As columnist David Brooks noted, "We used to have a certain framework of decency within which we held our debates,
and somehow we've lost our framework."[1] Brooks's comment
inspired me to search for that framework—where it thrives

and where it breaks down. I read classic works of European social critics who saw American democracy as a beacon of light to the world. I listened to the incredible story of Daryl Davis, the African-American blues musician whose friendship with members of the KKK inspired them to relinquish their robes. I found places where people discuss politics without rancor. And I talked with a West Virginia conservationist who looked to coal executives for help.

Narcissism vs. Democracy

What does Brooks's envisioned "framework of decency for debates" have to do with narcissism? In its pathological manifestations, narcissism renders individuals and groups incapable of the engagement crucial to shared problem-solving and collective governance. German philosopher Theodor Adorno said, "Democracy is nothing less than defined by critique." He elaborated, "The system of checks and balances, the reciprocal overview of the executive, the legislative, and the judiciary, means as much as that each of these powers subjects the others to critique and thereby reduces the despotism that each power, without this critical element, gravitates to."[2] Adorno also happens to be the scholar who, in his analysis of the rise of Nazism, first used the term *collective narcissism*.[3] Before we explore the ways we can promote democratic engagement, let's look at the role of narcissism in breaking it down.

Citing evidence of growing political polarization, such as increased political homogeneity among married couples and within residential neighborhoods, Shanto Iyengar and Sean Westwood set out to evaluate the level of animosity between members of opposing political parties. They wanted to look beyond the open hostility that often infuses political debates and see to what degree attitudes toward political differences infiltrate nonpolitical and personal domains. Their findings, published in the 2015 report, "Fear and Loathing across Party Lines: New Evidence on Group Polarization," offer a sobering perspective. Using the Implicit Associations Test—famous for exposing the unconscious biases of well-meaning people[4]— they reveal that unconscious hostility toward opposing party members is even stronger and more automatic than implicit hostility based on black-white racial polarization. While society places constraints on racial bias, partisan animosity is socially *encouraged*—as anyone can gather from a scan of social media posts. How often, for example, do we challenge fellow party members to check their facts and watch their assumptions? The study further showed that partisan animosity manifested in discriminatory practices, such as selecting students for scholarships based on cues to party membership instead of qualifications reflected in their resumes. Discrimination based on party affiliation exceeded discrimination based on race. Finally, the researchers found that discrimination was motivated more by animosity toward members of the opposing party than by favoritism toward members of their own party. The authors of the study noted that this deep hostility sends a clear signal to elected officials to stay within, rather than reach across, party lines.

The Dance of Collective Narcissism

What fuels this hostility between parties? Social psychologists have long identified a tendency to overvalue members of one's own group (*in-group love*) while devaluing members of other groups (*out-group hostility*). Psychologist Drew Westen and his associates discovered, through brain imaging, that people with strong partisan identifications use rationalizations to "turn off" neural circuits channeling threatening information about their own party. At the same time, Westen discovered, the brain activates reward circuits that offer partisans a "jolt of positive reinforcement for their biased reasoning."[5]

Though the brain does its part in protecting and enhancing in-group love, *collective narcissism* seems to have an important role in feeding out-group hatred. In 2009, Agnieszka Golec de Zavala and her colleagues launched an extensive project to quantify and study the characteristics of collective narcissism.[6] They have taken their research to diverse settings to look at timely concerns such as: attitudes toward out-groups in Poland, predictors of prejudice related to the Brexit vote, and conspiracy thinking during the 2016 U.S. presidential election. They defined collective narcissism as "an exaggerated in-group esteem contingent on external validation."[7] What this means is that individuals high in collective narcissism overvalue their own group but at the same time harbor unexpressed doubts about the group's superiority. These doubts manifest as defensive protectiveness of the group, hypersensitivity to perceived threats, and an insatiability regarding the recognition the group must receive. Interestingly, collective narcissism is associated with vulnerable individual narcissism but not with its grandiose counterpart.[8] In particular, researchers found that susceptible individuals lacked a sense of personal control and self-esteem. This is an important finding given what author Mark Manson refers to as "victimhood chic"—the modern tendency to leverage victimhood to one's sense of superiority. These observations seem apt here:

> "Victimhood chic" is in style on both the right and the left today, among both the rich and the poor. In fact, this may be the first time in human history that every single demographic group has felt unfairly victimized simultaneously. And they're all riding the highs of the moral indignation that comes along with it.[9]

As strident as Manson's remarks may seem, they expose the weaponizing of vulnerability so characteristic of collective narcissism. When collective victimhood is used as a weapon, it stops the conversation and undermines true empathy. The history of powerlessness and victimization is usually very real, but it works like that file cabinet Judith Siegel refers to. The victim pulls open the drawer and throws out its contents at an out-group member who then shields herself against the barrage rather than offering understanding. Then the vulnerable instigator feels dismissed, and the bruised recipient avoids the instigator, and the instigator feels more disenfranchised and powerless, and all of this gets stuffed back into that file cabinet—until the next provocation.

What Golec de Zavala's group found is that it is collective narcissism, not positive group identification, that breeds out-group hostility and conspiracy speculations.[10] A longitudinal study over the course of the 2016 presidential election found that when collective narcissism was high, liberals as well as conservatives demonstrated increases in conspiracy thinking.[11] By contrast, group members with low collective narcissism and high group regard do not show the same need

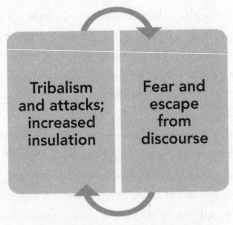

Mending the Narcissistic Divide

to lash out at other groups.[12] Just as individuals with sturdy self-esteem tend to be accepting of others, those with healthy group esteem can afford to be more magnanimous toward out-group members.

We seem a long way from magnanimous. What social and political commentators are calling *tribalism* sounds very similar to collective narcissism. Glenn Greenwald describes the sentiment behind tribalism: "The tribe that has defining beliefs that I share, we're justified in doing anything, because the other tribe is the bad, evil tribe."[13] Calling out this behavior on both sides is a start. Our increased awareness of the problem makes it harder to enjoy hiding in our corners. And this is the good news within the bad news. America is hurting, and hurt is often necessary to inspire change. In discussions about the dysfunction in American political discourse, people tend to blame one of two, seemingly opposed, problems: (1) The aggressive, attacking way in which we engage, and (2) our tendency to disengage and hide out in our ideological echo chambers. Through the lens of the vicious circle, we can see how the two tendencies interact: We attack or hide because there's a monster next door, and, as we attack or hide, we insulate ourselves, nursing more fear and anger in our isolation. So universities limit discussions to "safe" topics, and the venom goes underground. Or venom spews and reinforces negative expectations. Whether we are more comfortable with "fight" or "flight," we dance to the same music.

As I write, you may be thinking, "But the monsters are real. They are evil," or "Why are we always the ones who have to be understanding?" Let me assure you, the other side is saying the same thing. I was recently struggling with my perception that liberals listen better and work for common ground more than conservatives seem to. Then, while scanning through radio stations in the car, I came across a conversation on a conservative talk show. The commentator was saying, "We listen.

But we don't get the same back. It's the knee-jerk reactions—
xenophobic, racist."[14] David Brooks observes that forces on
multiple fronts—from big data to consumerism to identity
politics—have "amputated people from their own depths and
divided them into simplistic, flattened identities."[15] Where is
that "framework of decency" that allows room for filled-out
humans to productively engage?

Remembering Who We Are

In 1938, the novelist and Nobel Laureate, Thomas Mann,
embarked on a coast-to-coast U.S. lecture tour. He wasn't
promoting a book. Mann, who had relocated to America to
escape Nazi Germany, was promoting democracy. He defined
democracy as "that form of government and of society which is
inspired above every other with the feeling and consciousness
of the dignity of man."[16] His mission, however, was not to teach
Americans about democracy. He wanted to warn those gifted
with democracy to remember and protect what they had. He
said, "Instruction is one thing—and another is memory, reflection, re-examination, the recall to consciousness of a spiritual
and moral possession of which it would be too dangerous to
feel too secure and too confident."[17] His words are all too pro-
phetic at a time "consciousness of the dignity of man" seems to
be a diminishing capacity.

But that capacity is not dead. In fact, since I started to look
for frameworks of decency in America, I've begun to see more
of what Mann so appreciated. I see Daryl Davis sitting in a
club with a KKK member, giving him a platform instead of
reacting. I see the two hundred members of the Klan relinquish their robes due to this friendship and the understanding
that emerged from it.[18] I see a blossoming of social media and
fact-check sites that challenge participants to abandon blind

assumptions in a shared quest for truth.[19] I don't have room for all the evidence I see. Instead, I'll share a story from a place where America's hurt is deeply felt—the coalfields of West Virginia.

My husband and I lived in West Virginia for eighteen years and had close seats to that hurt. He, a criminal defense attorney and guardian ad litem, saw the increasing fallout of economic decline, drug addiction, and hopelessness. As a therapist, I listened to stories of former coal employees who had lost their livelihood but retained the stress imposed by a suffering industry. We also enjoyed the stunning beauty of "the mountain state," rafting on the rivers with our boys, skiing the mountain slopes, and hiking to vistas that astounded us. We saw hurt to these natural resources, too, and lived through an extended water contamination crisis that rendered our water unusable even for washing our hands.[20] Slogans across the state highlighted an increasing division between "Friends of Coal," and "Friends of the Mountains." After the 2016 election, I saw these interests lock in, mobilizing both the anger of those affected by the steep drop in the state's coal production and the despair of those facing deep cuts to conservation funding and infrastructure. This situation was ripe for a vicious circle of blaming and hostility.

Beth Wheatley grew up in West Virginia and found her calling as she played in the forests there as a child. Now director of external affairs and strategic initiatives for The Nature Conservancy of West Virginia, the shifting socioeconomic landscape was a cue to Wheatley to try something new. She said, "For The Nature Conservancy to advance its mission in West Virginia and the larger coalfields region, I knew we needed to figure out how to contribute more to a vibrant economic future." But she also knew that the organization needed to change its approach in order to get there. She continued, "I started by recognizing, 'I don't know what I don't know.' We had to get out of that mode of thinking that we must have a game plan or solution to present to enter into conversations. What if we went in not knowing the answers—and maybe not even knowing the full landscape of the problem?"

So she set up listening sessions inviting coal executives, economic development leaders, former government officials, and other stakeholders to share their perspectives on West Virginia's economic future. Wheatley and her colleagues approached everyone with a personal invitation: "We really want to have the chance to have a deep conversation with you." There were three ground rules. First, she said, "I was interviewing them…I assured them I would not be responding with my own thoughts. They were free to allow their ideas to flow." Second, Wheatley assured them she would not disclose the specific source of content shared in interviews. The third ground rule was the assurance that she would get back in touch with participants "to let them know how we've been using their thoughts to inform The Nature Conservancy's work."

Wheatley's bold experiment rested on her belief that if she engaged people personally, they would respect and embrace the opportunity. But even she was surprised what came of it. She told me one experience she had meeting with a high-level coal executive:

> I looked at this guy, his title, his role—all that could paint a picture of him focused first and foremost on bringing coal back. I asked him, "What do you want for West Virginia's economic future?" What I discovered is that he embraces diversifying the economy and sees the State's natural beauty—our forests and rivers—as important in this diversification. And he opened the door to working together to see nature contribute to economic growth. After we met, he told me, "Thank you for the opportunity to share. We never get to have these conversations—to get to the bottom

of it. There is never time or space for me to do this. We no longer are having true dialogue." We cannot go into our work making assumptions about what people are thinking and feeling [in regards to the State's economic future]...I realized that, before this moment, there just was no chance to build a bridge to a common effort.

Wheatley's interviews were so successful that the organization set up Nature and Economy Summits with the same ground rules only in a group context. "No media," she emphasized. She recalled, "One of my colleagues was walking away from the summit with his jaw dropped. He said to me, 'Did you see how people were leaning in to the conversation?' He had expected crossed arms and defensiveness." When I asked Wheatley what has emerged from these problem-solving sessions, I felt her excitement:

It totally changed our programming. It had a monster influence...For example, we historically would purchase land, and activities on the land would be largely limited to trail development and forest or stream restoration. Now we're looking at lands that would allow us to do economic development. There are 1.2 million acres of former mine lands across West Virginia and the Central Appalachian region. This is degraded land, and much of it is unproductive. Many owners are asking, "What's the next revenue stream for our land?" So the focus has become on developing partnerships with these landowners and others to answer this question and create new jobs. Healthy forests often surround the degraded land, so we can use both as a place for different kinds of economic development that are compatible with also maintaining the health of the land and water. Some of the mined land is perfect for solar development because it has been leveled and is near transmission lines. And then we can incorporate agroforestry practices across portions of former mine lands and forests. And we can undertake responsible forestry, resulting in carbon credits and timber. We can develop tourism and trails, providing public access that was not readily available in areas with large industrial ownerships. What's key is that the economic model can be profitable, providing opportunities for landowners and others to replicate and scale. The model is aimed at creating new jobs and revenue streams in addition to the environmental benefits from these nature-based economic activities—solar, forestry, agroforestry, and outdoor recreation. Many areas of West Virginia are so remote and lack infrastructure, but this economic model works in remote places.

As I reflected on the rancor I had observed between the interests Wheatley brought together in these conversations, I was a bit dumbfounded. I asked Wheatley, "Am I correct in concluding that there was no name-calling, nobody feeling slighted, no people walking out of the room in disgust?" She said she witnessed none of that. Though The Nature Conservancy's success is anchored in its ability to build bridges, Wheatley seemed a bit awestruck herself. She said, "It's one of the best things I have done." Though it took her just doing it—doors had been shut on her efforts in the past—once launched, "It got traction—tons of traction." When I asked about her inspiration, she responded, "Curiosity. I really wanted to find a bridge between nature and economy. I knew that if we didn't get out of our comfort zone, we'd just keep doing things the way we've done them. I wanted to find a way to bridge that gap—to advance both." Thinking of that image of people leaning into these conversations, I commented, "It seems you created comfort zones." She agreed: "Comfort zones where there were none before. Amazing how easy that is to do." This struck me too, the ease of it all. And as if she read my mind, she added, "By allowing the space for people to make connections, you can innovate. We, as a country, are missing the boat on that."

Changing the Conversation

One of the problems of group polarization is that people naturally have a better view of the depth and diversity of individuals within their own groups and are inclined to see members of the out-group in more uniform and stereotyped ways.[21] Wheatley's approach not only restored this missing depth but also offered personal control in place of hopelessness. As we've discussed, this is a key element in whether positive in-group feelings cross over into collective narcissism. In fact, new research reveals that collective narcissism is diminished when individuals simply reflect on positive ways in which they've exercised personal control.[22] What is interesting is that, while collective narcissism declined, non-narcissistic positive group feelings increased. In line with this finding, Yale Law professor Amy Chua argues that the point is not to undermine group identities but that, to move away from tribalism, we need to bond through our shared responsibility to a larger group that we call America.[23] How do we forge these bonds without undermining our commitment to our causes? Here are some ways to translate theory into action.

When our energies go toward defensively attacking the opposition, we have little left to focus on desired change. We also lash out when we feel helpless, and lashing out generates more of the same, feeding that helplessness. When we facilitate change, even in small ways, we strengthen our sense of personal control. When something triggers the desire to become defensive, we would do better to pause and focus on how we want things to improve. The good news is that this shift helps to mend the narcissistic divide even as we further our causes.

We can also start to ask different questions. On the evening after interviewing Wheatley, my husband was complaining about people's ignorance about a political issue—one he and I happen to disagree on. I wanted to understand his position, so I asked him what made him angry and got back more of the same complaints I already knew well. Then, taking a cue from Wheatley, I asked, "What do you care about?" His tone softened, and he shared a perspective I had never heard before, one more balanced—one that even acknowledged shared ground with the very people he had been complaining about.

Social science research has exposed the numerous shortcuts our brains use to save time. Unfortunately, the shortcuts contribute to many of our social ills, including stereotyping, racism, and misattribution of problems. For example, we commit the *fundamental attribution error* when we assume that the offensive actions of others are more due to internal factors than to life circumstances.[24] Research on *salience bias* demonstrates that we give more weight to what stands out, so we home in on a hateful outlier while neglecting the larger context of benign communications. Recognizing such errors can help us pause and remember what we don't know.[25] Physician Rachel Naomi Remen introduced the term "generous listening" as a part of a culture change she has been advancing in the medical field.[26] Building on the recognition of what we don't know, this means listening without assumptions, with a willingness to be surprised, and with an effort to understand the "the humanity behind the words."[27] As he reflected on his transformative conversations with KKK members, Daryl Davis noted, "The most important thing I learned is that when you are actively learning about someone else you are passively teaching them about yourself. So if you have an adversary with an opposing point of view, give that person a platform."[28]

Imagine the sea change that might occur if we collectively rejected cheap headlines—even the ones we agree with—in favor of intimate knowledge. Sensational news offers short-lived excitement without depth. Truth seeking in this way may seem unexciting at first but promises to open up new territory of thought and the delight of discovery.

Beyond all of the humanitarian implications of her project, Wheatley's efforts resulted in ideas that were better than they would have been had the groups involved worked in isolation. And this is the spirit of democracy—the idea that *the people— all of them,* not a leader or a group—are the nation's most valuable resource.

Getting Up

One hundred years before Thomas Mann delivered his lectures on democracy, another European toured the United States to witness the workings of democracy in America. Alexis de Tocqueville, a French lawyer and aristocrat, came to the United States to study American penitentiary systems. After touring for nine months, conducting more than two hundred interviews, and reading hundreds of books and documents, however, he ended up conducting a comprehensive survey of democracy. The young lawyer's resulting book, *Democracy in America,* the Oxford Research Encyclopedia of Literature notes, "continues to enjoy a prestige only slightly less than that of the actual founding documents of the nation."[29]

Though de Tocqueville is typically quoted for his lofty statements about America, his writing reveals a much more grounded perspective. "On arriving in the United States," he wrote, "I was surprised to discover how common talent was among the governed and how rare in government."[30] He saw democracy as an imperfect but worthy process, not a product.

He observed, "Democratic institutions awaken and flatter the passion for equality without ever being able to satisfy it to the full."[31] He saw the potential tyranny of the majority and the threat of despotism. He said, "Equality places men side by side without a common bond to hold them together. Despotism raises barriers to keep them apart." He also noticed how perpetually restless and dissatisfied Americans seemed to be, and predicted that if nothing keeps this in line, "we will then find men constantly changing course for fear of missing the shortest road to happiness."[32]

Despite these concerns—or perhaps because of them—de Tocqueville's affection for America infuses his tome. He saw America not as our narcissistic inclinations might prefer but as our humanity requires. In fact, his writings suggest that America is better positioned than most to withstand narcissistic injury. He wrote, "If democracy is more likely than a king or body of nobles to make a mistake, it is also more likely to correct that mistake."[33] More than anything, de Tocqueville saw greatness in our ability to fall, then get up, and try again.

ENDNOTES

Introduction

1. In case examples such as this one, names and circumstances have been changed sufficiently to keep identities private.
2. Lull, R. B., & Dickinson, T. M. (2016). Does television cultivate narcissism? Relationships between television exposure, preferences for specific genres, and subclinical narcissism. *Psychology of Popular Media Culture.* 7(1), pp. 47–60. See also Reiss, S., & Wiltz, J. (2004). Why People Watch Reality TV. *Media Psychology.* 6(4), pp. 363–378.
3. Watts, A. L., Lilienfeld, S. O., Smith, S. F., Miller, J. D., Campbell, W. K., Waldman, I. D., & Faschingbauer, T.J. (2013). The Double-Edged Sword of Grandiose Narcissism: Implications for Successful and Unsuccessful Leadership Among U.S. Presidents. *Psychological Science.* 24(12), pp. 2379–2389.
4. Malkin, C. (2015). *Rethinking Narcissism: The Secret to Recognizing and Coping with Narcissists.* New York: Harper Perennial.

Chapter One

1. Mahler, M. S. (1974). Symbiosis and Individuation—The Psychological Birth of the Human Infant. *The Psychoanalytic Study of the Child.* 29, pp. 89–106.
2. Mahler, p. 98.
3. Malkin, C. (2016, July 20). The Spectrum: From Echoism to Narcissistic Personality Disorder. Retrieved from http://www.drcraigmalkin.com/blog/narcissistic-personality-disorder.
4. American Psychiatric Association. (2013). *Diagnostic and Statistical Manual of Mental Disorders* (5th ed.). Arlington, VA: American Psychiatric Publishing, p. 669.
5. Cramer, P. (2017). Childhood Precursors of the Narcissistic Personality. *The Journal of Nervous and Mental Disease.* 205(9), pp. 679–684.

6. Morf, C. C., & Rhodewalt, F. (2001). Unraveling the paradoxes of narcissism: A dynamic self-regulatory processing model. *Psychological Inquiry. 12*, pp. 177–196.
7. American Psychiatric Association, pp. 767–768.
8. American Psychiatric Association, p. 670.
9. American Psychiatric Association, pp. 669–670.
10. Dhawan, N., Kunik, M. E., Oldham, J., & Coverdale, J. (2010). Prevalence and treatment of narcissistic personality disorder in the community: a systematic review. *Comprehensive Psychiatry. 51*, pp. 333–339.
11. Study finding 0% prevalence: Lenzenweger, M. F., Loranger, A. W., Korfine, L., & Neff, C. (1997). Detecting personality disorders in a nonclinical population. Application of a 2-stage procedure for case identification. *Arch Gen Psychiatry. 54*, pp. 345–351. Study finding 6.2% prevalence: Stinson, F. S., Dawson, D. A., Goldstein, R. B., Chou, S. P., Huang, B., Smith, S. M., & Grant, B. F. (2008). Prevalence correlates, disability, and comorbidity of DSM-IV narcissistic personality disorder: Results of the Wave 2 National Epidemiologic Survey on Alcohol and Related Conditions. *Journal of Clinical Psychiatry. 69*(7), pp. 1833–1845.
12. Malkin, C. (2015). *Rethinking Narcissism: The Secret to Recognizing and Coping with Narcissists.* New York: Harper Perennial, p. 35.
13. Alexander, F. (1949). *Fundamentals of Psychoanalysis.* London: George Allen and Unwin LTD, pp. 234–235.
14. Stinson F. S., Dawson, D. A., Goldstein, R. B., Chou, S. P., Huang, B., Smith, S. M., & Grant, B. F. (2008). Prevalence correlates, disability, and comorbidity of DSM-IV narcissistic personality disorder: Results of the Wave 2 National Epidemiologic Survey on Alcohol and Related Conditions. *Journal of Clinical Psychiatry. 69*(7), pp. 1833–1845.

Chapter Two

1. Levy, K. N. (2012). Subtypes, Dimensions, Levels, and Mental States in Narcissism and Narcissistic Personality Disorder. *Journal of Clinical Psychology: In Session. 68*(8), pp. 886–897. See also Gabbard, G. O. (2016). The many faces of narcissism. *World Psychiatry. 15*(2), pp. 115–116.

2. Dickinson, K. A., & Pincus, A. L. (2003). Interpersonal analysis of grandiose and vulnerable narcissism. *Journal of Personality Disorders. 17*(3), pp. 188–207.

3. Miller, J. D., Hoffman, B. J., Gaughan, E. T., Gentile, B., Maples, J., & Campbell, W. K. (2011). Grandiose and vulnerable narcissism: A nomological network analysis. *Journal of Personality. 79*(5), pp. 1013–1042. The authors review a number of divergent characteristics of the two subtypes, including inverse relationships between grandiose and vulnerable narcissism in relation to the Big 5 personality traits. Specifically, grandiose narcissism is positively correlated with Extraversion, while negatively correlated with Neuroticism and Agreeableness, and vulnerable narcissism is positively related to Neuroticism, while negatively correlated with Extraversion and Agreeableness. See also Miller, J. D., Lynam, D. R., Hyatt, C. S., & Campbell, W. K. (2017). Controversies in Narcissism. *Annual Review of Clinical Psychology. 13*(1), pp. 291–315.

4. Miller, J. D., Lynam, D. R., Hyatt, C. S., & Campbell, W. K. (2017). Controversies in Narcissism. *Annual Review of Clinical Psychology. 13*(1), pp. 291–315. See also Krizan, Z., & Herlache, A. D. (2017). The Narcissism Spectrum Model: A Synthetic View of Narcissistic Personality. *Personality and Social Psychology Review.* pp. 1–29.

5. Jauk, E., Weigle, E., Lehmann, K., Benedek, M., and Neubauer, A. C. (2017). The Relationship Between Grandiose and Vulnerable (Hypersensitive) Narcissism. *Frontiers in Psychology. 8*(Article ID 1600). Retrieved from https://www.ncbi.nlm.nih.gov/pmc/articles/PMC5601176/.

6. Jordan, C. H., Spencer, S. J., Zanna, M. P., Hoshino-Browne, E., & Correll, J. (2003). Secure and defensive high self-esteem. *Journal of Personality and Social Psychology. 85*(5), pp. 968–975.

7. Gabbard, G. O. (1989). Two Subtypes of Narcissistic Personality Disorder. *Bulletin of the Menninger Clinic. 53*(6), pp. 527–532.

8. Miller, J. D., Maples, L. M., Buffardi, L., Cai, H., Gentile, B., Kisbu-Sakarya, Y., & Campbell, W. K. (2015). Narcissism and United States' culture: The view from home and around the world. *Journal of Personality and Social Psychology. 109*(6), pp. 1068–1089.

9. Malkin, C. (2015). *Rethinking Narcissism: The Secret to Recognizing and Coping with Narcissists.* New York: Harper Perennial.

10. Yerkes, R. M., & Dodson, J. D. (1908). The relation of strength of stimulus to rapidity of habit-formation. *Journal of Comparative Neurology and Psychology. 18*, pp. 459–482.

11. American Psychiatric Association. (2013). *Diagnostic and Statistical Manual of Mental Disorders* (5th ed.). Arlington, VA: American Psychiatric Publishing, p. 646.

12. Krizan, Z., & Herlache, A. D. (2017). The Narcissism Spectrum Model: A Synthetic View of Narcissistic Personality. *Personality and Social Psychology Review*, pp. 1–29. Note that spectrum models go back to earlier conceptions, such as that of Gabbard, who in 1989 described a continuum between the oblivious and hypervigilant subtypes of narcissistic personality disorder. See also Gabbard, G. O. (1989). Two Subtypes of Narcissistic Personality Disorder. *Bulletin of the Menninger Clinic. 53*(6), pp. 527–532.

13. Miller, J. D., et al. (2015).

14. American Psychiatric Association, p. 646.

15. Frances, A. (2017, February 14). An Eminent Psychiatrist Demurs on Trump's Mental State [Letter to the Editor]. *New York Times*. Retrieved from https://www.nytimes.com/2017/02/14/opinion/an-eminent-psychiatrist-demurs-on-trumps-mental-state.html.

16. Frances, A. (2017). *Twilight of American Sanity: A Psychiatrist Analyzes the Age of Trump*. New York: HarperCollins, p. 4.

17. Lee, B. X. (Ed.). (2017). *The Dangerous Case of Donald Trump: 27 Psychiatrists and Mental Health Experts Assess a President*. New York: St. Martin's Press.; The American Psychiatric Association's Goldwater Rule states, "[I]t is unethical for a psychiatrist to offer a professional opinion unless he or she has conducted an examination and has been granted proper authorization for such a statement." This restriction was codified in 1973 due to concern about public comments made by psychiatrists on the mental state of senator and presidential candidate Barry Goldwater. These diagnostic opinions were offered without direct consultation or permission from Mr. Goldwater, and included such severe diagnoses as psychosis, megalomania and paranoid schizophrenia. For history and APA's position, see Levin, A. (2016, August 25). Goldwater Rule's Origins Based on Long-Ago Controversy. *Psychiatric News*. Retrieved from https://psychnews.psychiatryonline.org/doi/full/10.1176/appi.pn.2016.9a19.

18. Gartner, J. "Mental Health Professionals Declare Trump is Mentally Ill And Must Be Removed." Retrieved from https://www.change.org/p/trump-is-mentally-ill-and-must-be-removed.

19. Lee.

20. Shenk, J. W. (2005, October). Lincoln's Great Depression. *The Atlantic.* Retrieved from https://www.theatlantic.com/magazine/archive/2005/10/lincolns-great-depression/304247/. Joshua Wolf Shenk discusses the ways in which Lincoln's depression seems to have contributed to some of his great leadership qualities, such as his realism and clarity, his humility, and his creativity.

21. Lifton, R. J. (2017). Foreword: Our witness to malignant normality. In Lee, B. X. (Ed.), *The Dangerous Case of Donald Trump: 27 Psychiatrists and Mental Health Experts Assess a President* (pp. xv–xix). New York: St. Martin's Press.

22. Lasch, C. (1979). *The Culture of Narcissism: American Life in the Age of Diminishing Expectations.* New York: W.W. Norton & Co. See also Twenge, J. M., & Campbell, W. K. (2009). *The Narcissism Epidemic: Living in the Age of Entitlement.* New York: Atria Paperback.

23. Lasch, p. 239.

24. Twenge, pp. 18–39. The authors reference a cumulative database of Narcissistic Personality Inventory (NPI) scores for 49,818 college students who had completed the inventory between 1979 and 2008. They note not only a steady upward trend, but also an accelerating rate of increase in levels of narcissism.

25. Malkin, pp. 15–27. Malkin notes that, because the NPI includes admirable qualities, it is inaccurate to use a high score as an indicator of unhealthy narcissism. He also cites evidence that millennials have higher levels of altruism than youth of earlier generations. See also Pinkus, A. L., Ansell, E. B., Pimentel, C. A., Cain, N. M., Wright, A. G. C., & Levy, K. (2009). Initial construction and validation of the Pathological Narcissism Inventory. *Psychological Assessment. 21*(3), pp. 365–379.The Pathological Narcissism Inventory (PNI), designed to isolate and measure pathological manifestations of narcissism, was developed in response to concerns that the NPI primarily measures adaptive expressions of narcissism.

26. Lasch, p. 79.

27. Watts, A. L., Lilienfeld, S. O., Smith, S. F., Miller, J. D., Campbell, W. K., Waldman, I. D., & Faschingbauer, T. J. (2013). The

Double-Edged Sword of Grandiose Narcissism: Implications for Successful and Unsuccessful Leadership Among U.S. Presidents. *Psychological Science. 24*(12), pp. 2379–2389

Chapter Three

1. Ma, G., Fan, H., Shen, C., & Wang, W. (2016). Genetic and Neuroimaging Features of Personality Disorders: State of the Art. *Neuroscience Bulletin.* 32(3), pp. 286–306.
2. Malkin, C. (2015). *Rethinking Narcissism: The Secret to Recognizing and Coping with Narcissists.* New York: Harper Perennial, p. 65.
3. Tibbals, C. (n.d.). Psychoanalytic Perspectives on Narcissistic Personality Disorder: An Overview (unpublished literature review). University of Nevada, Reno, 6.
4. Kernberg, O. F., Yeomans, F. E., Clarkin, J. F., & Levy, K. N. (2008). Transference focused psychotherapy: Overview and update. *International Journal of Psychoanalysis. 89*(3), pp. 601–620.
5. Mahler, M. S. (1974). Symbiosis and individuation—The Psychological Birth of the Human Infant. *The Psychoanalytic Study of the Child. 29*, pp. 89–106.
6. Kohut, H. (1972). Thoughts on Narcissism and Narcissistic Rage. *Psychoanalytic Study of the Child. 27*, p. 363. The author notes this theory assumes "an independent line of development in the narcissistic sector of the personality, a development that leads to the acquisition of mature, adaptive, and culturally valuable attributes in the narcissistic realm."
7. Henschel, C. (2014). The Effects of Parenting Style on the Development of Narcissism. *Behavioral Health. 1*(1), pp. 1–8. Retrieved from http://www.sakkyndig.com/psykologi/artvit/henschel2014.pdf.
8. Associated Press. (2017, September 5). Putin says Trump 'not my bride, and I'm not his groom.' *AP News.* Retrieved from https://apnews.com/1f2127fb6bc34ffabe7085553b22a8d5.
9. Sherrill, S. (2001, December 9). The Year in Ideas: A to Z; Acquired Situational Narcissism. *New York Times.* Retrieved from https://www.nytimes.com/2001/12/09/magazine/the-year-in-ideas-a-to-z-acquired-situational-narcissism.html. Though the concept of acquired situational narcissism

(ASN) informed Millman's clinical work with celebrity patients, ASN is absent from the psychiatric literature and behavioral research studies. The idea of "state (vs. trait) narcissism" has been studied in its natural fluctuations as well as through experimental manipulation. For example, experimental enhancement of narcissism was associated with increased aggression in Li, C., Sun, Y., Ho, M. Y., Shaver, P. R., and Wang, Z. (2016). State narcissism and aggression: The mediating roles of anger and hostile attributional bias. *Aggressive Behavior. 42*(4), pp. 333–345. See also Giacomin, M., & Jordan, C. H. (2016). The Wax and Wane of Narcissism: Grandiose Narcissism as a Process or State. *Journal of Personality. 84*(2), pp. 154–64.

10. Wachtel, P. (1977). *Psychoanalysis and Behavior Therapy: Toward an Integration.* New York: Basic Books.

11. Chan, M. (2017, June 2). 'He broke me.' Kathy Griffin Says Trump Family Ruined Her Life Over Controversial Photo. *Time.* Retrieved from http://time.com/4803225/kathy-griffin-trump-photo-head/. See also Bernstein, J. (2017, September 23). Kathy Griffin: 'Trump went for me because I was an easy target.' *The Guardian.* Retrieved from https://www.theguardian.com/culture/2017/sep/23/kathy-griffin-trump-went-for-me-easy-target.

Chapter Four

1. For a brief background on Ovid (full Latin name, Publius Ovidius Naso), who lived from 43 BCE to 17 CE, see Kenney, E. J. Ovid. In *Encyclopædia Britannica.* Retrieved from https://www.britannica.com/biography/Ovid-Roman-poet.

2. Campbell, J., & Moyers, B. D. (1988). *The Power of Myth.* New York: Doubleday, p. 48.

3. Myth and quotations derived from these translations: Ovid. (2000). *Metamorphoses* (Book III). (A. S. Kline, Trans.). Retrieved from http://ovid.lib.virginia.edu/trans/Metamorph3.htm, and Ovid. (1964). *Metamorphoses* (Book III, pp. 339–509, R. Humphries, Trans.) In Godolphin, F. R. B. (Ed.) *Great Classical Myths* (pp. 352–357).

4. Theoi Project (n.d.). Liriope. Retrieved from http://www.theoi.com/Nymphe/NympheLiriope.html.

5. Online Etymology Dictionary. (n.d.) Narcissus (n.). Retrieved from https://www.etymonline.com/word/narcissus.

Chapter Five

1. Lin, D., Lord, P., Miller, C., & Lee, R. (Producers), & McKay, C. (Director). (2017). *The Lego Batman Movie* [Motion Picture]. United States: Warner Animation Group.
2. American Psychiatric Association. (2013). Diagnostic and Statistical Manual of Mental Disorders (5th ed.). Arlington, VA: American Psychiatric Publishing, pp. 667–669.
3. Horney, K. (1991). *Neurosis and Human Growth: The Struggle Toward Self-Realization.* New York: W. W. Norton & Company, pp. 23–24.
4. Horney, p. 194.
5. Horney, p. 18.
6. Kohut, H. (1972). Thoughts on Narcissism and Narcissistic Rage. *Psychoanalytic Study of the Child. 27*, p. 387.
7. Kohut, p. 381.
8. Kohut, p. 385.
9. Studies consistently identify higher levels of self-esteem among grandiose narcissists in comparison to vulnerable narcissists. For a recent discussion of these findings, see Rogoza, R., Zemojtel-Piotrowska, M., Kwiatkowska, M. M., and Kwiatkowska, K. (2018). The Bright, the Dark, and the Blue Face of Narcissism: The Spectrum of Narcissism in its Relations to the Metatraits of Personality, Self-Esteem, and the Nomological Network of Shyness, Loneliness, and Empathy. *In Frontiers in Psychology. 9*(Article ID 343). Retrieved from https://www.ncbi.nlm.nih.gov/pmc/articles/PMC5861199/.
10. Twenge, J. M., & Campbell, W. K. (2009). *The Narcissism Epidemic: Living in the Age of Entitlement.* New York: Atria Paperback, pp. 24–28.
11. See Jordan, C. H., Spencer, S. J., Zanna, M. P., Hoshino-Browne, E., & Correll, J. (2003). Secure and Defensive High Self-Esteem. *Journal of Personality and Social Psychology. 85*(5), pp. 968–975. See also Miller, J. D., & Campbell, W. K. (2010). The case for using research on trait narcissism as a building block for understanding narcissistic personality disorder: A clarification and expansion. *Personality Disorders: Theory, Research, and Treatment.*

1(3), pp. 200–201. See also Vater, A., Ritter, K., Schröder-Abé, M., Schütz, A., Lammers, C., Bosson, J. K., & Roepke, S. (2013). When grandiosity and vulnerability collide: Implicit and explicit self-esteem in patients with narcissistic personality disorder. *Journal of Behavior Therapy and Experimental Psychiatry*. *44*(1), pp. 37–47. See also Pierro, R. D., Mattavelli, S., & Gallucci, M. (2016). Narcissistic Traits and Explicit Self-Esteem: The Moderating Role of Implicit Self-View. *Frontiers in Psychology*. *7*(Article ID 1815). Retrieved from https://www.ncbi .nlm.nih.gov/pmc/articles/PMC5118622/.

12. Malkin, C. (2015). *Rethinking Narcissism: The Secret to Recognizing and Coping with Narcissists*. New York: Harper Perennial.

13. Horney, K. (1991). *Neurosis and Human Growth: The Struggle Toward Self-Realization*. New York: W. W. Norton & Company, pp. 26–28.

Chapter Six

1. Ovid. (2000). *Metamorphoses* (Book III). (A. S. Kline, Trans.). Retrieved from http://ovid.lib.virginia.edu/trans/ Metamorph3.htm.

2. Malkin, C. (2015). *Rethinking Narcissism: The Secret to Recognizing and Coping with Narcissists*. New York: Harper Perennial.

3. Parada, C. (n.d.). Echo. *Greek Mythology Link*. Retrieved from http://www.maicar.com/GML/Echo.html.

4. Del Vicario, M., Bessi, A., Zollo, F., Petroni, F., Scala, A., Caldarelli, G., & Quattrociocchi, W. (2016). The spreading of misinformation online. *Proceedings of the National Academy of Sciences of the United States of America*. *113*(3), pp. 554–559. Retrieved from http://www.pnas.org/content/113/3/554. full. The echo does not stop here. When the heat is on, we find refuge in our "echo chambers"—likeminded, polarized communities—on social media. A massive quantitative analysis of Facebook information found that, rather than challenging and correcting misinformation, the echo chamber phenomenon was responsible for proliferating unverified rumors. See also Rose-Stockwell, T. (2017, July 28). This is How Your Fear and Outrage are Being Sold for Profit. *Quartz*. Retrieved from https://qz.com/1039910/ how-facebooks-news-feed-algorithm-sells-our-fear-and-outrage-

for-profit/. Individualized Facebook channels fuel the fire of people's reactions, as advertisers count on engaging customers who are either angry or afraid.

5. Cameron, J. (2002). *The Artist's Way: A Spiritual Path to Higher Creativity.* New York: J.P. Tarcher/Putnam.

6. Ovid (A. S. Kline, Trans.).

7. Ovid. (1964). *Metamorphoses* (Book III, pp. 339-509, R. Humphries, Trans.) In Godolphin, F. R. B. (Ed.) *Great Classical Myths* (pp. 352–357).

8. Gottfried, J. (2016, July 14). Most Americans already feel election coverage fatigue. *Pew Research Center.* Retrieved from http://www.pewresearch.org/fact-tank/2016/07/14/most-americans-already-feel-election-coverage-fatigue/.

9. Wear, M., and Davis, C. (2016, November 1). This election has made Americans angry and sick. Here's how we can recover. *The Washington Post.* Retrieved from https://www.washingtonpost.com/posteverything/wp/2016/11/01/this-election-has-made-americans-angry-and-sick-heres-how-we-can-recover/?utm_term=.d247dcf9e84b.

10. Itkowitz, C. (2016, October 13). People are so stressed by this election that the American Psychological Association has coping tips. *The Washington Post.* Retrieved from https://www.washingtonpost.com/news/inspired-life/wp/2016/10/13/people-are-so-stressed-by-this-election-that-the-american-psychological-association-has-coping-tips/?utm_term=.b8a81945fd21. See also APA Stress in America™ Survey: US at "Lowest Point We Can Remember;" Future of Nation Most Commonly Reported Source of Stress. (2017, November 1). *American Psychological Association.* Retrieved from http://www.apa.org/news/press/releases/2017/11/lowest-point.aspx.

11. Clifford, C. (2016, November 14). Online therapy start-up sees a 7-fold spike in traffic after Trump victory. *CNBC.* Retrieved from https://www.cnbc.com/2016/11/14/online-therapy-startup-sees-a-7-fold-spike-in-traffic-after-trump-victory.html.

12. Helgoe, L. (2013). *Introvert Power: Why Your Inner Life is Your Hidden Strength.* Naperville, IL: Sourcebooks.

13. This hijacking of processing time may be a factor in sexual exploitation where the initiator claims innocence because the victim, reflecting or seeking the right words, did not utter a clear and strong "no."

Chapter Seven

1. Wachtel, P. L. (1977). *Psychoanalysis and Behavior Therapy: Toward an Integration.* New York: Basic Books.
2. Wachtel, p. 5.
3. Wachtel, P. L. (2005). An (inevitably) self-deceiving reflection on self-deception. In M. R. Goldfried (Ed.), *How Therapists Change: Personal and Professional Reflections.* Washington, DC: American Psychological Association, pp. 83–101.
4. See Wachtel, P. L. (1999). *Race in the Mind of America.* New York: Routledge. See also Wachtel, P. L. (2017). *The Poverty of Affluence: A Psychological Portrait of the American Way of Life.* New York: Rebel Reads. (Original work published 1983).
5. Wachtel, P. L. (2000). Reclaiming the disavowed: The evolution of an integrative point of view. In J. Shay & J. Wheelis (Eds.), *Odysseys in psychotherapy.* New York: Irvington, pp. 359–392.
6. Alexander, F. (1980). The principle of corrective emotional experience. In Alexander, F., and French, T. M. (Eds.), *Psychoanalytic Therapy: Principles and Application.* Lincoln, NE: University of Nebraska Press, pp. 66–70. (Original work published 1946). According to Franz Alexander, to facilitate a "corrective emotional experience" meant "to reexpose the patient, under more favorable circumstances, to emotional situations which he could not handle in the past."
7. Wachtel, P. L. (2014). *Cyclical Psychodynamics and the Contextual Self: The Inner World, the Intimate World, and the World of Culture and Society.* New York: Routledge, p. 32.
8. Wachtel, P. L. (2013, October 10). Race relations: Vicious Circles, Virtuous Circles, and the Path Toward Resolution. Presentation for the Clinton School of Public Service [Video file]. Retrieved from https://www.youtube.com/watch?v=t-JwKIQceNU.
9. This response begs the question, "what is reinforcing about being snapped at?" Behavior analysts define reinforcers by what perpetuates the behavior, and this is not always obvious. In this case, she was lonely and the reward may simply be the fact that he has responded. She is no longer alone.
10. Gibson, L. C. (2015). *Adult Children of Emotionally Immature Parents: How to Heal from Distant, Rejecting, or Self-Involved Parents.* Oakland, CA: New Harbinger, pp. 30–40.

Chapter Eight

1. Freud, A. (1993). *The Ego and the Mechanisms of Defence.* London: Karnac Books. (Original work published 1936).
2. Freud, p. 113.
3. Freud, p. 110.
4. Wanis, P. (2013, June 3). Holocaust—Jews informing— "Identification with the aggressor"; a love for power [Web log transcript of interview with P. Zimbardo]. Retrieved from https://www.patrickwanis.com/holocaust-jews-informing-identification-aggressor-love-power/.
5. Ferenczi, S. (1949). Confusion of the Tongues Between Adults and the Child—(The Language of Tenderness and Passion). *The International Journal of Psychoanalysis. 30,* p. 228.
6. Ferenczi, S. (1949). Confusion of the Tongues Between Adults and the Child—(The Language of Tenderness and Passion). *The International Journal of Psychoanalysis. 30,* pp. 225–230.
7. Fink, K. (2007). *Silent No More: Speaking Out About Domestic Violence.* Terra Alta, WV: Headline Books.
8. Fink, p. 21.

Chapter Nine

1. Duncan, S. M. (2013). *Only the Most Able: Moving Beyond Politics in the Selection of National Security Leaders.* New York: Rowman & Littlefield, p. 229. "When he was serving as Churchill's minister of defense in 1952, Harold Alexander, a formal field marshal, declared that Churchill 'hated yes-men—he had no use for them.'"
2. Robertson, L., & Farley, R. (2017, January 24). Fact check: The controversy over Trump's inauguration crowd size. *USA Today.* Retrieved from https://www.usatoday.com/story/news/politics/2017/01/24/fact-check-inauguration-crowd-size/96984496/.
3. Velocci, C. (2017, September 17). Emmys: Sean Spicer Parodies His Inflated Inauguration Crowd Claims in Surprise Appearance. *The Wrap.* Retrieved from https://www.thewrap.com/emmys-sean-spicer-parodies-inflated-inauguration-crowd/.
4. Seeking reassurance is what behavior therapists call a "safety behavior."

5. Hoefle, V. (2015, May 14). The Difference Between Praise and Encouragement. *PBS*. Retrieved from http://www .pbs.org/parents/expert-tips-advice/2015/05/difference-praise-encouragement-matters/. See also Hoefle, V. (2015). *Straight Talk on Parenting: A No-Nonsense Approach on How to Grow a Grown-Up*. New York: Bibliomotion.

6. Benjamin, J. (1988). *The Bonds of Love: Psychoanalysis, Feminism, & the Problem of Domination*. New York: Pantheon Books.

7. Brummelman, E., Nelemans, S. A., Thomaes, S., & de Castro, B. O. (2017). When Parents' Praise Inflates, Children's Self-Esteem Deflates. *Child Development. 88*(6), pp. 1799–1809.

8. Rogers, F. (Creator/Producer), & Walsh, B., Chen, D. F., Moates, B., Lally, P., Silberman, S., & Muens, B. (Directors). (1968–2001). *Mister Rogers' Neighborhood*. [Television series]. Pittsburgh, PA: Family Communications, Inc.

9. Archival footage in Capotosto, C., & Ma, N. (Producers), & Neville, M. (Director). (2018). *Won't You Be My Neighbor?* [Documentary motion picture]. USA: Focus Features.

10. May 1, 1969: Fred Rogers testifies before the Senate Subcommittee on Communications. [Video file]. Retrieved from https://www.youtube.com/watch?v=fKy7ljRr0AA.

11. Gottman, J. M., & Levenson, R. W. (1999). What predicts change in marital interaction over time? A study of alternative models. *Family Process. 38*(2), pp. 143–158.

12. Malkin, C. (2015). Change and recovery. In *Rethinking Narcissism: The Secret to Recognizing and Coping with Narcissists*. New York: Harper Perennial, pp. 113–136. See also Giacomin, M., & Jordan, C. H. (2014). Down-regulating narcissistic tendencies: Communal focus reduces state narcissism. *Personality and Social Psychology Bulletin. 40*(4), pp. 488–500. See also Hepper, E. G., Hart, C. M., & Sedikides, C. (2014). Moving Narcissus: Can Narcissists Be Empathic? *Personality and Social Psychology Bulletin. 40*(9), pp. 1079–1091.

13. Malkin, p. 117.

Chapter Ten

1. Kitman, M. (2009, May 1). How Reality Works. *The New Leader*, pp. 35-36.

2. Jewell, H. (2018, February 14). Is "The Bachelor' making me dumb? I hopped in an MRI to find out. *The Washington*

Post. Retrieved from ttps://www.washingtonpost.com/news/ soloish/wp/2018/02/14/is-the-bachelor-making-me-dumb- i-hopped-in-an-mri-to-find-out/?utm_term=.e5596d4c6c27.

3. FMRI, or functional magnetic resonance imaging, maps changes in brain activity (indicated by blood flow) when a subject is exposed to various stimuli. This makes it a valuable tool in psychology research.

4. Chester, D. S., & DeWall, C. N. (2016). The pleasure of revenge: Retaliatory aggression arises from a neural imbal- ance toward reward. *Social Cognitive and Affective Neuroscience. 11*(7), pp.1173–1182.

5. Melas, C. (2018, February 8). Omarosa: 'Big brother' costars want to stab me in the back' like at the White House. *CNN.* Retrieved from https://www.cnn.com/2018/02/07/ entertainment/omarosa-celebrity-big-brother-premiere/index .html.

6. Noble, O. (2017, February 22). 24 Things Trump Does Better Than Anybody (According to Trump). *Vice News.* Retrieved from https://news.vice.com/en_us/article/nedxnm/24-things- nobody-does-better-than-trump-according-to-trump.

7. Fan, C., Chu, X., Zhang, M., & Zhou, Z. (2016). Are Narcis- sists More Likely to be Involved in Cyberbullying? Examining the Mediating Role of Self-Esteem. *Journal of Interpersonal Violence,* pp. 1–24.

8. Lull, R. B., & Dickinson, T. M. (2016). Does Television Culti- vate Narcissism? Relationships Between Television Exposure, Preferences for Specific Genres, and Subclinical Narcissism. *Psychology of Popular Media Culture. 7*(1), pp. 47–60.

9. Garber-Paul, E. (2016, August 19). Naked Trump Statues: Meet Anarchist Artists Behind 'Emperor Has No Balls.' *Rolling Stone.* Retrieved from https://www.rollingstone.com/culture/ culture-features/naked-trump-statues-meet-anarchist-artists- behind-emperor-has-no-balls-249522/.

10. JimCarrey (2018, March 29). Dear Smithsonian National Portrait Gallery @NPG, I know it's early but I'd like to submit this as the official portrait of our 45th President, Donald J. Trump. It's called, 'You Scream. I Scream. Will We Ever Stop Screaming?' [Twitter post]. Retrieved from https://twitter .com/JimCarrey?lang=en.

11. Santiago, C., & Criss, D. (2017, October 17). "An activist, a little girl, and the heartbreaking origin of 'Me too.'" *CNN.*

Retrieved from https://www.cnn.com/2017/10/17/us/
me-too-tarana-burke-origin-trnd/index.html.

12. Alyssa_Milano (2017, October 15). If you've been sex-
ually harassed or assaulted write 'me too' as a reply to
this tweet. [Twitter post]. Retrieved from https://twitter.
com/Alyssa_Milano/status/919659438700670976?ref_
src=twsrc%5Etfw&ref_url=http%3A%2F%2Fwww.cnn.
com%2F2017%2F10%2F15%2Fentertainment%2Fme-too-twit-
ter-alyssa-milano%2Findex.html.

13. Burke, L. (2018, March 9). The #MeToo shockwave: how the
movement has reverberated around the world. *The Telegraph.*
Retrieved from https://www.telegraph.co.uk/news/world/
metoo-shockwave/.

14. Goldberg, L., Hashimoto, R., Schneider, H., & McNall, B.
(Producers), & Badham, J. (Director). (1983). *WarGames*
[Motion picture]. United States: MGM.

Chapter Eleven

1. Online Etymology Dictionary. (n.d.) Hell (n.). Retrieved from
https://www.etymonline.com/word/hell.

2. A skilled therapist may willingly become that mirror, or "part
object," and work to help the fragile bully tolerate the presence of someone separate.

3. Hornblow Jr., A. (Producer), & Cukor, G. (Director).
(1944). *Gaslight* [Motion picture]. United States:
Metro-Goldwyn-Mayer Studios.

4. Gibson, L. C. (2015). *Adult Children of Emotionally Immature
Parents: How to Heal from Distant, Rejecting, or Self-Involved Parents.* Oakland, CA: New Harbinger, p. 11.

5. Cacioppo, J. T., & Patrick, W. (2008). *Loneliness: Human Nature
and the Need for Social Connection.* New York: W.W. Norton
& Co., p. 83. "Loneliness, like hunger, is a warning to do
something to alter an uncomfortable and possibly dangerous
condition."

6. Eisenberger, N. I. (2012). The pain of social disconnection:
examining the shared neural underpinnings of physical and
social pain. *Nature Reviews Neuroscience. 13,* pp. 421–434.

7. Norcross, J. C. (2011). *Psychotherapy Relationships That Work:
Evidence-Based Responsiveness* (2nd ed.). New York: Oxford
University Press.

8. Cameron, J. (2002). *The Artist's Way: A Spiritual Path to Higher Creativity.* New York: J.P. Tarcher/Putnam.

Chapter Twelve

1. Malkin, C. (2015). *Rethinking Narcissism: The Secret to Recognizing and Coping with Narcissists.* New York: Harper Perennial, p. 34. According to Craig Malkin, the drive to help can represent a type of grandiosity associated with *communal narcissism,* a more recently identified narcissism subtype. Communal narcissists, he notes, "regard themselves as especially nurturing, understanding, and empathetic."
2. Sky, T. (2018, January 3). The myth of the ideal woman and the worthiness wound [Blog post]. Retrieved from https://www.thaissky.com/blog/the-myth-of-the-ideal-woman.
3. Waites, E. A. (1982). Fixing women: devaluation, idealization, and the female fetish. *Journal of the American Psychoanalytic Association. 30*(2), p. 458.
4. Hepper, E. G., Hart, C. M., & Sedikides, C. (2014). Moving Narcissus: Can Narcissists Be Empathic? *Personality and Social Psychology Bulletin. 40*(9), pp. 1079–1091. See also Giacomin, M., & Jordan, C. H. (2014). Down-regulating narcissistic tendencies: communal focus reduces state narcissism. *Personality and Social Psychology Bulletin. 40*(4), pp. 488–500.
5. Links, P. S., & Stockwell, M. (2002). The role of couple therapy in the treatment of narcissistic personality disorder. *American Journal of Psychotherapy. 56*(4), pp. 522–538.
6. Gottman, J. M., & Levenson, R. W. (1999). What predicts change in marital interaction over time? A study of alternative models. *Family Process. 38*(2), pp. 143–158.
7. Archer, D. (2017, March 6). The Danger of Manipulative Love-Bombing in a Relationship. *Psychology Today* [Blog entry]. Retrieved from https://www.psychologytoday.com/us/blog/reading-between-the-headlines/201703/the-danger-manipulative-love-bombing-in-relationship.

Chapter Thirteen

1. Jones, R., Schur, M., & Brooker, C. (Writers), & Wright, J. (Director). (2016). Nosedive. [Television series episode]. In C. Brooker (Creator/Producer). *Black Mirror.* UK: Netflix.

2. Tamir, D. I. & Mitchell, J. P. Disclosing information about the self is intrinsically rewarding. Proc. Natl. Acad. Sci. USA 109, 8038–8043 (2012). See also Meshi, D, Mamerow, L, Kirilina, E. Morawetz, C., Margulies, D. S., & Heekeren, H. R. (2016). Sharing self-related information is associated with intrinsic functional connectivity of cortical midline brain regions. *Scientific Reports, 6*(Article number 22491). Retrieved from https://www.nature.com/articles/srep22491.

3. Dunbar, R. I., Marriott, A., & Duncan, N. D. (1997). Human conversational behavior. *Human Nature. 8*(3), pp. 231–246.

4. Naaman, M., Boase, J., & Lai, C-H. (2010, February 6–10). Is it Really About Me? Message Content in Social Awareness Streams. *Proceedings of the 2010 ACM Conference on Computer Supported Cooperative Work,* pp. 189–192. A systematic analysis of posts generated by over 350 Twitter users resulted in categorization of 20% of users as "Informers," and the remaining 80% as "Meformers," or self-disclosers. See also Nguyen, M., Bin, Y. S., & Campbell, A. (2012). Comparing online and offline self-disclosure: A systematic review. *Cyberpsychology, Behavior, and Social Networkin. 15*(2), pp. 103–111. Though studies generally reveal higher levels of self-disclosure in online communications, contradictions are present in the literature.

5. Cacioppo, J. T., Cacioppo, S., Gonzaga, G. C., Ogburn, E. L., & VanderWeele, T. J. (2013). Marital satisfaction and break-ups differ across on-line and off-line meeting venues. *Proceedings of the National Academy of Science U.S.A.. 110*(25), pp. 10135–10140. Retrieved from http://www.pnas.org/content/pnas/early/2013/05/31/1222447110.full.pdf. University of Chicago researchers found that romantic relationships that began online resulted in happier and more enduring marriages than those initiated offline.

6. Davidow, B. (2013, June 10). Skinner Marketing: We're the Rats, and Facebook Likes are the Reward. *The Atlantic.* Retrieved from https://www.theatlantic.com/technology/archive/2013/06/skinner-marketing-were-the-rats-and-facebook-likes-are-the-reward/276613/.

7. Nicas, J. (2018, February 7). How YouTube Drives People to the Internet's Darkest Corners. *The Wall Street Journal.* Retrieved from https://www.wsj.com/articles/how-youtube-drives-viewers-to-the-internets-darkest-corners-1518020478.

8. Rothman, L. (2013, April 10). *Buckwild* Update: MTV Cancels Show; Producer Speaks Out. Retrieved from http://entertainment.time.com/2013/04/10/buckwild-update-mtv-cancels-show-producer-speaks-out/. MTV cancelled *Buckwild* in response to the off-screen death of Shain Gandee, one of the show's stars.

9. Reiss, S., & Wiltz, J. (2004). Why people watch reality TV. *Media Psychology. 6*, pp. 363–378.

10. Lull, R. B., & Dickinson, T. M. (2018). Does Television Cultivate Narcissism? Relationships Between Television Exposure, Preferences for Specific Genres, and Subclinical Narcissism. *Psychology of Popular Media Culture. 7*(1), pp. 47–60. Narcissism is also positively correlated with preferences for sports, thriller/horror genres, and negatively correlated with a preference for news. See also Mehdizadeh, S. (2010). Self-Presentation 2.0: Narcissism and Self-Esteem on Facebook. *Cyberpsychology, Behavior, and Social Networking. 13*(4), pp. 357–364. See also Andreassen, C. S., Pallesen, S., & Griffiths, M. D. (2017). The relationship between addictive use of social media, narcissism, and self-esteem: Findings from a large national survey. *Addictive Behavior. 64*, pp. 287–293.

11. Errasti, J., Amigo, I., & Villadangos, M. (2017). Emotional Uses of Facebook and Twitter: Its Relation with Empathy, Narcissism, and Self-Esteem in Adolescence. *Psychological Reports. 0(0)*, pp. 1–22. [Epub ahead of print].

12. Gonzales, A. L., & Hancock, J. T. (2011). Mirror, mirror on my Facebook wall: Effects of exposure to Facebook on self-esteem. *Cyberpsychology, Behavior, and Social Networking. 14*(1-2), pp. 79–83.

13. Andreassen.

14. Metzler, A., & Scheithauer, H. (2017). The Long-Term Benefits of Positive Self-Presentation Via Profile Pictures, Number of Friends and the Initiation of Relationships on Facebook for Adolescents' Self-Esteem and the Initiation of Offline Relationships. *Frontiers in Psychology. 8*(Article 1981), pp. 1–15.

15. Williams, A. (2013, December 13). The Agony of Instagram. *The New York Times.* Retrieved from https://www.nytimes.com/2013/12/15/fashion/instagram.html. Terms like "Instagram envy" and "Facebook envy" now litter the Internet.

16. Errasti.

17. Clark, J. L., Algoe, S. B., & Green, M. C. (2018). Social Network Sites and Well-Being: The Role of Social Connection. *Current Directions in Psychological Science. 27*(1), pp. 32–37.

18. Of note is Reddit's "Neutral Politics" forum. See r/ NeutralPolitics. (n.d.). *reddit.* Retrieved from https://www .reddit.com/r/NeutralPolitics/.

19. Tromholt, M. (2016). The Facebook Experiment: Quitting Facebook Leads to Higher Levels of Well-Being. *Cyberpsychology, Behavior, and Social Networking. 19*(11), pp. 661–666. This effect was particularly notable for heavy Facebook users, passive users, and users prone to envy.

20. Kidd, D. C., & Castano, E. (2013). Reading Literary Fiction Improves Theory of Mind. *Science. 342*(6156), pp. 377–380.

Chapter Fourteen

1. Rattray, E., Lucas, G., Lazer, D., & Baker, M. G. (Producers), & Henson, J. (Director). (1986). *Labyrinth* [Motion picture]. United States: TriStar Pictures.

2. National Domestic Violence Hotline. (2013, June 10). 50 Obstacles to Leaving: 1–10. Retrieved from https://www .thehotline.org/2013/06/10/50-obstacles-to-leaving-1-10/.

3. DiClemente, C. C., & Prochaska, J. O. (1982). Self-change and therapy change of smoking behavior: A comparison of processes of change in cessation and maintenance. *Addictive Behavior. 7*(2), pp. 133–142. See also Prochaska, J. O., Norcross, J. C., & DiClemente, C. C. (1994). *Changing For Good.* New York: Morrow. The authors refer to their stages of change model as the Transtheoretical Model (TTM), because it incorporates a range of psychological theories, activating those most applicable to each stage of change.

4. Individual therapy can help one partner understand and shift his or her steps, which then shifts the couple dynamic. When both partners are willing and able to change, a couples' therapist can get a front-row view of the dance and help interpret it from a more neutral vantage point.

5. For basics on mindfulness practice, see Mindful.org. (n.d.). Getting started with mindfulness. Retrieved from https://www .mindful.org/meditation/mindfulness-getting-started/. There are numerous apps that provide guided mindfulness

training and meditation. See Fischer, K. (2018, April 20). Best meditation apps of 2018. *Healthline.* Retrieved from https:// www.healthline.com/health/mental-health/top-meditation-iphone-android-apps.

6. Weiss, J. (1952). Crying at the Happy Ending. *Psychoanalytic Review. 39*(4), p. 338.

7. Jung, C. (1955). *Modern Man in Search of a Soul.* New York: Harcourt Brace, p. 234. (Original work published 1933).

8. Oliver, M. (2004). The Journey. In Mary Oliver, *New and Selected Poems, Volume One.* Boston: Beacon Press, pp. 114–115.

9. Perls, F.S. (1969). *Gestalt Therapy Verbatim.* Moab, UT: Real People Press, p. 57.

Chapter Fifteen

1. The origin of the French word, "rapprochement," can be broken down to "re," meaning "back, again" and "aprochier," meaning "approach. Online Etymology Dictionary. (n.d.) Rapprochement (n.). Retrieved from https://www .etymonline.com/word/rapprochement#etymonline_v_ 3365.

2. Mahler, M. S. (1974). Symbiosis and Individuation—The Psychological Birth of the Human Infant. *The Psychoanalytic Study of the Child. 29*, p. 101.

3. Siegel, J. P. (2006). Dyadic splitting in partner relationships. *Journal of Family Psychology.* 20(3), pp. 418–422 (quote p. 421). Siegel's research has demonstrated the presence of dyadic splitting among domestic abusers, as well among victims who return to abusive relationships. See also Siegel, J. P., & Forero, R. M. (2012). Splitting and emotional regulation in partner violence. *Clinical Social Work Journal.* 40(2), pp. 224–230.

4. Siegel, J. P. (2010). *Stop Overreacting.* Oakland, CA: New Harbinger.

5. Siegel, J. P. (2008). Splitting as a focus of couples treatment. *Journal of Contemporary Psychotherapy. 38*, pp. 161–168.

6. Gottman, J. M., & Silver, N. (2015). *The Seven Principles for Making Marriage Work: A Practical Guide from the Country's Foremost Relationship Expert.* New York: Harmony Books, p.16.

7. Gottman, pp. 44–47.

8. Winnicott, D. W. (1960). The Theory of the Parent-Infant
    Relationship. *International Journal of Psychoanalysis. 41*, pp.
    585–595.
9. Siegel, p.165.
10. Gottman, p. 88.

Chapter Sixteen

1. Kopp, S. B. (1972). *If You Meet the Buddha on the Road, Kill
    Him! The Pilgrimage of Psychotherapy Patients.* New York: Bantam
    Books, p. 41.
2. Twenge, J. M., & Campbell, W. K. (2009). *The Narcissism Epi-
    demic: Living in the Age of Entitlement.* New York: Atria Paperback.
3. This story does not include my numerous falls on the way to
    getting an agent.
4. Wickman, F. (2013, October 18). Who really said you should
    "Kill your darlings"? Slate. Retrieved from http://www.slate
    .com/blogs/browbeat/2013/10/18/_kill_your_darlings_
    writing_advice_what_writer_really_said_to_murder_your.html.
    Though many authors have used this advice, the source
    goes back to the reprinted Cambridge lectures of Arthur
    Quiller-Couch, and his advice, "Murder your darlings."
5. Quote found in Moore, D. W. (2012). *The Mindful Writer: Noble
    Truths of the Writing Life.* Somerville, MA: Wisdom Publica-
    tions, p. 13. Describing Mann's alter ego in his novel *Tristan*,
    the author Arnold Bauer comments that he, "conveys the
    impression that writing comes harder to a writer than anyone
    else." See also Bauer, A. (1971). *Thomas Mann* (A. Henderson,
    & E. Henderson, Trans.). New York: Frederick Ungar Pub-
    lishing, p. 26.
6. Orwell, G. (1984). *Why I Write.* New York: Penguin, p. 10.
    (Original work published 1946).
7. See Helgoe, L. (2013). *Introvert Power: Why Your Inner Life is
    Your Hidden Strength*, p. 123.
8. Gottman, J. M., & Silver, N. (2015). *The Seven Principles for
    Making Marriage Work: A Practical Guide from the Country's Fore-
    most Relationship Expert.* New York: Harmony Books,
    pp. 97–102.

Chapter Seventeen

1. Brooks, D. (2017, December 14). The Glory of Democracy. *The New York Times.* Retrieved from https://www.nytimes.com/2017/12/14/opinion/democracy-thomas-mann.html.

2. Adorno, T. W. (1998). *Critical Models: Interventions and Catchwords.* (H. W. Pickford, Trans.). New York: Columbia University Press, p. 281.

3. Adorno, T., & Levin, T. (1985). On the Question: "What Is German?" *New German Critique.* (36), pp. 121–131.

4. Iyengar, S., & Westwood, S. J. (2015). Fear and Loathing Across Party Lines: New Evidence on Group Polarization. *American Journal of Political Science. 59*(3), pp. 690–707.

5. See Westen, D. (2008). *The Political Brain: The Role of Emotion in Deciding the Fate of the Nation.* New York: PublicAffairs, p. xiv. Westen's research was more recently cited as support for Donald Trump's statement at a campaign rally, "I could stand in the middle of 5th Avenue and shoot somebody and I wouldn't lose voters." See Westen, D., & Israel, S. (2018, January 15). This is your brain on Trump. *The Hill.* Retrieved from https://thehill.com/opinion/white-house/368980-this-is-your-brain-on-trump.

6. Collective narcissism [Website]. Retrieved from http://collectivenarcissism.com/.

7. Golec de Zavala, A., & Federico, C. M. (2018). Collective narcissism and the growth of conspiracy thinking over the course of the 2016 United States presidential election: A longitudinal analysis. *European Journal of Social Psychology.* [ePub ahead of print].

8. Collective narcissism and individual vulnerability. Collective narcissism [Website]. Retrieved from http://collectivenarcissism.com/#1497002848473-ad1ae1c6-93dc.

9. Manson, M. (2016). *The Subtle Art of Not Giving a F*ck: A Counterintuitive Approach to Living a Good Life.* New York: HarperCollins, pp. 110–111.

10. Cichocka, A., Marchlewska, M., Golec de Zavala, A., & Olechowski, M. (2015). 'They will not control us': Ingroup positivity and belief in intergroup conspiracies. *British Journal of Psychology. 107*, pp. 556–576.

11. Golec de Zavala, A., & Federico, C. M. (2018).

12. Golec de Zavala, A., Cichocka, A., & Bilewicz, M. (2013). The paradox of in-group love: Differentiating collective narcissism advances understanding of the relationship between in-group and out-group attitudes. *Journal of Personality. 81*(1), pp.16–28.

13. Greenwald, G. (2016, December 23). Glenn Greenwald on Bill Maher, Keith Olbermann, Tribalism, and "The Resistance." The Jimmy Dore Show [Video file]. Retrieved from https://www.youtube.com/watch?v=qofqmWXNkYA.

14. Wachtel, P. L. (1999). *Race in the Mind of America.* New York: Routledge. Paul L. Wachtel discusses the way in which careless accusations of racism feed the vicious cycle contributing to the racial divide.

15. Brooks, D. (2018, June 14). Personalism: The Philosophy We Need. *The New York Times.* Retrieved from https://www.nytimes.com/2018/06/14/opinion/personalism-philosophy-collectivism-fragmentation.html.

16. Mann, T. (1938). *The Coming Victory of Democracy.* New York: Alfred A. Knopf, p. 19.

17. Mann, p. 8.

18. Van der Kolk, N., & Baker, B. (Producers). (2014, February 27). The Silver Dollar. *Love + Radio* [Audio podcast]. Retrieved from http://loveandradio.org/2014/02/the-silver-dollar/.

19. Examples: (a.) Reddit's *NeutralPolitics* forum is a heavily moderated site that lists ten rules for contributors, including requirements that users are courteous in their interactions, address the argument and not the person, and back their statements with sources. For example, the rule on "substantive content" states, "We do not allow bare expressions of opinion, low effort one-liner comments, jokes, memes, off topic replies, or pejorative name calling." See r/NeutralPolitics. (n.d.). *reddit.* Retrieved from https://www.reddit.com/r/NeutralPolitics/. (b.) *Factcheck.org,* operated by the Annenberg Public Policy Center of the University of Pennsylvania, regularly monitors and checks the accuracy of political claims. See Annenberg Public Policy Center. (n.d.). *Factcheck.org.* Retrieved from https://www.factcheck.org/about/our-mission/. The Center is now working with Facebook to find and expose "viral fake news." See Annenberg Public Policy Center. (2016,

December 15). FactCheck.org to work with Facebook on exposing viral fake news. Retrieved from https://www .annenbergpublicpolicycenter.org/factcheck-org-to-work-with-facebook-on-exposing-viral-fake-news/. (c.) *Votesmart.org* offers voters factual, nonpartisan information on political candidates. Their website describes the project's guiding vision, "Picture this: thousands of citizens (conservative and liberal alike) working together, spending endless hours researching the backgrounds and records of thousands of political candidates and elected officials to discover their voting records, campaign contributions, public statements, biographical data (including their work history) and evaluations of them generated by over 400 national and 1300 state special interest groups." Vote Smart. (n.d.). About Vote Smart. Retrieved from https://votesmart.org/about#.W41SjOhKg2w.

20. Gabriel, T. (2014, January 10). Thousands Without Water After Spill in West Virginia. *The New York Times*. Retrieved from https://www.nytimes.com/2014/01/11/us/ west-virginia-chemical-spill.html.

21. Brewer, M. B. (2007). The social psychology of intergroup relations: Social categorization, ingroup bias, and outgroup prejudice. In A. W. Kruglanski & E. T. Higgins (Eds.), *Social Psychology: Handbook of Basic Principles*. New York: Guilford Press. pp. 695–715.

22. Cichocka, A., Golec de Zavala, A., Marchlewska, M., Bilewicz, M., Jaworska, M. & Olechowski, M. (2018). Personal control decreases narcissistic but increases non-narcissistic in-group positivity. *Journal of Personality. 86*, pp. 465–480.

23. Chua, A. (2018). *Political Tribes: Group Instinct and the Fate of Nations*. New York: Penguin.

24. Grinnell, R. (2016). Fundamental Attribution Error. *Psych Central*. Retrieved from https://psychcentral.com/ encyclopedia/fundamental-attribution-error/. The *fundamental attribution error* refers to "People's tendency to overemphasize internal explanations for the behavior of others, while failing to take into account the power of the situation."

25. For a helpful summary of this phenomenon, see The Decision Lab. Salience bias. Retrieved from https://thedecisionlab .com/bias/salience-bias/.

26. Remen, R. N. (2013, January 9). Generous Listening. Retrieved from http://www.rachelremen.com/generous-listening/.
27. Tippett, K. (2016). *Becoming Wise: An Inquiry Into the Mystery and Art of Living.* New York: Penguin, p. 29.
28. Van der Kolk, N., & Baker, B. (Producers). (2014, February 27). The Silver Dollar. *Love + Radio* [Audio podcast]. Retrieved from http://loveandradio.org/2014/02/the-silver-dollar/.
29. Kemp, Kathryn W. (2017, July). de Tocqueville, Alexis. *Oxford Research Encyclopedias.* Retrieved from http://literature.oxfordre.com/view/10.1093/acrefore/9780190201098.001.0001/acrefore-9780190201098-e-579.
30. de Tocqueville, A. (2004) *Democracy in America: A New Translation by Arthur Goldhammer.* New York: Library of America, p. 225. (Original work published in two volumes, the first in 1835, and the second in 1840).
31. de Tocqueville, A., p. 590.
32. de Tocqueville, A., p. 626.
33. de Tocqueville, A., p. 258.

ABOUT THE AUTHOR

Laurie Helgoe, PhD, is a clinical psychologist, educator, and author, with a special interest in the relationship between personality and culture. Dr. Helgoe is an Associate Professor of Behavioral Sciences at the Ross University School of Medicine. She is the author of six books, including the critically acclaimed *Introvert Power: Why Your Inner Life is Your Hidden Strength* (2013, 2008), which is published in six languages.

The views expressed in this book are the author's own and do not represent the policies or positions of the Ross University School of Medicine.